T0213630

Communications
in Computer and Information Science 785

Commenced Publication in 2007
Founding and Former Series Editors:
Alfredo Cuzzocrea, Xiaoyong Du, Orhun Kara, Ting Liu, Dominik Ślęzak,
and Xiaokang Yang

Editorial Board

More information about this series at http://www.springer.com/series/7899

Andrzej Dziech · Andrzej Czyżewski (Eds.)

Multimedia Communications, Services and Security

9th International Conference, MCSS 2017
Kraków, Poland, November 16–17, 2017
Proceedings

 Springer

Editors
Andrzej Dziech
AGH University of Science and Technology
Krakow
Poland

Andrzej Czyżewski
Gdańsk University of Technology
Gdansk
Poland

ISSN 1865-0929   ISSN 1865-0937 (electronic)
Communications in Computer and Information Science
ISBN 978-3-319-69910-3   ISBN 978-3-319-69911-0 (eBook)
https://doi.org/10.1007/978-3-319-69911-0

Library of Congress Control Number: 2017957545

Printed on acid-free paper

This Springer imprint is published by Springer Nature
The registered company is Springer International Publishing AG
The registered company address is: Gewerbestrasse 11, 6330 Cham, Switzerland

Preface

It is not obvious among technical sciences to find a second equally diverse and multidisciplinary one, such as multimedia communication technology. The richness of this discipline is growing rapidly when we consider its connection with telecommunications and security issues. This year's edition of the International Conference on Multimedia Communications, Services and Security (MCSS; the ninth event in this series), which stands out for its long tradition, was characterized by a unique diversity of topics that perfectly illustrate the wealth of issues that are positioned at the center of the scientific interest of researchers who have demonstrated their commitment to this broad area.

Consequently, according to the MCSS conference principles, and the call for papers, in these proceedings the reader will find a discussion of the issues associated with classic telecommunications, such as: quality demands for servers, distribution of voice messages in crisis and emergency situations, logging flows for the SDN-WAN optimization and others. Multimedia technology comprises sounds, images, and alphanumeric data processing, and therefore some of the papers presented here cover such topics as: sound direction determination employing MEMS microphones and digital signal processing, object re-identification applicable to multi-camera surveillance systems, cameras calibration, video summarization for newscasts, parallel object detection and tracking algorithms in video, contour extraction and compression, as well as other topics reflecting the researchers' effort to extract information embedded or hidden within multimedia data.

It is well known that multimedia technology constitutes a very practical field, and hence among the presented papers the reader can find reports on experimental implementations concerning a quite broad range of applications, such as those applied to traffic monitoring (especially to automatic vehicle counting and classification), semantically enhanced navigation employing augmented reality, advanced multimodal biometrics, and even to the musical acoustics field in terms of recording the bowed string.

Some of the topics relate to signals and images that are inherently not entirely repeatable, or reproducible, so that by nature their representations are remaining unique. That is why some of the authors used soft computing methods or machine learning techniques to solve practical problems within the scope of their applied research. In particular, the interrelation between multimedia technology and the security domain contributes to an area that requires special consideration. This connection distinguishes the thematic scope of the MCSS conference distinguishing itself from many hitherto existing fora established for the exchange of scientific thoughts in both research areas. This feature, being reflected in the majority of the presented papers, is particularly visible in the works devoted to the intrusion prevention system following the paradigm of SAS (Security-as-a-Service Solutions), steganography using routing protocols, and proposed solutions concerning crisis and emergency situations.

As Chairs of the 9th MCSS conference we hope that the participants of this conference as well as the readers of the proceedings will broaden their knowledge thanks to the detailed and careful presentation of ideas, methods, and results.

November 2017

Andrzej Dziech
Andrzej Czyżewski

Organization

The International Conference on Multimedia Communications, Services and Security (MCSS 2017) was organized by AGH University of Science and Technology and the University of Computer Engineering and Telecommunications (WSTKT).

Executive Committee

General Chairs

Andrzej Dziech	AGH University of Science and Technology, Poland
Andrzej Czyżewski	Gdańsk University of Technology, Poland

Committee Chairs

Remigiusz Baran	Kielce University of Technology
Mikołaj Leszczuk	AGH University of Science and Technology, Poland
Paweł Korus	AGH University of Science and Technology, Poland
Jan Derkacz	AGH University of Science and Technology, Poland
Andrzej Matiolański	AGH University of Science and Technology, Poland
Wojciech Chmiel	AGH University of Science and Technology, Poland

Technical Program Committee

Christof Brandauer	Salzburg Research Forschungsgesellschaft M.B.H., Germany
Antonio Cataliotti	University of Palermo, Italy
Adam Dąbrowski	Poznan University of Technology, Poland
Andrzej Duda	Grenoble Institute of Technology, France
Grzegorz Dobrowolski	AGH University of Science and Technology, Poland
Marek Domański	Poznan University of Technology, Poland
Andrzej Duda	Grenoble Institute of Technology, France
Michał Grega	AGH University of Science and Technology, Poland
Christophe Gonzales	Pierre et Marie Curie University in Paris, France
Lucjan Janowski	AGH University of Science and Technology, Poland
Denis Jouvet	Inria, France
Marek Kisiel-Dorohinicki	AGH University of Science and Technology, Poland
Anton Kummert	University of Wuppertal, Germany
David Larrabeiti	Universidad Carlos III de Madrid, Spain
Antoni Ligęza	AGH University of Science and Technology, Poland

Charles Loomis	SixSQ Sarl, Switzerland
Karolina Marciniuk	Gdansk University of Technology, Poland
Piotr Odya	Gdansk University of Technology, Poland
Andrzej Pach	AGH University of Science and Technology, Poland
George Papanikolaou	Aristotle University of Thessaloniki, Greece
Zbigniew Piotrowski	Military technical Academy (WAT), Poland
Stefano Salsano	University of Rome Tor Vergata, Italy
Kamel Smaili	Lorraine Research Laboratory in Computer Science and Its Applications, France
Piotr Szczuko	Gdansk University of Technology, Poland
Olga Szmit	Gdansk University of Technology, Poland
Ryszard Tadeusiewicz	AGH University of Science and Technology, Poland
Cedric Tavernier	Assystem E&OS, France
Manuel Uruena	Universidad Carlos III de Madrid, Spain
Joerg Velten	University of Wuppertal, Germany
Miroslav Vozňák	VSB-Technical University of Ostrava, Czech Republic
Jakob Wassermann	University of Applied Sciences, Technikum Wien, Austria
Zygmunt Wróbel	University of Silesia, Poland
Jaroslav Zdralek	VSB, Technical University of Ostrava, Czech Republic
Tomasz Zieliński	AGH University of Science and Technology, Poland

Organizing Committee

Remigiusz Baran	Kielce University of Technology, Poland
Tomasz Ruść	University of Computer Engineering and Telecommunications (WSTKT), Poland
Jarosław Biała	AGH University of Science and Technology, Poland
Jan Derkacz	AGH University of Science and Technology, Poland
Sabina Drzewicka	AGH University of Science and Technology, Poland
Michał Grega	AGH University of Science and Technology, Poland
Piotr Guzik	AGH University of Science and Technology, Poland
Agnieszka Kleszcz	AGH University of Science and Technology, Poland
Paweł Korus	AGH University of Science and Technology, Poland
Mikołaj Leszczuk	AGH University of Science and Technology, Poland
Piotr Bogacki	AGH University of Science and Technology, Poland
Rouhollah Kian Ara	AGH University of Science and Technology, Poland
Andrzej Matiolański	AGH University of Science and Technology, Poland

Sponsors

- Security In trusted SCADA and smart-grids (SCISSOR Project)
- INPREDO project (Choosing acceptable road speeds on roads with include dynamic traffic management)
- AGH University of Science and Technology, Department of Telecommunications
- University of Computer Engineering and Telecommunications (WSTKT)

Contents

Contour Extraction and Compression Scheme Utilizing Both the Transform and Spatial Image Domains

Remigiusz Baran[1(✉)], Andrzej Dziech[2], and Jakob Wassermann[3]

[1] Department of Computer Science, Electronics and Electrical Engineering, Kielce University of Technology, al. 1000-lecia P.P. 7, 25-314 Kielce, Poland
r.baran@tu.kielce.pl
[2] Department of Telecommunications, AGH University of Science and Technology, al. Mickiewicza 30, 30-059 Kraków, Poland
dziech@kt.agh.edu.pl
[3] Department of Electronics and Telecommunications, University of Applied Sciences, Höchstädtplatz 6, 1200 Vienna, Austria
jakob.wassermann@technikum-wien.at

Abstract. Two new simple but fast and pretty efficient approaches for contour data detection, extraction and approximation are presented in this paper. The High-Pass Filter (HPF) method, designed to detect and extract contours from greyscale images is the first presented method. It operates in spectral domains either of the Periodic Haar Piecewise-Linear (PHL) transform or the Haar Wavelet one. The other presented method, known as the Segments Distances Ratios (SDR) approach, is used, in turn, to approximate the contour lines given by the HPF method. Its spatial approximation accuracy is carefully investigated and reported as well as referred to the universally recognized Ramer algorithm. Efficiency of both presented methods as well as their performance aspects are finally discussed and concluded.

Keywords: Contour detection and extraction · Contour compression · Haar wavelet · PHL transform · Bit-plane slicing · Spatial approximation

1 Introduction

Contour processing finds a widespread use in many applications. Contour extraction and compression are also required in topographic and weather maps preparation, medical imaging and diagnosing as well as in image compression. In addition, contours are important image features for both image coding and object detection and recognition [1]. Therefore, they are also utilized in various computer vision applications, as e.g. in robot guidance as well as character, license plate [2] and pattern recognition.

Placing an object of interest in a scene is the goal of the object detection. However, to obtain the outline of an object, a given edge detection method must be followed by an appropriate contour extraction method. A variety of edge detection and contour extraction algorithms have been presented in the literature [3]. In general, there are two

© Springer International Publishing AG 2017
A. Dziech and A. Czyżewski (Eds.): MCSS 2017, CCIS 785, pp. 1–15, 2017.
https://doi.org/10.1007/978-3-319-69911-0_1

main categories of contour detection and extraction methods. These are the Multiple Step Contour Extraction (MSCE) methods and the Object Contour Following (OCF) ones [4]. The MSCE category includes techniques where edges are identified as a result of the edge detection procedure carried out in parallel. This mainly includes different discrete operators which are applied to compute the gradient approximation of the image intensity function [5]. However, this also includes The Single Step Parallel Contour Extraction (SSPCE) method proposed in [4]. While the gradient approximation methods returns a binary image where object boundaries are foregrounded, the SSPCE algorithm results in a direct contour line description given e.g. as a set of Cartesian co-ordinates of the following contour line vertices.

The SSPCE method uses a 3 × 3 window and the 8-connectivity scheme [6] to check if a given image pixel ($P_{i,j}$) belongs to the traced contour line, as illustrated in Fig. 1.

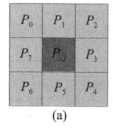

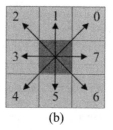

(a)   (b)

Fig. 1. A 3 × 3 window (a) and the Freeman chain coding system [6] related to the 8-connectivity scheme (b).

The decision on this subject is made with regard to 8 neighborhood pixels ($P_0 \div P_7$) and the identification rules given as follows:

$$\mathbf{B}(i,j) = C_k \quad \text{if} \quad \left\{ P(i,j) \cap P_{3-k} \cap (P_{4-k} \cup P_{5-k}) \cap \overline{P_{1-k}} \cap \overline{P_{2-k}} \right\} = 1 \tag{1}$$
$$\text{for } k = 0, 2, \ 4 \text{ i } 6;$$

$$\mathbf{B}(i,j) = C_k \quad \text{if} \quad \left\{ P(i,j) \cap P_{4-k} \cap P_{3-k} \cap \overline{P_{2-k}} \right\} = 1 \tag{2}$$
$$\text{for } k = 1, 3, \ 5 \text{ i } 7;$$

where:

$\mathbf{B}(i, j)$ – coded edge direction;
$C_k = 2^k$ – code of edge direction for $k = 0, 1, 2, 3, 4, 5, 6, 7$;
$P(i, j)$ – tested pixel;
P_k – pixel from the $P(i, j)$ pixel neighborhood.

The goal of contour approximation/compression is to reduce the bit rate for transmission and storage without introducing significant distortion to the contour line. One of the main approaches solving this problem is the spatial domain approach. Most of the spatial domain methods are based on the polygonal approximation scheme [7] which stands in general for searching for the polygon that approximates the original contour line as close as possible regarding the given fit criterion. Majority of polygonal approximation methods use Cartesian co-ordinates to represent the contour lines. However, there are also schemes and applications where polar or Freeman's (also generalized) [6] chain coding representations are utilized.

One of the most appreciated examples of such scheme is the Ramer algorithm [8], which uses the maximum distance of the curve from the approximating polygon as the fit criterion. The Ramer idea for approximating the curve is illustrated in Fig. 2.

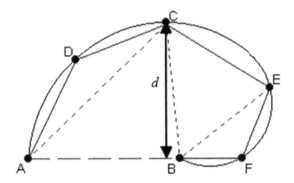

Fig. 2. The Ramer method for fitting the curve by line segments [8].

The Ramer algorithm for fitting the AB curve proceeds as follows:

- first, the distance d from the furthest curve point C to the line segment AB is computed;
- then, if the distance d is greater than a predetermined threshold, new line segments - AC and BC, of approximating polygon are created,

The above procedure is repeated for approximating polygon until the desired accuracy, regarding each new segment, is reached.

The fit criterion in the Minimum Area Error (MAE) [7] approach is the area error caused by the approximating polygon. The area error A between the new approximating polygon and the original one, within the scope of analyzed segments, is given as follows:

$$A = \frac{1}{2} \sum_{i=1}^{N-1} (x_{i+1} - x_i)(y_{i+1} - y_i) \tag{3}$$

where: x and y are the Cartesian co-ordinates of vertices of the triangles drawn by the approximating polygon and the original one.

Another approach, known as the Minimum Mean Square Error (MMSE) one [7], looks for the polygon that minimizes the mean square error ε given, in turn, as follows:

$$\varepsilon = \frac{1}{L_c} \sum_{i=1}^{L_c} d_i^2 \tag{4}$$

where:

L_c – is the length of the analyzed segment,
d_i – stands for the distance between i vertex of the input contour and the edge of the approximating polygon.

Fit criterion of the next appreciated polygonal approximation scheme, known as the Tangent Method [7], is the tangent of an angle between two lines - the opening line and the closing one, respectively, regarding the procedure illustrated in Fig. 3.

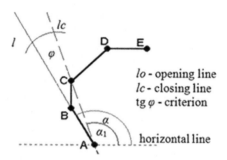

Fig. 3. Fit criterion of the Tangent Method [7].

The opening line – l_o, is the line determined by the first two points (A and B) of the analyzed part of the contour line, while the closing line – l_c, is the one that passes through the first (A) and the next point - the third (C), fourth (D), etc., of a new line segment under investigation, consecutively. The closing line is shifted to a new position if the tangent of the φ angle is less than a given threshold value. Otherwise, the current closing line determines the new opening line.

Some other acknowledged polygonal approximation methods were also proposed by Pavlidis [9], Sirjani [10], as well as de Carvalho et al. [11].

The remaining part of this paper is to present two new simple but fast and pretty efficient approaches for contour data detection, extraction and approximation. The first of this approaches, known as the High-Pass Filter (HPF) method detects and extracts contours from greyscale images, exploiting the advantages either of Periodic Haar Piecewise-Linear (PHL) or Haar transforms. The HPF method as well as the PHL transform are presented in Sect. 2. Contours obtained as a result of the HPF method require further processing steps, e.g. to find their effective - compressed representation. The other presented method, known as the Segments Distances Ratios (SDR) approach is used to achieve this goal. Presentation of the SDR method is given in Sect. 3. Efficiency of both presented methods is finally discussed and concluded in Sect. 4.

2   High-Pass Filter for Contour Extraction

High-Pass Filter (HPF) for contour extraction is a spectral domain approach carried out on spectrum coefficients of selected transforms, e.g. either the Haar Wavelet transform or the Periodic Haar Piecewise-Linear (PHL) one [12]. The basic idea of the HPF contour extraction is just to filter out (set to zero) these spectrum coefficients that are related to "low frequencies" within an image content. This can be achieved regarding decomposing properties of both the aforementioned transforms. The Haar transform decomposes an input image on sub-images being sequential approximations of an input data. In other words, the Haar transform creates a hierarchical representation of an input image, as depicted in Fig. 4b, wherein the top-left sub-images are the results of low-pass filtering (LL sub-images) while the bottom-right ones – of the high-pass filtering (HH sub-images). Similar results can be obtained using the PHL transform, as illustrated in Fig. 4c. In that case, the simplest way to carry out the HPF extraction is to reject selected LL sub-images (like in zonal compression methods [13]), as, for example, depicted in Fig. 4d.

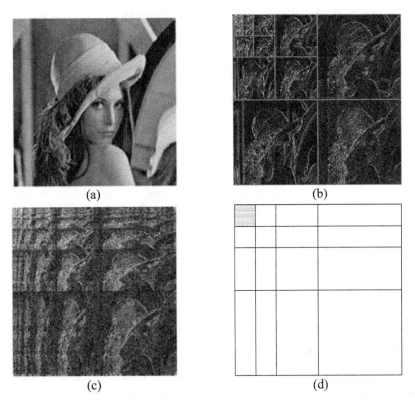

Fig. 4. Haar spectrum – at decomposition level 8 (b) and PHL spectrum [14] (c) of an image (a) and exemplary rejection zone for HPF filtering (d).

2.1 PHL Transform

The Periodic Haar Piecewise-Linear kernel [12] – the basic linearly independent and non-orthogonal functions of the PHL transform, are obtained by integration of the Haar functions [14]. The set of PHL functions is defined as follows:

$$PHL(0,t) = 1, \quad PHL(1,t) = \left[\frac{2}{T} \int\limits_{mT}^{t+mT} har(i,\tau)d\tau \right] + \frac{1}{2},$$

$$PHL(i,t) = \frac{2^{k+1}}{T} \int\limits_{mT}^{t+mT} har(i,\tau)d\tau, \tag{5}$$

where:

i – number of the Haar function, m – number of period;
k – group index of PHL functions;
$i = 2, 3, \ldots, N - 1; \quad k = 1, 2, \ldots, (\log_2 N) - 1; \quad m = 0, 1, 2, \ldots;$
$t \in (-\infty, +\infty);$
2^{k+1} – factor applied to normalize the maximum amplitude of the PHL functions.

Matrix equations of the forward and inverse PHL transform, respectively, are given as follows:

$$[C(N)] = \left[-\frac{1}{2^{k+1}} \right] [PHL(N)][X(N)] \tag{4}$$

$$[XN] = [IPHL(N)][C(N)] \tag{5}$$

where:

$[C(N)]$ – vector of PHL coefficients (PHL spectrum),
$[X(N)]$ – vector of sampled signal,
$[PHL(N)]$ – matrix of forward transform,
$[IPHL(N)]$ – matrix of inverse transform,
$\left[-\frac{1}{2^{k+1}} \right]$ – diagonal matrix of normalization.

2.2 Results of Experiments

To illustrate selected results of experiments, a set of three test 256 level greyscale images has been chosen. Test images and related results of performed examinations are depicted, in turn, in Figs. 5a, b and c, respectively.

2.3 Bit-Planes Decomposition

In fact, results of HPF filtering presented in Fig. 5. Are the grey-level images, as the original ones. To extract the contours' polygons and finally represent them as vectors of vertices described in the Cartesian coordinate system, an additional step of bit-planes decomposition has been proposed. Slicing an input 256 gray-levels image into 8

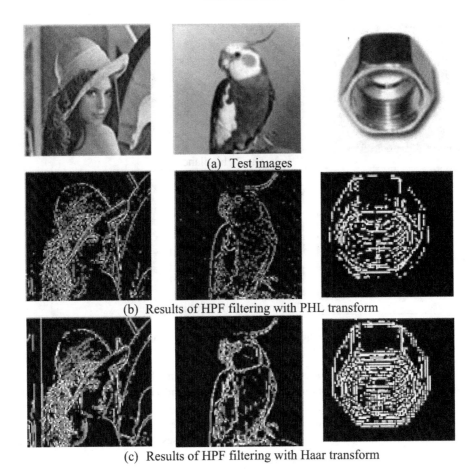

(a) Test images

(b) Results of HPF filtering with PHL transform

(c) Results of HPF filtering with Haar transform

Fig. 5. Selected results of HPF filtering for contour extraction.

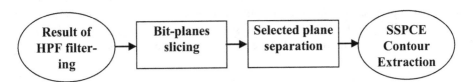

Fig. 6. Flowchart of bit-plane decomposition for contour extraction.

distinct bit-planes and SSCPE contour extraction carried out on the selected bit-plane
are the key stages of this step, as depicted in Fig. 6.

Binary images obtained as results of bit-plane slicing stage, represented by the 7th
and the most significant bit planes of test images from Fig. 5a are presented in Fig. 7a
and b, respectively.

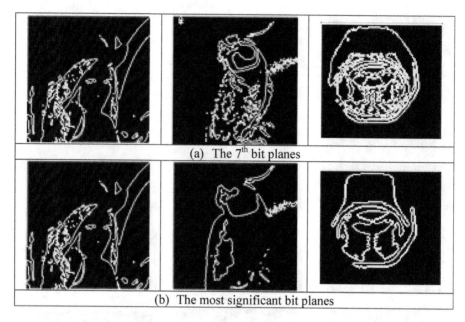

Fig. 7. Selected results of bit-plane slicing stage following the HPF filtering.

Regarding the results presented in Fig. 7, separation of the most significant bit planes can be useful for contour extraction when an individual, especially artificial object, as e.g. in the case of the nut image, accounts for an entire image content. Separation of the 7th bit plane, in turn, is more advisable, for contour extraction from natural scenes or natural objects, as in the remaining cases of Lena and bird pictures.

3　Segments Distances Ratios

Segments Distances Ratios (SDR) approach for contour compression belongs to the polygonal approximation methods. The fit criterion of the SDR approach is the ratio between the direct (*LD*) and the real (*LR*) distances of analyzed segments, as illustrated in Fig. 8. The fit criterion for the SDR approach is given as follows:

$$\frac{LD}{LR} > th \tag{6}$$

where:

th – a predetermined threshold value of the SDR ratio.

The flowchart of the SDR algorithm is presented in Fig. 9. The first point of analyzed segment is known as the starting point *SP*, while the last one – as the ending point *EP*. To calculate the direct distance *LD* an appropriate trigonometric formula is used. If the SDR ratio is greater than a given threshold *th*, the *EP* point is set to the

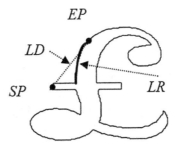

Fig. 8. Direct (*LD*) and real (*LR*) distances for a given segment.

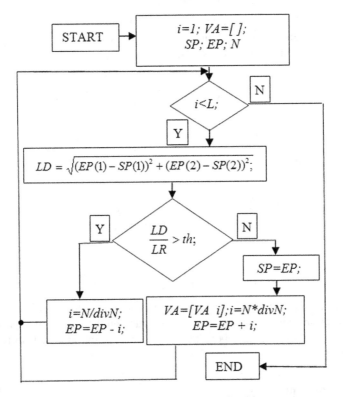

Fig. 9. Flowchart of the SDR algorithm.

value given by the length of the analyzed segment *N* divided by the scaling factor *divN*. Otherwise, the *SP* point is shifted to position of the *EP* one, while the *EP* point is set to new value being a result of multiplying the length of the line segment *N* by the scaling factor *divN*. This causes that a new line segment is drawn. Final positions of the *SP* and *EP* points determine vertices of approximating polygon *VA*.

The SDR algorithm scans contour points only once. In addition, it requires to store no information, e.g. about the contour points coordinates while they are processed.

3.1   Applied Measures

The proposed approximating method is related to the data compression problem. To evaluate its compression abilities, the compression ratio given by the equation as follows has been applied:

$$CR = \frac{(L_{CC} - L_{AC})}{L_{CC}} \cdot 100\% \tag{7}$$

where:

L_{CC} – the length of the input contour,
L_{AC} – the length of the approximating polygon.

To evaluate the distortion introduced by the SDR approximation, the Mean Square Error (MSE) and Signal-to-Noise Ratio (SNR) measures have been used. The MSE and SNR measures are defined as follows, respectively:

$$MSE = \frac{1}{l_{CC}} \sum_{i=1}^{l_{CC}} d_i^2 \tag{8}$$

where:

d_i – the distance between i point of the approximating polygon and the original contour line.

$$SNR = -10 * \log_{10} \left(\frac{MSE}{VAR} \right) \tag{9}$$

where:

VAR – variance of the input sequence.

Earlier research [15] proved that SNR should not be less than 30 dB to receive the expected compromise between the compression ratio and the quality of approximation. If the SNR measure exceeds the above thresholds, level of introduced distortion cannot be accepted.

3.2   Results of Experiments

To illustrate the performed experiments and to report their outcomes, a set of three test contour lines, obtained as a result of HPF contour extraction approach, has been selected. Test contours and related results of SDR approximation are depicted in Figs. 10a, b and c, respectively.

Performed experiments have been also used to compare compression abilities of the SDR approach with other contour approximation methods. Effects of this comparison, done with regard to the *SNR* and *CR* measures, for the case of the Ramer Method and with the use of test contours illustrated in Fig. 10a, are presented in Fig. 11.

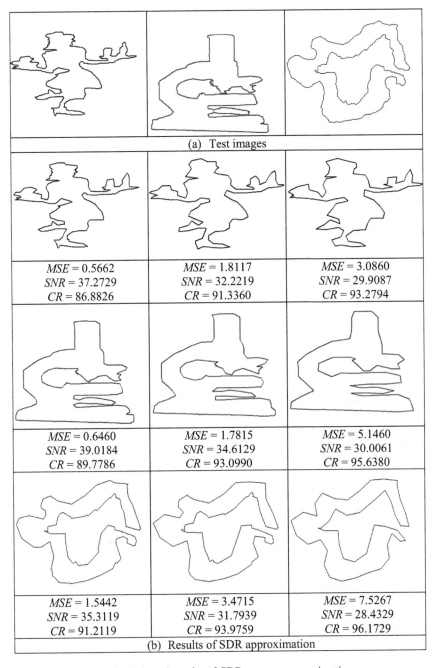

(a) Test images

MSE = 0.5662
SNR = 37.2729
CR = 86.8826

MSE = 1.8117
SNR = 32.2219
CR = 91.3360

MSE = 3.0860
SNR = 29.9087
CR = 93.2794

MSE = 0.6460
SNR = 39.0184
CR = 89.7786

MSE = 1.7815
SNR = 34.6129
CR = 93.0990

MSE = 5.1460
SNR = 30.0061
CR = 95.6380

MSE = 1.5442
SNR = 35.3119
CR = 91.2119

MSE = 3.4715
SNR = 31.7939
CR = 93.9759

MSE = 7.5267
SNR = 28.4329
CR = 96.1729

(b) Results of SDR approximation

Fig. 10. Selected results of SDR contour approximation.

Results presented in Fig. 10b show that the SDR method for contour approximation has good compression abilities. Maintaining assumptions related distortions that can be accepted (regarding the acceptable *SNR* level), it can be noticed that compression ratio for SDR approach, in selected cases, can be even greater than 95%.

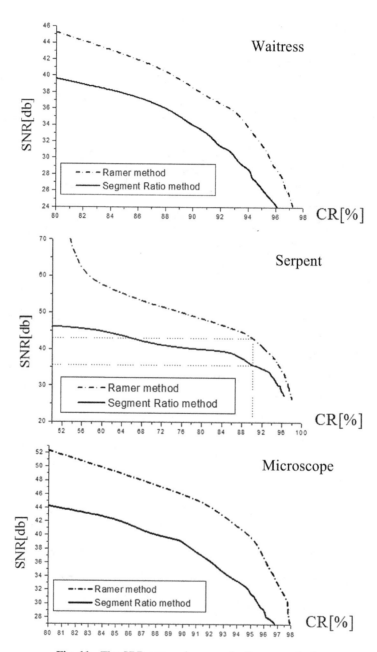

Fig. 11. The SDR approach versus the Ramer method.

Figure 11 shows that the SDR approach is slightly worse than the Ramer method in respect to the SNR method. The effectiveness of this two approaches is almost comparable only when the compression ratio is going high. On the other hand, the SDR method is much faster than the Ramer one. Plots depicted in Fig. 12 prove the SDR superiority within this aspect.

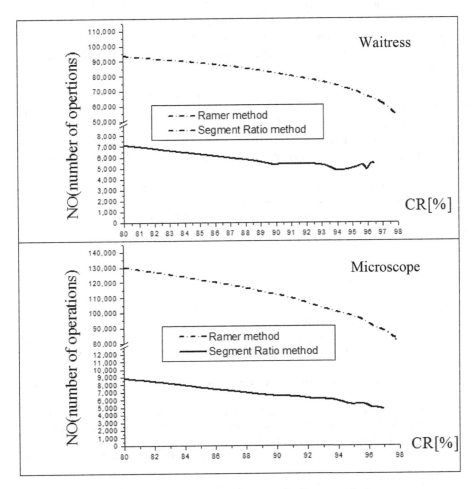

Fig. 12. The SDR approach versus the Ramer method.

4 Summary and Final Conclusions

Two new approaches: (*i*) the High-Pass Filtering (HPF) for contour detection and extraction and (*ii*) the Segments Distances Ratios (SDR) for polygonal spatial approximation of contour lines are presented in this paper. Presented methods, when used consecutively – one after another, can be applied as an entire complete scheme for contour extraction and approximation. Results of its application to selected test images and contour lines, respectively, are reported and analyzed in reference to its approximation accuracy. Carried out investigations let us to draw the conclusions as follows:

- the HPF method, followed by a bit-plane slicing step, can be especially useful – efficient, when applied for contour extraction of objects individually presented on a given picture, e.g. in the case of industrial computer vision systems (regarding mainly its simplicity and easy of implementing as an embedded system) designed to control the quality of artificial items on the product line,
- the SDR approach, although is slightly worse than the well-known Ramer method in respect of approximation accuracy, outperforms the Ramer algorithm in terms of computational complexity and processing times.

Taking the above into consideration and regarding especially an aspect of computational complexity, the final conclusion is that the HDF approach followed by the SDR one can be successfully utilized in numerous applications where contour extraction and approximation plays an essential role, for example in object identification and localization, evaluation of objects parameters (e.g. size, dimensions, area), etc.

Acknowledgements. This work was partially supported by The Horizon 2020 project SCISSOR - Security In trusted SCADA and smart-grids (Grant agreement no: 644425) and also by The Polish National Centre for Research and Development (NCBR), as a part of the Project no. DZP/RID-I-68/14/NCBIR/2016 (RID - InPreDo).

References

1. Wei, H., Yang, C.Z., Yu, Q.: Contour segment grouping for object detection. J. Vis. Commun. Image Represent. **48**, 292–309 (2017)
2. Baran, R., Ruść, T., Rychlik, M.: A smart camera for traffic surveillance. In: Dziech, A., Czyżewski, A. (eds.) MCSS 2014. CCIS, vol. 429, pp. 1–15. Springer, Cham (2014). doi:10.1007/978-3-319-07569-3_1
3. Parker, J.R.: Algorithms for Image Processing and Computer Vision. Wiley, New York (1997)
4. Dziech, A., Besbas, W.S., Nabout, A., Nour Eldin, H.A.: Fast algorithm for closed contour extraction. In: Proceedings of the 4th International Workshop on Systems, Signals and Image Processing, Poznan, Poland, 28–30 May 1997, pp. 203–206 (1997)
5. Jain, A.K.: Fundamentals of Digital Image Processing. Prentice-Hall, Englewood Cliffs (1989)
6. Freeman, H.: Computer processing of line drawing images. Comput. Surv. **6**, 57–98 (1974)
7. Baran, R., Kleszcz, A.: The efficient spatial methods of contour approximation. In: Proceedings of the 18th IEEE Conference on Signal Processing: Algorithms, Architectures, Arrangements, and Applications, pp. 116–121 (2014)
8. Ramer, U.: An iterative procedure for the polygonal approximation of plane curves. Comput. Graph. Image Process. **1**, 244–256 (1972). Academic Press
9. Pavlidis, T., Ali, F.: Computer recognition of handwritten numerals by polygonal approximations. IEEE Trans. Syst. Man Cybern. (SMC-5), 610–614 (1975)
10. Sirjani, A., Cross, G.: An algorithm for polygonal approximation of digital objects. Pattern Recogn. Lett., 299–303 (1988). Elsevier Science Publishers

11. Carvalho, J.D., Guliato, D., Santiago, S.A., Rangayyan, R.M.: Polygonal modeling of contours using the turning angle function. In: Canadian Conference on Electrical and Computer Engineering (CCECE 2007), pp. l090–1093, 22–26 April 2007
12. Slusarczyk, P., Baran, R.: Piecewise-linear subband coding scheme for fast image decomposition. Multimedia Tools Appl. **75**(17), 10649–10666 (2016)
13. Dziech, W., Baran, R., Wiraszka, D.: Signal compression based on zonal selection methods. In: Proceedings of the International Conference on Mathematical Methods in Electromagnetic Theory, vol. 1, pp. 224–226 (2000)
14. Belgassem, F., Dziech, A.: Fast algorithms for the periodic haar piecewise linear transforms. In: Proceedings of the AMSE International Conference on Signal and Systems, Brno, Slovakia, vol. 1 (1996)
15. Ukasha, A., Dziech, A., Elsherif, E., Baran, R.: An efficient method of contour compression. In: International Conference on Visualization, Imaging and Image Processing, pp. 213–218 (2009)

The Project IDENT: Multimodal Biometric System for Bank Client Identity Verification

Andrzej Czyżewski, Piotr Bratoszewski, Piotr Hoffmann[✉],
Michał Lech, and Maciej Szczodrak

Multimedia Systems Department, Faculty of Electronics, Telecommunications
and Informatics, Gdańsk University of Technology, 80-233 Gdańsk, Poland
ident@multimed.org

Abstract. Biometric identity verification methods are implemented inside a real banking environment comprising: dynamic handwritten signature verification, face recognition, bank client voice recognition and hand vein distribution verification. A secure communication system based on an intra-bank client-server architecture was designed for this purpose. Hitherto achieved progress within the project is reported in this paper with a focus on the design and implementation of the developed biometric authentication system. Implemented multimodal biometric client identity verification methods are briefly outlined and results of hitherto obtained biometric sample acquisition and analysis are reported.

Keywords: Biometrics · Verification · Digital handwritten signature · Voice verification · Face verification · Hand veins scanning

1 Introduction

As it is projected by one the leading research institutes – Gartner – the on-going digital transformation, fintech sector development and IoT (Internet of Things) megatrends will drive the need for new identity and access management (IAM) solutions, with new biometrics to emerge in a key role. According to Gartner, by 2020 new biometric methods will displace passwords and fingerprints for access to endpoint devices across 80% of the market [1]. Global biometrics market in the government sector, is forecasted to grow at a CAGR of over 11% until 2020 or of 16% by 2022 according to different analyses and will surpass USD 31 billion by 2023. Global mobile biometrics market growth is forecast to be primarily driven by banking and healthcare industry and software segment along with support from growing demand for smart devices, government initiatives, and increasing penetration of e-commerce and particularly mobile transactions. In Gartner's 2014 Hype Cycle for Emerging Technologies, biometric authentication methods were identified as 2–5 years from market entry.

Based on hitherto co-operation with the largest Polish bank (PKO Bank Polski), the authors of this paper have developed relations that enable both, technical cooperation and assessment of implementation potential of biometric solutions. Having in mind discussions currently taking place in Poland and in Europe on solutions of future universal electronic document (ID card, passport) or an electronic signature (not only

A. Dziech and A. Czyżewski (Eds.): MCSS 2017, CCIS 785, pp. 16–32, 2017.
https://doi.org/10.1007/978-3-319-69911-0_2

for corporate but also for individual use), it was decided to plan a research project covering different to the existing range of development and implementation works being done in biometrics. Meanwhile, the most popular means of verification methods require users to remember a password or PIN or have special identifiers (access cards and electronic tokens). Both methods are used successfully in numerous banks, however, their overall performance does not reach what the biometric methods may offer in terms of an increased security and a unrivalled convenience. Especially the elderly people are particularly prone to frauds and extortion of passwords or PIN codes, due to the multiplicity of authorization systems in which they cannot remember all the access data. As a result, they often write them on the piece of paper, which considerably decreases the safety. Additionally, there is a risk of so-called identity theft. Some of the banks trying to use voice biometrics with good effect. The sample of that solution can be Voicepin [2], but it's worth to remember that in noise environment voice biometrics can be hard to use with success. Because of growing need for new means of verification and identification of a person carrying out the operations, methods based on natural features of clients provide both data security and ease of use. Consequently, the currently available biometric solutions face several challenges:

- there are no universal methods of biometrics suited for multiple areas of use
- convenience of use and reliability of biometrics are far from perfect
- known and used solutions may fail to be effective in the long term
- currently, the most popular biometric solutions for verification in banking industry are, according to studies, which examine the situation in 121 banks around the world: fingerprint (48%), verification using the distribution of blood vessels in a finger (12%) and voice verification (11%). These solutions are burdened with numerous imperfections, e.g. Characteristics of the fingerprint are changing with age and the impact on the result of authentication of dirty fingertips or the humidity is too high. Verification with vein distribution in fingers is flawed by a negative impact on the effectiveness of changes in body temperature, humidity of the surrounding and calibration matrix. Verification by voice is a relatively cheap solution, with the biggest cost driver and weakest link being the software responsible for processing and analyzing signals (i.e. breach to database with recordings and personal data)
- inability to identify a single, fully universal and adequately safe method covering potentially all areas (identification, authentication, verification) and various fields of application (banking, e-government, healthcare, corporate)
- the need to prevent digital divide od elderly or impaired person, since as it results from hitherto gained experience on authentication methods and solutions, in many occasions they may cause practical problems to elderly or disabled people.

Consequently, the authors have identified an urgent need to design an integrated, secure and at the same time convenient multimodal technology, as an answer to limited, fragmentary approaches. The new method, should allow for:

- authentication of transactions and operations in electronic banking,
- access to business applications and data transferred electronically,
- signing documents as well as the reduction of paper documents in offices.

The achieved progress in the project realization is outlined in this paper.

2   Biometric System Architecture

The biometric system was implemented as a distributed client-server software archi-tecture depicted schematically in Fig. 1. The system is composed of: the client stations, the server station and the separate database. The client station consists of two com-puters – one is a standard PC computer operated by the bank employee (serving also as the bank cashier's terminal), whereas the second one mounted additionally at the bank cashier stand is a proprietary micro PC-based machine used for bank clients' biometric data acquisition and parametrization. Whenever the parametrization of the acquired signals and images is done, parameters are inserted into the remote database. The server-side application's main tasks are related to the controlling of the process of biometric samples registration of multiple clients that can use the system simultane-ously, as well as to the verification of authenticity of biometric samples upon requests from the bank teller.

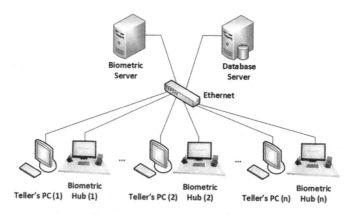

Fig. 1. Biometric system overview

The architecture of the proposed solution has been selected in to best adapt it to the banking environment. The performance of the system achieved so far justifies its conformity to the principal demands. The main disadvantage of the implemented solution pertains to the lack of any redundant infrastructure, which, in the case of a failure of the server, would support the functioning of the system. An enhancement of the system with some additional infrastructure elements (including redundant infras-tructure) will take place during further development of the solution.

The proposed and implemented biometric system consists of a set of biometric sensors used for recording biometric samples plus a compact industrial computer (referred to as "Biometric Hub") with 2 attached monitors to it: one monitor for providing visual feedback for bank client (displaying guidance and progress of biometric signal acquisition) and the second one constituting also a touch screen allowing for easy interaction of the client with the system as well as for submitting a handwritten signature with the digital pen. The bank advisor (teller) has an access to the biometric system and to his or her authorized terminal used for making financial transactions. Thanks to the prepared network application, the teller's computer allows for the control of the biometric identity verification process directly from the bank teller's PC over the banking intranet. Biometric sensors that were made available on the stand include: the biometric pen; the Time of Flight (ToF) camera with a built-in RGB-D sensor and the stereo microphone, as well as the scanner of hand blood vessels. The developed extension is presented in Fig. 2. The part (a) of the figure shows a preview of the extension together with the sensors used, the part (b) contains a photograph of the developed system installed at a bank counter. The proposed biometric system was built in such a way that it would be possible to add in the future other modalities not included at this time, such as iris scanning, which is recently becoming increasingly popular.

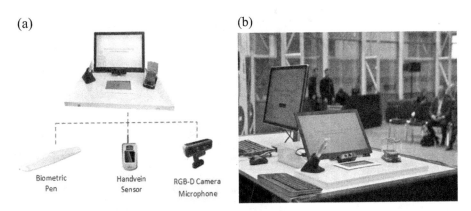

(a)

(b)

Biometric
Pen

Handvein
Sensor

RGB-D Camera
Microphone

Fig. 2. Biometric identity verification station: schematic diagram showing connected sensors (a); photo of the experimental biometric stand installed inside bank outlet (b)

The control of above devices is possible thanks to the developed software solution that consists of 3 distributed applications:

- IDENTBioServer – server application that supervises the process of collecting biometric samples,
- IDENTBioHub – biometric overlay application that enables collecting biometric samples,
- IDENTBioDoradca – application for the banking advisor's computer, allowing for the control of the entire process of collecting biometric samples.

The developed system has a distributed architecture; hence its individual components communicate with each other using data transmission over Ethernet. The most important element of the system is the biometric server with an implemented database which stores biometric samples. The database server consists of 6 databases containing the registered modalities and the collective IDENT Maintenance database where the summarized information is stored separately under individual client ID number registered in the system. The biometric server, in addition to communicating with the database server, monitors all operations performed in the biometric system, and distributes control messages to individual clients. Clients of the server application are both: the consultants' workstations and the biometric hubs developed within the project task, where the system's client applications are installed, namely IDENTBioDoradca and IDENTBioHub, respectively. The biometric stations, installed in a bank branch, consist of two system clients which communicate with a biometric server. The target number of biometrics stations that will communicate with the biometric server in this project will be around 100. The stations will be installed in 60 branches of the PKO Bank Polski bank in the Pomeranian Voivodeship. The developed system communicates with the banking network via the ESB bank information bus, employing the architecture presented in Fig. 3.

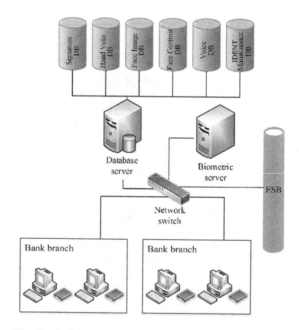

Fig. 3. Architecture of developed communication system

Figure 4 contains a diagram of interactions in the developed system for integrating, exchanging, and storing biometric information. This diagram applies to the case of registering a new client and carrying out two trial verifications (attempts). The registration involves an acquisition of 3 biometric samples to be recorded and two more for verification. The server-side application is responsible for controlling the process by sending the appropriate triggers and waiting for the response of each module (BH - Biometric Hub, TPC - cashier's PC terminal) in the form of information concerning the

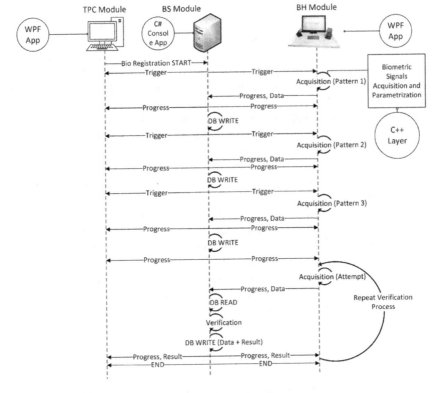

Fig. 4. Data integration diagram

expected Progress or the expected Data. Proprietary message format was developed to support the flow of information between server and clients. Write and Read operations present in Fig. 4. denote writing data into and reading data from the appropriate modality databases. Acquisition process refers to registration and subsequent parametrization of biometric signals from the given sensor attached to BH module.

3   Biometric System Services

3.1   Signature Verification

Digital Pen Communication Layer
According to results by other authors [3], the frequency of hand movements during putting down the signature adopts the values in the range of 20 and 30 Hz. In order to confirm this, a simple experiment was conducted in which a signature was put down using a graphical tablet. The sampling frequency of the tablet equaled to 126 S/s. A participant was asked to put down his/her signature the fastest he/she can. Next, the acceleration curve was derived from the time-stamped samples of the signature line and

its periodogram was calculated. The maximum power in the periodogram occurred near the 32 Hz. Therefore, assuming a safety margin and increasing the value to 40 Hz, according to Kotielnikow-Shannon law, the biometric pen should obtain signals from sensors with the sampling frequency equal to at least 80 S/s. However, meeting such a requirement would demand using high speed or EDR (Enhance Data Rate) versions of the Bluetooth protocol (the Biometric pen communicates with the Biometric Hub in this way), which would in turn entail a shortening of recharging cycles of the battery mounted inside the pen. Therefore, a trade-off between the data transmission speed and the biometric pen operation time duration has to be made, i.e. the wireless communication between the biometric pen and the hub was based on the low-energy Bluetooth 4.0 + LE standard. It was assumed that the protocol should ensure transmission speed corresponding to 50 Sa/s, which is sufficient for a reliable acquisition of signatures put down with a typical tempo.

The experiment aiming at assessment of influence of receiver – transmitter distance on communication latency has been conducted. In the experiment, the distance between the biometric pen and the receiver, in the range of 0–150 cm, was being increased with a variable hop (5, 10 and 20 cm). The delay between the time of receiving two following data packages was measured in the receiver software layer of the signature acquisition subsystem, using cv::getTickCount() function of the OpenCV library. In Fig. 5 the distribution of delay averaged over 420 measurements, for each distance, is presented. The dashed line represents values averaged over all the measurements, the dotted line represents a third quartile, and the solid line represents the values averaged over values higher than 10 ms (in practice, values around 77 ms), for each distance. The delay changes periodically in cycle ~ 77 ms$-\sim 1$ ms$-\sim 1$ ms$-\sim 1$ ms which corresponds to the biometric pen transmission rate equal to 50 packets per second. Occasional lags in communication were especially noticeable for distances equal to 20 cm and 90 cm. This phenomenon is associated with the application of a chip antenna with radiation pattern in the form of side lobes interfering with the nearby obstacles.

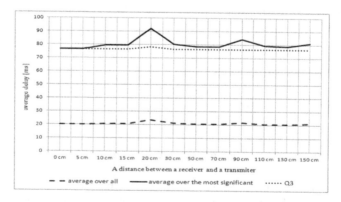

Fig. 5. Average delay in transmission in relation to receiver-transmitter distance for the Bluetooth link between Biometric pen and Biometric Hub

Signature Verification Method

The signature verification has been based on 6 dynamic measures, which are shortly described later on in the paper, employing the dynamic time warping (DTW) algorithm. The method is based on the assumption that time-domain functions of two arbitrary authentic signatures entail less warping than the functions of the authentic and the forged signature. Therefore, the information derived from the DTW method and then used for the verification process represents the convergence of a "diagonal" and an optimal cost path in the accumulated cost matrix. The matrix is created in the manner given by Eq. 1, where $\gamma_{i,j}$ is the accumulated cost in cell (i, j), d is the distance (Eq. 2) between the elements of functions F and G (Eqs. 3 and 4) representing values of a particular parameter, such as acceleration or angular position, of two arbitrary signatures of lengths m and n:

$$\gamma_{i,j} = d(f_i, g_j) + \min(\gamma_{i-1,j-1}; \gamma_{i-1,j}; \gamma_{i,j-1}) \tag{1}$$

$$d(f_i, g_j) = |f_i - g_j| \tag{2}$$

$$F = f_1, f_2, \ldots, f_i, \ldots, f_n \tag{3}$$

$$G = g_1, g_2, \ldots, g_j, \ldots, g_m \tag{4}$$

The distance metric given by Eq. 2 has been chosen empirically and it turned out that it outperformed other popular metrics, providing the best relation of FRR to FAR measure during experiments. The standard back tracing manner [4] of finding the optimal path w, given by Eqs. 5 and 6, in the accumulated cost matrix has been used:

$$\mathbf{w} = \{w_k, w_{k-1}, \ldots, w_0\} \quad \max(m; n) \le k < m + n - 1 \tag{5}$$

$$w_k = \begin{cases} (i-1, j-1) & \gamma_{i-1,j-1} = \min(\gamma_{i-1,j-1}; \gamma_{i-1,j}; \gamma_{i,j-1}) \\ (i-1, j) & \gamma_{i-1,j} = \min(\gamma_{i-1,j-1}; \gamma_{i-1,j}; \gamma_{i,j-1}) \\ (i, j-1) & \gamma_{i,j-1} = \min(\gamma_{i-1,j-1}; \gamma_{i-1,j}; \gamma_{i,j-1}) \end{cases} \tag{6}$$

In the previous work by the authors [5] another path tracing method had been proposed which performed well with the measures representing in the time domain the shape of the signature put down on the graphic tablet using an ordinary tablet stylus. In the work presented herein, for the 3-axis acceleration (ax, ay, az) and 3-axis angular position from a gyroscope (gx, gy, gz), 6 measures have been defined, denoted respectively by $c_{ax}, c_{ay}, c_{az}, c_{gx}, c_{gy}, c_{gz}$, representing a degree of convergence of DTW matrix "diagonal" and the optimal path. The convergence c for any of the six measures is defined as the sum of absolute differences of y positions of pixel belonging to the matrix "diagonal" d and pixel belonging to the optimal cost path $\mathbf{w}$, for the same x position, according to (Eq. 7):

$$c = \sum_{x=0}^{k} |y(d_x) - y(w_x)| \tag{7}$$

The assessment of the degree of signature authenticity p, within a range [0; 1], using the 6 measures involves a comparison of their values c' with threshold values c_{THR}, according to (Eq. 8):

$$p = \begin{cases} 1 & c' < c_{THR} \\ \frac{c_{THR}}{c'} & c' > c_{THR} \end{cases} \tag{8}$$

where c' is a value of measure c obtained from DTW method after rescaling, according to (Eq. 9), where n and m define the size of the accumulated cost matrix:

$$c' = 10000 \frac{c}{nm} \tag{9}$$

Thus, the thresholds c_{THR} could be set empirically to fixed values, and for convergence of the path and the diagonal equaled 300. The global similarity ratio value is the average value of all the p values. The measures: FRR (false rejection rate) and FAR (false acceptance rate) have been evaluated for the presented method and the results are given in Sect. 4.1.

3.2 Face Image Verification

The verification of face image has been based on a vector of 768 parameters calculated for each face image sample. Face detection is followed by the algorithm for matching face landmarks which consists of 68 feature points [6, 7]. Correspondingly to detected points, regions of eyes, nose, mouth and face are selected. After the size normalization of each region, HoG and LBP methods are applied. The obtained feature vector is a result of concatenation of the HoG and LBP features and dimension reduction by linear discriminant analysis [8]. The algorithms implementing the face image recognition modality and some of other modalities used for the proposed solution have been selected on the basis of authors' past experiences and upon the literature review.

In the verification phase the distance between samples is calculated as L2 norm. In practice, face detection algorithms efficiency in the banking client visual verification system strongly depends on lighting conditions met in bank operating outlets [9].

Results of the implemented face image verification algorithm performance in real banking environments are discussed briefly in Sect. 4.2

3.3 Voice Verification

Vocal modality in the proposed identity verification system uses the GMM method (Gaussian Mixture Model)/UBM (Universal Background Model) [10]. Alize Framework [11] and mel-frequency cepstral coefficients (MFCC) are used for voice samples parametrization. Data for UBM model training came from recordings made in real banking environments. Recordings took place in three Pomeranian branches of PKO Bank Polski, where each branch had different acoustic conditions. Recorded speech samples contained read speech, free-form speech and acoustic background. It was necessary to adapt the developed method to difficult acoustic conditions prevailing in bank branches.

The basic parameter that needs to be adjusted to the conditions is the appropriate choice of the number of GMM. To determine their optimum amount, EER (equal error rate) was measured depending on the amount of GMM used in the process of creating speaker models. Three series of data were used in the studies, which differed in the way the model of individual speakers was generated. The first data series used recordings with the same acoustic background as the recordings used to create universal background model. The second data series contained so-called short recordings up to 10 s long. The third data series contained a 30 s long speech. The second and third series were recorded with different background than the recordings used to develop universal background model.

Figure 6 shows a graph presenting the impact of GMM amount on the EER error. Increasing the number of mixtures to 256 causes the EER to drop for all 3 data series. Increasing the number of mixtures above 256 leads to stabilization of the results. Further increasing of the number of mixtures causes the increase in EER. Value of 256 was used as the final value of the quantity of GMM mixtures.

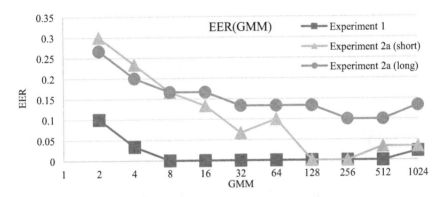

Fig. 6. EER index values versus number of Gaussian mixtures used in GMM

The second key issue in creating a speech verification system was the issue of selecting the appropriate length of recordings involved in the speaker verification process. For this purpose, an experiment was conducted in which the effectiveness was assessed of the speech verification system using 15 and 30 s long speech for recording the speaker model and 5 and 10 s long speech for verification. Speech samples for recording speaker model were repeated by each speaker 3 times. Universal background model was generated based on 30 recordings done in the branch of the bank. The first series of tests was conducted employing 50 persons.

For the version with 15 s long speech used to create speaker model and 5 s long verification sample, the achieved error rate was 0.02 EER. For the version with 30 s long speech used to create a speaker model and 10 s long verification sample, the error amounted to 0.56. The results of the experiment are shown in Fig. 7. Finally it was decided to use 18 s long speech sample repeated 3 times and the 8 s long verification sample.

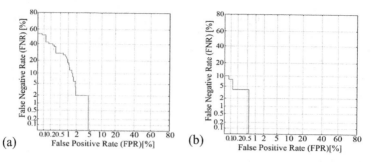

Fig. 7. GMM-UBM speaker verification method performance: (a) short utterance variant; (b) long utterance variant

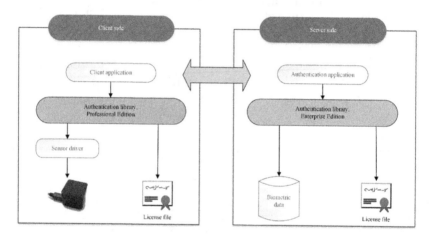

Fig. 8. Hand vein subsystem configuration

3.4   Hand Vein Distribution Verification

The consumer version of Hand Vein sensor, namely the Fujitsu PalmSecure device [12], is used for experiments, providing a part of the developed stand for multimodal verification of bank clients. The assumed scale of the experimental solution (i.e. 100 stations using PalmSecure to identify customers) was solved in the client-server architecture using client-side (Professional Edition - PE) licensing and processing library licenses for Enterprise Edition (EE). The diagram in Fig. 8 illustrates the PalmSecure software configuration. The client application is responsible for reading the biometric data through a connected PalmSecure sensor and processing them into the format required by the authentication process. The data are transferred to the server running a multi-threaded identification process based on a biometric data repository stored on the server. Then the server-side application returns the identification/verification result to the client application.

The method based on the commercial sensor is used principally as a reference for the remaining identity verification modalities which were designed by the team working on the IDENT project, especially since the hand vein scanning & recognition is known for comparatively low false acceptance rates.

4 Experiments

Initially, the biometric system described in the paper has been tested on a group of 156 people—employees of PKO Bank Polski. The people testing the stations were the first group of people to use the stations even before they are installed at the bank branches. The tests were conducted during PKO Bank Polski in-house training for advisers who would later operate the biometric stations in branch offices during the system's target research.

Each trainee registered biometric patterns for each modality during the course of experiment. The registration employed biometric stations identical to those that are to be installed at bank branches. The complete registration of biometric patterns included the recording of 3 patterns of signature, two patterns of blood vessel layout (one pattern for each hand), 10 patterns of the face image and 3 voice patterns 17-second long each (the text included oral consent for the use of biometric data).

Once the registration of biometric patterns has been completed for each modality, verification of their conformity was carried out by submitting yet another, verification sample. After completing the pattern registration process, each participant completed a questionnaire regarding the tested system and the propensity to use biometrics at the bank and in everyday life. Surveys were presented to participants in the developed biometric system, simultaneously for the person acting as the adviser and for the client. The last step of the procedure was an attempt at forging the submitted patterns made by observers. The biometric samples recorded during the experiment were saved on the biometric server of the PKO Bank Polski bank, in accordance with the specification described in Sect. 2. In overall, an individual comprehensive biometric registration process generated at least 30 biometric samples per person.

The registration of biometric samples was performed in a typical 30 m^2 training and conference room, at three identical biometric stations at the same time. The system configuration was compliant with the one described in Sect. 2. It includes 3 Biometric Hubs, 3 advisor's PCs and a central server hosting the engineered biometric database. The devices communicate with each other through a 16-port TCP/IP switch. An analysis concerns the results obtained for the sample group of 50 people is included in this paper. Since the IDENT project is still in progress, the full set of results will be analysed in future publications.

4.1 Handwritten Signature Verification Results

The FRR (false rejection rate) and FAR (false acceptance rate) measures were calculated for the set containing 50 persons. The FRR was equal to 0.05 (17/333) and FAR was equal to 0.09 (30/333). The data has been divided into 3 sets, regarding the particular biometric stations on which they were acquired, and the distribution of FRR and FAR measures has been checked. The results are presented in Table 1, in which for each person the relation of false rejected samples (FRR) and false accepted samples (FAR) to all the samples obtained in the particular verification session have been given. Cases in which the signatures were false rejected or false accepted have been marked with a bolded font. The sole zeros in Table 1 denote lack of forgeries for the particular person. The relation of FRR to FAR measure coherent with the one obtained in the earlier experiments was obtained only on one of the biometric stations (station 2). The FRR for this station was equal to 0.08 (8/101) and FAR was equal to 0.02 (2/101). It is unlikely that the distribution of forgeries on 3 stations, equal to 14/2/14, was accidental and the hardware mounted on each station was performing identically. As the software and hardware elements were of the same type, the reason for obtaining distorted data on stations 1 and 3 must have been associated with the positioning of the transmitter in the biometric pen in relation to the receiver of Biometric Hub and its influence to the communications effectiveness (see Sect. 3.1).

Table 1. The distribution of false rejected handwritten authentic signature samples and false accepted forged samples for each biometric station

Authentic trials			Forgeries		
Station 1	Station 2	Station 3	Station 1	Station 2	Station 3
0/2	0/2	0/2	0/7	0/4	**2/4**
0/2	0/2	0/2	0/4	0	0/8
0/2	0/2	0/2	0/4	**2/6**	0/4
0/2	0/2	0/2	**1/5**	0/4	**1/2**
0/2	0/2	0/2	0/4	0	**2/2**
0/2	0/2	**1/5**	**1/6**	0	**2/2**
0/2	**1/5**	0/2	0/4	0/8	0
0/2	**3/5**	0/2	0/4	0/2	0
0/2	**4/6**	**3/6**	**2/2**	0	0/4
0/2	0/2	0/2	**1/6**	0/1	**2/5**
0/2	0/2	0/2	**1/7**	0/4	**1/6**
0/2	0/2	0/2	**5/6**	0/4	**2/9**
0/4	0/4	0/3	0/4	0/4	0/4
0/2	0/2	**1/3**	**2/7**	0/7	0/4
0/2	0/2	0/2	0/4	0/4	**2/3**
0/2	0/2	**4/6**	0/4	0/3	0/4
0/2	0/2	0/2	**1/6**	0/4	0/4
0/36	**8/46**	**9/47**	**14/84**	**2/55**	**14/65**

4.2   Face Image

In the initial experiment, biometric samples acquired from 50 persons were selected for analysis, including face image recordings. The tests were organized in such a way that pairs of persons, were working at 3 different biometric stands simultaneously. Each person enrolled 10 reference samples and 5 verification attempt samples. Among about half of the population (22 persons) fraud attempts in this modality were simulated. The total number of acquired samples was equal 380. In this experimental set, 2 persons identities were false accepted and one person's identity was false rejected. Obtained FAR result for face image modality in the preliminary experiment equals 0.03 and FRR 0.01. The results are presented in Table 2.

Table 2. Results of face verification for samples acquired from 50 persons

	Genuine	Impostor
Decision accept	49	2
Decision reject	1	20

In the first case of false acceptance, the genuine person did not maintain neutral face expression, moreover the impostor person wore similar characteristic frame glasses. In the second case, the images where person keeps eyes closed should be rejected in order to achieve sufficient distance between genuine and fraud attempter. Based on obtained results, further analysis will be done towards defining an optimized decision threshold, which will in turn not affect significantly the false rejection rate.

4.3 Voice

The results of voice verification process are presented in Table 3. Each person registered 17 s of voice for three times in order to develop the speaker-specific model. For the verification purpose a single 7-second long voice sample was used. The FRR in the experiment is equal to 0.09 and the FAR equals 0.03. FRR and FAR results can be explained by the fact of high level of babble noise presence in the room where the experiment took place. Since all biometric stations worked simultaneously in the training room, it affected the received speech signal, because speakers were occasionally uttering at the same time while registering their biometric samples of a different kind. The detailed analysis of the SNR values and its influence on the verification results are to be found in the previous paper by Bratoszewski et al. [13].

Table 3. Results of voice verification for samples acquired from 50 people

	Genuine	Impostor
Decision accepts	41	3
Decision rejects	9	47

4.4 Discussion

The achieved results of the verification for each modality currently are in progress. The modality of the signature achieved FAR and FRR of 0.02 and 0.08, respectively. It should be noted that the obtained results differed depending on the station at which the registration took place. The FAR and FRR rates for image modality are at the levels of 0.03 and 0.01 respectively. The main factor negatively influencing the obtained results is the lighting at the place where the application is used. Partially controlled head and face setup as opposed to hand placement in handvein device leads to difficult situations such as rapid head movements, which disrupts the obtained parameters.

Voice modality has FAR and FRR measures of 0.06 and 0.22. In case of this modality, noise in the environment of the person being verified had a negative impact on the effectiveness of identity verification. The reference point for the obtained results is the only commercial subsystem used in the system, Fujitsu PalmSecure. In the experiment which was conducted this modality obtained FAR and FRR measures correspondingly at the level of 0.00 and 0.0265, allowing for the participants of the study to sign-in or verify their biometric patterns in an effective way.

5 Training Program

A proper use of engineered biometric stations requires the trained staff to operate them. For the needs of using 100 stations intended for installation, a series of training sessions of the bank advisors was organized. The bank employees acquired knowledge of biometrics in general during the sessions, the operation principles of the bank PKO Bank Polski Documents Identification and Monitoring System, operation of the biometric stations, the way of maintaining a dialogue and providing encouragement for the clients to register their biometric samples in the station. In the course of the training sessions, during 17 meetings, 156 advisors were prepared to use the developed biometric stations.

Each person taking part in the training registered their biometric samples in one of 3 stations for each modality in the system. Owing to that, it was possible to collect an extensive data of biometric samples of 5 modalities coming from more than 150 people. The present paper analyses only a part of the obtained samples. In the future, all the results will be analyzed to eventually conduct tests on some 10.000 samples collected after the solution is installed in 100 stations in 60 bank outlets. Apart from registration of biometric samples, the employees also tried to imposter their colleagues in fraud samples. At the end of the software use session, each person sitting at the stations filled in a survey which, apart from questions concerning the evaluation of the station, included also space for remarks and attitude towards the use of biometrics in the bank.

The organization of the conducted training sessions was reflected in the participants' evaluation, summary of which is presented in Fig. 9. The average note of the training as granted by the participants amounted to 5.16 on the scale from 1 to 6. None of the training blocks received a note lower than 5. Such high notes also advocate to

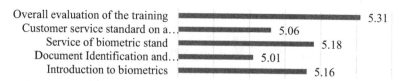

Fig. 9. Result of opinion poll concerning the training effectiveness organized with the participation of 156 trained bank employees (subdivided into 17 sub-groups)

friendliness and intuitiveness of the developed system, as the block of questions in which the participants assessed the usability of the system was granted one of the highest notes.

6 Conclusions

The results achieved so far reveal the need for the development of a data fusion method that would allow for combining the best features of individual biometric modalities in terms of their accuracy and convenience. This subject will underlie the future research planned within the project. It is authors' opinion that in the case of multimodal biometric identification the data fusion should be performed on the decision level instead of the feature level.

Combining the biometric methods should be beneficial for the person being verified, both in terms of improving safety and convenience of using the transaction services. The central element of the data fusion process will employ a server application for an intelligent management of the acquired biometric features and the content of the biometric patterns database.

Acknowledgements. This work was supported by the grant No. PBS3/B3/26/2015 entitled "Multimodal biometric system for bank client identity verification" co-financed by the Polish National Center for Research and Development.

References

1. Gartner: Internet of Things will redefine identity management. http://www.planetbiometrics.com/article-details/i/2534/. Accessed 06 Sept 2017
2. VoicePIN - Voice authentication. http://voicepin.com. Accessed 06 Sept 2017
3. Ortega-Garcia, J., Fierrez-Aguilar, J., Martin-Rello, J., Gonzalez-Rodriguez, J.: Complete signal modeling and score normalization for function-based dynamic signature verification. In: Kittler, J., Nixon, Mark S. (eds.) AVBPA 2003. LNCS, vol. 2688, pp. 658–667. Springer, Heidelberg (2003). doi:10.1007/3-540-44887-X_77
4. Piyush Shanker, A., Rajagopalan, A.N.: Off-line signature verification using DTW. Pattern Recogn. Lett. **28**, 1407–1414 (2007)
5. Lech, M., Czyżewski, A.: A handwritten signature verification method employing a tablet. In: Signal Processing: Algorithms, Architectures, Arrangements, and Applications (SPA), Poznań, Poland, pp. 45–50 (2016)
6. Sagonas, C., et al.: 300 faces in-the-wild challenge: the first facial landmark localization challenge. In: Proceedings of IEEE International Conference on Computer Vision (ICCV-W), 300 Faces in-the-Wild Challenge (300-W), Sydney, Australia, December 2013
7. Baltrušaitis, T., et al.: Constrained local neural fields for robust facial landmark detection in the wild. In: IEEE International Conference on Computer Vision Workshops, 300 Faces in-the-Wild Challenge (2013)
8. Klontz, J., et al.: Open source biometric recognition. In: Proceedings of the IEEE Conference on Biometrics: Theory, Applications and Systems (BTAS) (2013)
9. Szczodrak, M., Czyżewski, A.: Evaluation of face detection algorithms for the bank client identity verification. Found. Comput. Decis. Sci. **42**(2), 137–148 (2017)

10. Chen, W., et al.: GMM-UBM for text-dependent speaker recognition. In: 2012 International Conference on Audio, Language and Image Processing, Shanghai, pp. 432–435 (2012)
11. Alize, Open Source Recognition. http://mistral.univ-avignon.fr. Accessed 06 Sept 2017
12. WhitePaper Fujitsu PalmSecure. https://www.fujitsu.com/au/Images/PalmSecure_white_paper-eu-en.pdf. Accessed 06 Sept 2017
13. Bratoszewski, P., Czyżewski, A., Hoffmann, P.: Pilot testing of developed multimodal biometric identity verification system. In: 2017 Signal Processing: Algorithms, Architectures, Arrangements, and Applications (SPA), Poznan (2017)

Application of Logistic Regression for Background Substitution

Michał Grega[✉], Paweł Donath, Piotr Guzik, Jakub Król,
Andrzej Matiolański, Krzysztof Rusek, and Andrzej Dziech

AGH University of Science and Technology,
al. Mickiewicza 30, 30-059 Kraków, Poland
grega@kt.agh.edu.pl

Abstract. The paper presents application of multinomial logistic regression for color segmentation. The common problem in the subject of image understanding is creation of a large enough corpus for algorithm training. Especially when a large set of classes has to be recognized or if using convolutional neural networks the size and diversity of the training set strongly influences the quality of the resulting system. We present a method of automated generation of training samples by combining a well-known green box technique with multinomial logistic regression for background substitution. We show the encountered problems and their solutions. We present numerous examples of algorithm performance in background substitution. We conclude the paper with presentation of other examples of application of logistic regression for image understanding.

Keywords: Logistic regression · Color model · Color detection · Background substitution

1 Introduction

Machine learning in image recognition is now a significant topic for both research and market applications. One of the world leader in CCTV, Axis has named smart monitoring one of 2017 leading trends. While the commercially available systems offer rather simplistic solutions in image understanding, much more sophisticated tools are a hot topic of ongoing research. One of the limiting factors of the most promising tools used for machine learning is the amount of training data required in order to obtain satisfactory results.

Creation of datasets for machine learning is tedious and often expensive. It is required to gather both visual data and required metadata. It often leads to manual tagging of images or video. On the other hand such promising tools as convolutional neural networks need from thousands to hundreds of thousands of both positive and negative examples per class if tasked with object detection. This calls for high level of automation in dataset creation. While some part of this

A. Dziech and A. Czyżewski (Eds.): MCSS 2017, CCIS 785, pp. 33–46, 2017.
https://doi.org/10.1007/978-3-319-69911-0_3

process can be easily automated when using simple morphological operations on images, it cannot be used extensively as it does not add to the required diversity of the dataset. It is still required to create an overwhelming amount of data for training and testing.

In this paper we show that it is feasible and effective to use logistic regression for background substitution for simple, highly automated and effective generation of training and testing samples. We describe our approach to sample generation, describe the problems related to blurring on the edge of the objects and propose the solution. We support our method with visual examples of both artificial and natural backgrounds. We also describe other applications in which we have successfully applied logistic regression, such as traffic lights detection, skin detection and object detection.

The remainder of this paper is structured as follows. In Sect. 2 an overview of works focusing on background substitution. In Sect. 3 logistic regression is formalized. Section 4 we present the application of logistic regression and obtained results – focusing mainly on background substitution. The paper is concluded in Sect. 5.

2   Related Work

For various computer vision applications, background subtraction (BS) is quick way of localizing moving objects in a video sequence from static camera. It is often first step of a multi-stage computer vision systems [3,11,16]. Most BS methods label every pixel at time as a background or foreground which is very useful in further processing.

We can distinguish several classes of algorithms dedicated to solve BS problem. Basic motion detection is the easiest way to model background. The foreground is estimated based on difference between current and previous frames [5] where low probability pixels are more likely to correspond to foreground moving objects. For instance, background pixels can be modeled with Gaussian distribution [23] or maximum inter-frame difference [9] over specified matrix of pixels (e.g. 3×3). To deal with fast changing background Stauffer and Grimson [22] proposed use of multimodal PDFs as mixture of K Gaussians. Gaussian Mixture Model (GMM) is now very popular method which was improved, for example in [13,24]. PDF is also used in Kernel Diversity Estimation (KDE) where pixels are divided between those from distribution and the others [6].

Another approach whose is designed to cope with multimodal backgrounds is one called *codebook* proposed by Kim in [14]. The method assigns each pixel sequence of color values based on training images and store it in *codebook*. To estimate background each pixel is compared with stored information with precisement to ilumination changes. The method can be parametrized by choosing how fast background can change.

The last mentioned algorithm is eigen backgrounds proposed by Oliver in [20]. It is non-pixel method which learn over unconstraint video sequences. When previous approaches use pixel-level statistics eingen takes into account neighbour statistics. This causes build of more global background model which is robust to unstable backgrounds.

In our case BS is done over static background with changing light conditions and shadows. Our greenbox scenario is dedicated to cut foreground objects as close as possible, without any additions from background image. Such distortion can affect on machine learning algorithm and cause false detections. This fact is important limitation in order to use previously mentioned approaches.

There are also some algorithms dedicated to background substitution in green screen scenarios. Such methods include chroma keying, luminance keying or 3D (differencial) keying. Those methods are common and included in many post-processing software.

3   Proposed Approach

We assume there are K types of color objects in the image and background is treated as an additional kind of object. Proposed approach originates in the development of a system for automatic recognition of traffic lights. There are two colorful objects: red, and green (yellow is ignored) and the background, thus $K = 3$.

3.1   Logistic Regression

Multinomial logistic regression represents a class of models known as generalized linear models (GLM). Unlike in the linear model, where output variable is a linear combination of predictors, in GLM, the response variable is related to linear combination of predictors by an activation function [2]

$$y = f(\beta \cdot x).$$

Its inverse $g(\cdot)$ is called the link function and the model has the form

$$g(y) = \beta \cdot x + \varepsilon,$$

where, ε represents the error term. This form is better for generalization since, the additional structure of the error term can be introduced in Generalized Mixed Effects Models [19].

GLM allow to apply linear model for problems where the response variable does not have normal distribution. An example is a classification problem where the output variable has Bernoulli distribution. Activation function maps the linear combination of predictors to the interval $(0, 1)$, thus the model can predict multinomial class probability. The typical choice for the activation function in multinomial logistic regression, is the *softmax* function. This function arises from the representation of multinomial distribution in exponential family form and the class probabilities take the form [17]:

$$\mathbb{P}(\mathcal{C}_k|x) = y(x) = \frac{e^{\beta_k \cdot x}}{\sum_{j=1}^{K} e^{\beta_j \cdot x}}. \tag{1}$$

Note that because of probability normalization condition, only $K - 1$ vector parameters β are required. To be consistent with MATLAB notation, we assume, that $\beta_K \cdot x = 0$.

3.2 Model Estimation

To make predictions one needs to find the model, i.e. find parameters β of multinomial logistic regression. For GLM a maximum likelihood estimators [10] are commonly used and implemented in various software packages. Thus combined with a modern feature selection and regularization method like lasso [10] they allow the model to be easily fitted to the collected data. Regularization prevents model from over-fitting and unique properly of lasso method removes unused predictors from the model. This results in an accurate, efficient and automatically constructed model of the color.

3.3 Implementation and Performance

Simplicity of (1) makes it possible to implement the prediction in many programming languages an computational environments including graphic shading language such as GLSL[1]. Thus the graphic processing can be used even if the device does not provide computation API.

Implementation gets even simpler and more efficient if only three basic components (r,g,b) are used. In such case linear part is a dot product of two four-vectors and it can be efficiently calculated in a single SIMD, or GLSL instruction. Nonlinear term of (1) in form the exponential the most computationally intense part of the prediction. However, there are numerous efficient and accurate approximation of exponential function e.g. [18].

The term "linear" in the name does not imply that the model is limited only to the linear decision boundaries in the feature space. When classification accuracy on basic components is not satisfactory the polynomial features (or any nonlinear basis) as well as interactions presented in Eq. (2) can be used to construct nonlinear decision boundary. However, the performance may decrease as more computations are required.

$$b^2 + gb + g^2 + rb + rg + r^2 + b^3 + gb^2 + g^2b + g^3 + rb^2 + rgb + rg^2 + r^2b + r^2g + r^3 \quad (2)$$

In the paper the features up to the power 3 (including interactions) were investigated. Dimension is motivated by two factors. The first is a general suggestion to avoid of degree higher than 3 in regression [12]. The second comes from the implementation point of view as the quadratic term for three features can be easily expressed as a quadratic form involving 3×3 matrix operations. Such operation can be very fast when implemented using modern SIMD instruction sets as SSE or NEON. Of course Eq. (2) together with original features r, g and b is just a starting point of the model and in reality only few components would end up with nonzero coefficients found by the lasso.

---

[1] Authors have GLSL implementation achieving real time speed processing of full HD images on Samsung galaxy S III.

4   Applications

The main application of GLM for color classification reported in this paper is background substitution. However, the same principle can be applied to many object detection problems, where object has a characteristics color distribution.

Later in the paper we report few examples where logistic regression has proven to be a good choice for preliminary objects selection. Combined with a strong ROI classifier like e.g. SVM it can make an accurate object detection algorithm that can be an alternative to widely used deep learning when only a small number of training samples is available.

Color of an object can be either due to emission or absorption of radiation. Objects that emit light of a given spectrum (electron excitation or black body radiation) tend to be easier to classify, as the spectrum does not highly depend on the environment. Examples of such objects are traffic lights with two well defined colors an the background. High temperature bodies also fall into this category.

On the other hand the color of an object absorbing radiation depends on the light in the environment. Thus the model gets more complicated, and usually nonlinear and interaction terms are required. Typical example is the color of a human skin or any painted object.

4.1   Background Substitution

Background subtraction in video sequences is widely studied and the effective algorithms were developed. However, still image pose a problem how to distinguish between object and its background. Extraction of an object of interest could be relatively easy if the object is set against the known background that has a homogeneous color, significantly different than the color of an object. Obviously, usually we can met such a circumstances only if the scene was previously properly prepared. A common approach is to use green background (called greenbox), commonly used in movie industry for CGI.

We used logistic regression to extract a uniform background and an object from an image. To assess an effect of our method we used 4 images with 2 different backgrounds (Fig. 1). First we had to compute regression factors. We choose one image for every background, which became our pattern, and manually split it into 2 parts: a background and an object. We noticed that some pixels on the border of the object and the background are difficult to classify (Fig. 2). Thus we could add them to both groups or add to none. We opted for the first option.

Next we treated a regression as an artificial neural network and computed the regression factors. By computing probability of a test object for all pixels in the image we got a map of probability P1 (Fig. 3).

The map look as we expected. Some of blur was classified as background but changes are acceptable. Thus we could substitute the background. The main equation to do this is:

$$newImage = oldImage * P1 + newBgnd * (1 - P1). \tag{3}$$

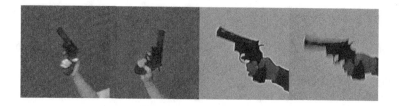

Fig. 1. Test images.

Fig. 2. Zoom on the blurred part of image.

Fig. 3. Probability P1.

After using this equation we got a result shown in Fig. 4.

As demonstrated object borders are not satisfying. We can still notice what was the colour of the old background. When we tried to change the division of the pattern, the object was cut too much so it is not the right way. Thus before using the Eq. (3) we had to remove background color from the blur. We were checking what characteristic features blur has. We found the main one when we transformed the image from RGB (Red Green Blue) model to HSV (Hue Saturation Value) model. This model represents a colour in a way much more similar to human perception. Hue close to the background almost does not change. Closer to the object it smoothly changes into the object's hue. Our idea was to restore the hue to what it would be without the background influence. However every attempt to remove background hue from blur hue ended with failure. The next, correct, idea was to extend object hue to neighbour pixels.

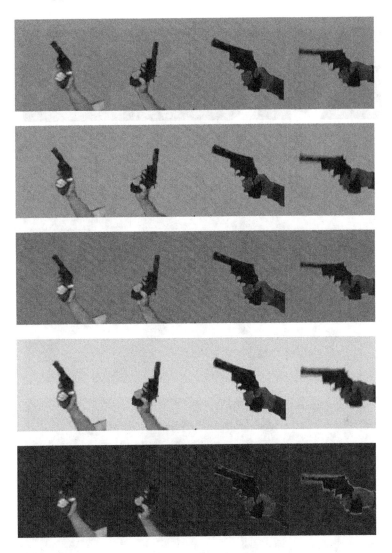

Fig. 4. The first results. (Color figure online)

For this purpose we had to mark an object without background influence. We created another map of probability - P2 (Fig. 5) by adding the blurred part of pattern only to background and computing regression factors one more time.

As we expected, more pixels were classified as background. We cut a part of image where P2 was below an established threshold (0.1) and used a gaussian filter with a small kernel (5 × 5) a few times. We were doing this until the blurred image filled the whole area where P1 was above another established threshold (0.05). After each use the filter we had to increase the brightness so that the object could blur to next pixels. If we used filter with bigger kernel, we would

Fig. 5. Probability P2.

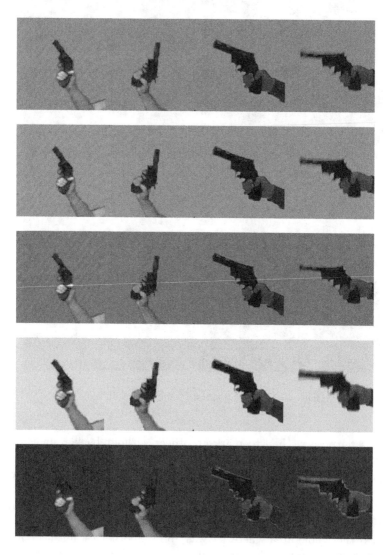

Fig. 6. The second results.

receive a result in shorter time, but colors from different parts of the object would interfere. Finally, we computed an image with adjusted hue using an equation:

$$imageWithAdjustHue = oldImage * P2 + blurredImage * (1 - P2). \qquad (4)$$

After using the Eq. (3) we obtained a result shown in Fig. 6.

As we can see, we successfully removed original background hue. However, edges of the image have incorrect brightness. The perfect way to minimize this effect would be to use light intensity from the original image and the new background. Unfortunately we do not have this information. Therefore we computed

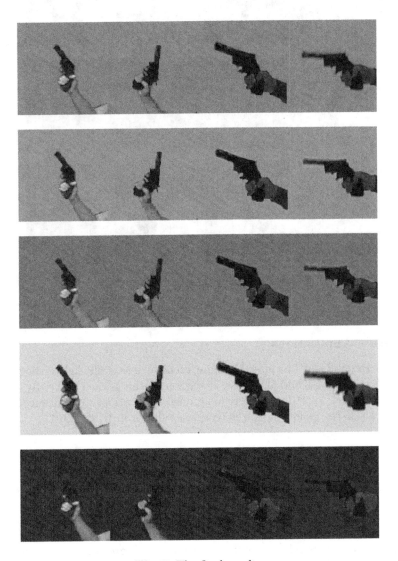

Fig. 7. The final results.

how much the background's brightness influenced on the blurred object's brightness and using P1 we adjusted the brightness. Finally we used the Eq. (3) and we received a result shown in Fig. 7.

As shown, the effect is satisfying. We present some examples with real backgrounds (the object is scaled) in Fig. 8.

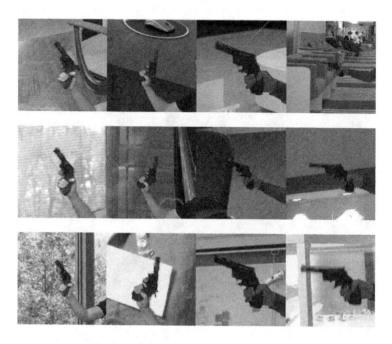

Fig. 8. Examples with real backgrounds.

4.2   Other Applications

Logistic regression may be applied in many areas such as traffic lights recognition, red eye effect detection and 3D glasses detection. In this section we briefly present such applications. Apart from before mentioned applications we have successfully applied logistic regression to skin detection as shown in [1,8] and [7].

Traffic Lights. Autonomous vehicles and digital assistants are the hot topics in applied machine learning. Recognition of traffic lights is crucial part of any autonomous driving system or digital assistant for visually impaired person. For this problem MLR is a natural candidate and it was used in the INSGIMA project [4]. Since the traffic light is a glowing object, the MLR models tend to be quite simple and only basic R, G and B components are used for prediction. Dependent variable is a factor representing red light, green light and the background (mostly gray and blue). Given an input RGB image, the model produces two probability maps: one for red and one for green light. Because background contains reds and greens (e.g. leaves or rear lights of the vehicles) additional strong classifier has to be used to filter objects. In our approach, the recognition pipeline goes as follow:

1. Probability maps from MLR.
2. Thresholding probability maps at high probability (e.g. 0.8 - this controls specificity).
3. Morphological operations (or Gaussian blur before thresholding) to make object smooth.
4. Candidate object extraction (contour extraction).
5. Candidate filtration by an SVM classifier on DCT coefficients used as features, in the similar way as in [21].

Further details about traffic light recognition by MLR are out of scope of this paper, however, for interested reader, in Table 1 we report the learned numerical values of the model coefficients.

Table 1. Numerical values for learned MLR color models (β).

	Skin	Red light β_0	Green light β_1	Unshave face	Red eye
Range	$<0,1>$	$<0,255>$	$<0,255>$	$<0,1>$	$<0,255>$
r	-3.35	0.0642	-0.0728	-5.09	0.16
g	23.26	-0.0894	0.1246	-24.29	-0.23
b	-8.58	0.0319	-0.0544	16.04	0.06
r^2	$-10,69$	-	-	25.29	-
g^2	-45.23	-	-	-74.0	-
b^2	108.52	-	-	-908.71	-
rg	-25.71	-	-	-149.58	-
gb	96.62	-	-	$748,4$	-
rb	77.51	-	-	640	-
r^3	4.42	-	-	-310.5	-
g^3	0.96	-	-	-69.19	-
b^3	8.75	-	-	134.93	-
1	-10.96	-5.3224	-3.6763	-21.62	-4.30

Red Eye. Red eye effect appears when the camera flash light is reflected in the eyes and makes them glowing in red. This effect decreases quality of a photography and digital cameras apply algorithm for removing the effect. However, algorithm may fail. Checking large number of images for this effect requires large amount of human interaction. However, having color samples of skin, lips hairs and background, one can construct a MLR by putting them into single negative class and samples of red eye effect color into positive class. This combined with pupils detection [21] makes an accurate red eye effect detector. This approach was used in the IMCOP project and again in Table 1 we report the learned numerical values of the model coefficients.

Object Detection. Object detection and classification is one of the most important application of computer vision. In general it is complicated task requiring powerful machine learning tools. However, the task gets simplified if the object to be detected can be distinguished from the background by its color.

Such a case when the object detection takes place in a controlled environment and the designer is free to select color of the object. This was the case in the SARACEN project [15] demonstration application.

The objective was to detect weather person watching a movie wears 3D glasses or not. In order to make segmentation from the background as simple as possible vivid orange colored glasses were used. Simple logistic regression on RGB components did the job of object extraction efficiently and accurately.

In most cases we are not allowed to prepare object for detection. But still there are situations where color model is the best first step in object detection.

Consider an object detection system designed for a corporate. Companies quite often introduce visual identity. Logos, documents, uniforms and tools have unified color palette. In such case color model trained for this particular corporate palette finds all objects of interest such as worker in a uniform.

Despite model being tailored for a particular company. It is still flexible as the new visual identity requires only retraining color model, the application logic stays the same.

5   Summary

In this paper we have shown the applicability of logistic regression in the task of background substitution. The specific problem we have solved was automated generation of samples for training of machine learning algorithms. We have identified problems encountered in the task of background substitution related to the distortion on the borders of the objects. The proposed solution was to extend the object hue to neighboring pixels using a Gaussian filter with a small kernel.

In future work we will focus on proving the positive effect on the effectiveness of machine learning algorithms when trained on a set consisting of a mixture of natural and CGI generated samples.

Acknowledgment. This work was supported by the Polish National Center for Research and Development under the LIDER Grant (No. LIDER/354/L-6/14/NCBR/2015).

References

1. Baran, R., Zeja, A.: The imcop system for data enrichment and content discovery and delivery. In: 2015 International Conference on Computational Science and Computational Intelligence (CSCI), pp. 143–146, December 2015
2. Bishop, C.: Pattern Recognition and Machine Learning. Information Science and Statistics. Springer, New York (2006)
3. Cheng, V., Kehtarnavaz, N.: A smart camera application: Dsp-based people detection and tracking. J. Electron. Imaging **9**(3), 336–346 (2000). http://dx.doi.org/10.1117/1.482749
4. Chmiel, W., Szwed, P.: Learning fuzzy cognitive map for traffic prediction using an evolutionary algorithm. In: Dziech, A., Leszczuk, M., Baran, R. (eds.) MCSS 2015. CCIS, vol. 566, pp. 195–209. Springer, Cham (2015). doi:10.1007/978-3-319-26404-2_16
5. Cucchiara, R., Grana, C., Prati, A., Vezzani, R.: Probabilistic posture classification for human-behavior analysis. IEEE Trans. Syst. Man Cybern. Part A: Syst. Hum. **35**(1), 42–54 (2005)
6. Elgammal, A., Harwood, D., Davis, L.: Non-parametric model for background subtraction. In: Vernon, D. (ed.) ECCV 2000. LNCS, vol. 1843, pp. 751–767. Springer, Heidelberg (2000). doi:10.1007/3-540-45053-X_48
7. Eshkol, A., Grega, M., Leszczuk, M., Weintraub, O.: Practical application of near duplicate detection for image database. In: Dziech, A., Czyżewski, A. (eds.) MCSS 2014. CCIS, vol. 429, pp. 73–82. Springer, Cham (2014). doi:10.1007/978-3-319-07569-3_6
8. Grega, M., Bryk, D., Napora, M.: Inact-indect advanced image cataloguing tool. Multimedia Tools Appl. **68**(1), 95–110 (2014). http://dx.doi.org/10.1007/s11042-012-1164-3
9. Haritaoglu, I., Harwood, D., Davis, L.S.: W4: real-time surveillance of people and their activities. IEEE Trans. Pattern Anal. Mach. Intell. **22**(8), 809–830 (2000)
10. Hastie, T., Tibshirani, R., Friedman, J.: The Elements of Statistical Learning: Data Mining, Inference, and Prediction. Springer Series in Statistics, 2nd edn. Springer, New York (2009). https://books.google.pl/books?id=tVIjmNS3Ob8C
11. Inaguma, T., Saji, H., Nakatani, H.: Hand motion tracking based on a constraint of three-dimensional continuity. J. Electron. Imaging **14**(1), 013021-1–013021-9 (2005). http://dx.doi.org/10.1117/1.1867473
12. James, G., Witten, D., Hastie, T., Tibshirani, R.: An Introduction to Statistical Learning: with Applications in R. Springer Texts in Statistics. Springer, New York (2014). https://books.google.pl/books?id=at1bmAEACAAJ
13. KaewTraKulPong, P., Bowden, R.: An improved adaptive background mixture model for real-time tracking with shadow detection. In: Remagnino, P., Jones, G.A., Paragios, N., Regazzoni, C.S. (eds.) Video-Based Surveillance Systems, pp. 135–144. Springer US, Boston (2002). https://doi.org/10.1007/978-1-4615-0913-4_11
14. Kim, K., Chalidabhongse, T.H., Harwood, D., Davis, L.: Real-time foreground-background segmentation using codebook model. Real-Time Imaging **11**(3), 172–185 (2005). http://dx.doi.org/10.1016/j.rti.2004.12.004
15. Leszczuk, M., Juszka, D., Janowski, L., Grega, M., Cruz, R., Nunes, M., Patrikakis, C., Papapanagiotou, S.: Quality aware, adaptive, 3D media distribution over P2P architectures. In: 2013 IEEE Globecom Workshops (GC Wkshps), pp. 1133–1138, December 2013

16. Makris, D., Ellis, T.: Learning semantic scene models from observing activity in visual surveillance. IEEE Trans. Syst. Man Cybern. Part B (Cybern.) **35**(3), 397–408 (2005)
17. MathWorks: Statistics and machine learning toolbox user's guide. Technical report, MathWorks, Inc. (2015). http://www.mathworks.com/help/releases/R2015a/pdf_doc/stats/stats.pdf
18. Mineiro, P.: fastapprox - fast approximate functions. https://code.google.com/archive/p/fastapprox/
19. Neves, C.: Categorical Data Analysis, 3rd edn., p. 41 (2014)
20. Oliver, N.M., Rosario, B., Pentland, A.P.: A bayesian computer vision system for modeling human interactions. IEEE Trans. Pattern Anal. Mach. Intell. **22**(8), 831–843 (2000)
21. Rusek, K., Guzik, P.: Two-stage neural network regression of eye location in face images. Multimedia Tools Appl. **75**(17), 10617–10630 (2016). https://doi.org/10.1007/s11042-014-2114-z
22. Stauffer, C., Grimson, W.E.L.: Adaptive background mixture models for real-time tracking. In: Proceedings of the 1999 IEEE Computer Society Conference on Computer Vision and Pattern Recognition (Cat. No PR00149), vol. 2, p. 252 (1999)
23. Wren, C., Azarbayejani, A., Darrell, T., Pentland, A.: Pfinder: real-time tracking of the human body. IEEE Trans. Pattern Anal. Mach. Intell. **19**, 780–785 (1997)
24. Zivkovic, Z.: Improved adaptive gaussian mixture model for background subtraction. In: Proceedings of the 17th International Conference on Pattern Recognition, ICPR 2004, vol. 2, pp. 28–31, August 2004

Intrusion Prevention System Decision Diagram in Security-as-a-Service Solutions

Tytus Kurek$^{(\boxtimes)}$, Marcin Niemiec, Artur Lason, and Andrzej R. Pach

AGH University of Science and Technology, Mickiewicza 30, 30-059 Krakow, Poland
{kurek,niemiec,lason,pach}@kt.agh.edu.pl

Abstract. Intrusion prevention systems are widely used as one of the core security services deployed by the majority of contemporary organizations. Although simple in operation, they tend to be difficult to configure due to the wide range of vendors using different algorithms to implement intrusion prevention system security policies. The most popular, rule-based representation of intrusion prevention system security policies frequently suffers from redundant, conflicting and deficient security rules which may lead to confusion and misconfigurations. This article introduces and presents the intrusion prevention system decision diagram as a new and formal representation of signature-based intrusion prevention system security policies. It is shown that in this diagram the issue of redundant, conflicting and deficient security rules is fully eliminated. Thanks to a tree-based structure the intrusion prevention system decision diagram is also well suited for use in privacy-preserving solutions for cloud-based security services. Finally, with fewer computationally-expensive pattern-matching operations, the intrusion prevention system decision diagram is a better performing packet examination engine than the rule-based engine. This finding was confirmed by experimental results.

Keywords: IPS · Decision tree · SecaaS · Cloud computing · Privacy

1 Introduction

IPS (*Intrusion Prevention Systems*) are widely used by the majority of contemporary organizations [1]. In 2014, the IPS market was valued at US$ 500 000 000 in the Asia/Pacific region alone [2]. As the numbers of IPS appliances in use grow, their percentage among other security systems also increases, making IPS services almost as important as network firewall services. Of the two main types of IPS as described later, signature-based IPS are the most prevalent [3]. Using regularly updated databases of know attack patterns, signature-based IPS appliances detect intrusion events as well as being capable of taking preventive actions in order to minimize the risk of a security violation; becoming a key element of the security infrastructure [4].

© Springer International Publishing AG 2017
A. Dziech and A. Czyżewski (Eds.): MCSS 2017, CCIS 785, pp. 47–61, 2017.
https://doi.org/10.1007/978-3-319-69911-0_4

Signature-based IPS security policies are generally implemented as a set of programmable security rules similar to those used in firewalls. ACL (*Access Control Lists*) consist of multiple ACE (*Access Control Entries*) which compromise elements representing particular fields in packet headers to be examined and actions to be taken. In signature-based IPS, ACE are extended with an additional object known as the signature representing a known attack pattern. Although this method of implementing signature-based IPS security policies does not seem to be complex, implementations are vendor-specific and differ across various platforms. Moreover, in contrast to firewall services whose security policies are always processed top-down from the ACL, actual algorithms used to process signature-based IPS security policies are also vendor-specific and sometimes closed-source [5]. Thus signature-based IPS suffer from a lack of a formal representation of their security policies.

Another problem with security policies represented as ACL is redundant, conflicting and deficient security rules. According to research performed in [6,7], the majority of ACL deployed by organizations are poorly implemented and have configuration errors in their ACE. This applies to both firewall and signature-based IPS services. Redundant rules in signature-based IPS result from compactness problems and occur if the security rules are simply doubled. In turn, conflicting rules are result from consistency problems and occur if the order in which security rules should be processed is changed accidentally. Finally, deficient rules result from completeness problems and occur if the programmed security rules do not take into account all possible traffic types.

Although easy to program, the rule-based representation of signature-based IPS security policies is not an optimal packet examination engine in terms of performance. This is because the rule-based engine requires many computationally-expensive pattern-matching operations to be performed in order to conduct the signature-matching operations. As such, the vast majority of IPS vendors use either modified or completely different algorithms to implement the packet examination engine [4]. For example, the Snort software – the most popular open-source IDS (*Intrusion Detection System*) software – uses a method of grouping programmed security rules by protocol type, ports and IP (*Internet Protocol*) addresses [8]. The fewer pattern-matching operations are performed, the better the performance of the IPS.

This article introduces the IPSDD (*Intrusion Prevention System Decision Diagram*) as a new representation of signature-based IPS security policies. The IPSDD is universal and scalable, so it can be used to represent all existing and future signature-based IPS security policies regardless of the vendor. Therefore, the IPSDD is assumed to be a formal representation of signature-based IPS security policies, and it can be regarded as an open source framework for all signature-based IPS implementations. Additionally, by addressing the compactness, consistency and completeness problems, it is shown that the IPSDD fully eliminates the issue of redundant, conflicting and deficient security rules.

Another important feature of the IPSDD is its applicability for privacy-preserving solutions for SecaaS (*Security-as-a-Service*) services [9]. It is shown that thanks to its tree-based structure the IPSDD is well suited to preserving confidentiality of cloud-based IPS security policies for signature-based IPS. The solution is based on an existing privacy-preserving framework for cloud-based firewall services, referred to as the LHC (*Ladon Hybrid Cloud*) [10]. Finally, the article demonstrates that the IPSDD can also be used as a high-performance packet examination engine. This is because fewer pattern-matching operations are performed in the IPSDD compared to the rule-based engine. To confirm this, an experiment in which the same packet set was examined against the signature-based IPS security policy implemented in the rule-based and IPSDD representation was conducted. The hypothesis is verified by experimental results.

The main contribution of this article is an introduction of decision-tree-based representation of signature-based IPS security policies which can be characterized by the following features compared to the existing solutions of this type:

- It can be used to represent all existing and future signature-based IPS security policies,
- It eliminates the issue of redundant, conflicting and deficient security rules,
- It can be used in existing privacy-preserving frameworks for SecaaS services like the LHC,
- It achieves better performance results than the rule-based engine.

The rest of the article proceeds as follows. Related work is reviewed in Sect. 2. In Sect. 3, the IPSDD is introduced and presented with its definition and generation algorithm. An example usage of the IPSDD for preserving confidentiality of cloud-based IPS security policies for signature-based IPS is shown in Sect. 4, including directions for future work on this topic. Experimental results concerning the IPSDD performance follow in Sect. 5. Finally, Sect. 6 concludes the article.

2   Related Work

Although the issue of formal, universal and scalable representation of signature-based IPS security policies is important, no research has been carried out on this topic thus far. There is also no research related to redundant, conflicting and deficient security rules in the rule-based representation of signature-based IPS security policies. However, some research has been conducted into how the representation of signature-based IPS security policies affects the performance of the packet examination engine. The most important items are discussed below.

In [11], Alsubhi et al. examine the impact of enforcement levels of signature-based IPS security policies on the performance of the packet examination engine. By applying different security policies with varying degrees of restrictiveness, they found a relationship and a tradeoff between the complexity of the security policies and the IPS performance. Similar studies were performed in [12]. In [13], Chen and Yang propose a new framework known as the ARM (*Attack-Response Matrix*) to transform the IDS security policies to the IPS security policies in firewalls with intrusion prevention capabilities. The show that this structure performs better compared to passive intrusion detection.

Other fields of study related to the topic of this article are these related to decision trees. In [14], Gouda and Liu introduce and present a mathematical structure known as the FDD (*Firewall Decision Diagram*) as a formal representation the firewall security policies. In contrast to the ACL, the FDD represents firewall security policies in a form similar to the BDD (*Binary Decision Diagram*) [15] where packets are examined top-down with contents of individual fields examined on different levels of the FDD. They show that by dealing with compactness, consistency and completeness problems, the FDD fully eliminates the issue of redundant, conflicting and deficient security rules. Detailed algorithms for generating, reducing, marking, compacting and simplifying the FDD are also presented there. Other notable studies related to the BDD, decision trees and privacy-preserving of outsourced data are [16–20].

In [9], the authors introduced a framework, referred to as the LHC, for preserving confidentiality of cloud-based firewall security policies. By leveraging an anonymized firewall based on BFFDD (*Bloom Filter Firewall Decision Diagram*) and a hybrid cloud model they showed that in this framework a high level of privacy is provided. They also demonstrated that it is possible to find a trade-off between the LHC privacy level, its congestion probability and efficiency. Although the LHC was originally designed as a privacy-preserving framework for cloud-based firewall services, it is applicable for preserving confidentiality of security policies of cloud-based service of any type as long as its security policies can be represented as a decision tree. Privacy-preserving solutions for cloud-based IDS (*Intrusion Detection System*) services were studied by the authors in [21]. To the best knowledge of the authors, there has been no previous research on privacy-preserving solutions for cloud-based IPS services.

3   IPSDD

This section introduces and presents the IPSDD as a new and formal representation of signature-based IPS security policies. The IPSDD is a decision tree structure based on the FDD presented in [13], but extended with additional characteristics specific to the signature-based IPS. These characteristics are an additional field representing the signature ID and a set of actions on terminal nodes instead of a single action. Similarly to the FDD, in the IPSDD packets are examined top-down with contents of individual fields and matched signature IDs examined on different levels of the IPSDD. As a result, a set of actions is returned representing preventive actions to be taken by the IPS. Before examining the IPSDD in more depth, it is important to review the most important facts regarding the signature-based IPS, principles of its operations and the rule-based representation of its security policies.

3.1   IPS Background

The signature-based IPS operates on the basis of signatures which represent know attack patterns [22]. In practice, the signatures are written as regular expressions and kept in a regularly updated database in a numbered order [23]. Each signature has a unique ID. During packet examination, content of the packet is examined against signatures defined in the IPS security policy. For each defined signature, a separate pattern-matching operation is performed. Another, less popular type of IPS, which operates on the basis of baselines generated during regular network operations, is an anomaly-based IPS. Moreover, some vendors offer hybrid solutions, and new intrusion detection methods are being researched. This article focuses on signature-based IPS only as it is the most prevalent type of IPS; signature-based IPS will be referred to as simply IPS in the remainder of the article.

According to [24], IPS security policies define the desired properties of the IPS based on the value of the assets that should be protected, the expected threats, and the cost of protection mechanisms. They state which behavior of the potential intruder is considered to be malicious and what actions should be taken in an event of an intrusion. IPS security policies are usually implemented as a set of programmable security rules similar to the ACL used in firewalls. The main difference is that although in firewalls ACL are used for security policy representation and packet examination, in the IPS the security rules are used for security policy representation only. The algorithms used for packet examination are vendor-specific and often closed-source. IPS security policies are usually implemented in an open format. In this case, only some of the traffic examined by the IPS is assumed to be malicious, with adequate security rules in place to deal with this. The remainder of the traffic is assumed to be non-malicious and it is allowed to pass without any actions being taken.

A sample IPS security policy is shown in Listing 1. Each security rule consists of four elements representing actions to be taken, with values of individual packet fields matching source IP address, destination IP address, and signature ID. In practice, the IPS security policy usually consists of more fields and individual implementations are vendor-specific; however, to facilitate the following discussion only two fields were assumed here. The values of the fourth field, representing the signature ID, were taken from the Snort signatures database [7]. An additional signature with an ID of 0 matching any packet content was assumed. In the presented security policy, the IPS:

- logs all packets sourced in the 149.156.0.0/16 network and destined to the 10.0.0.0/9 network
- logs all packets sourced in the 149.156.0.0/16 network and destined to the 10.128.0.0/9 network if they contain potential SSL Heartbleed attempts
- terminates all packets sourced in the 149.156.0.0/16 network and destined to the 10.128.0.0/9 network if they contain SQL injection attempts
- attempts to reset the TCP connection for all packets sourced in the 149.156.0.0/16 network and destined to all networks other than the 10.0.0.0/8 network if they contain the keyword "/bash"

Listing 1. Sample rule-based IPS security policy

```
log-attacker-packets
149.156.0.0/16
10.0.0.0/9
0-32608
log-attacker-packets
149.156.0.0/16
10.128.0.0/9
30514-30517,30777-30788
deny-packet-inline
149.156.0.0/16
10.128.0.0/9
2063
reset-tcp-connection
149.156.0.0/16
0.0.0.0-9.255.255.255,11.0.0.0-255.255.255.255
885
deny-packet-inline,produce-alert
0.0.0.0-149.155.255.255,149.157.0.0-255.255.255.255
0.0.0.0/0
213
```

– raises an alert and terminates all packets sources in all networks other than the 149.156.0.0/16 network and destined to all networks if they contain Linux rootkit attempts

All other traffic passes without any action being taken.

As already shown, both packet content, and packet fields are examined against the IPS security policy. While packet field examination operations are simple, packet content examination operations are complex. This is because packet content examination operations run computationally-expensive pattern-matching operations in the background [25–27]. Therefore, an effective IPS packet examination engine should run as few pattern-matching operations as possible.

3.2 IPSDD Definition

The following section introduces and presents a mathematical description of the IPSDD. Further discussion shows how the IPSDD deals with the problems of rule-based representation of the IPS security policy described above.

Field F_j is a variable whose domain, denoted as $D(F_j)$, is a finite interval of non-negative integers. *Signature S_k* is an association of *pattern t_k* and *ID d_k*. The *pattern t_k* is a finite array of characters. The *ID d_k* is a non-negative integer. *Actions A* is a set of finite arrays of characters. A *packet* over fields $F_1,...,F_d$ is a d-tuple $(p_1, ..., p_d)$ where each p_j ($1 \leq j < d$) is an element of $D(F_j)$ and p_d matches at least one t_k. A d_k associated with t_k is an element of $D(F_d)$.

An *intrusion prevention system decision diagram* (IPSDD) i over fields $F_1,...,F_d$ is an acyclic and directed graph that has the following five properties:

1. There is exactly one node in i that has no incoming edges. This node is called the *root* of i. The nodes in i that have no outgoing edges are called *terminal nodes* of i.
2. Each node n in i is labelled with a field, denoted as F_n, such that $F_d \in F_1,...,F_d$ if n is non-terminal and $F_n \subseteq A$ if n is terminal.
3. Each edge e in i is labelled with a non-empty set of integers, denoted as $I(e)$, such that if e is an outgoing edge of node n, then $I(e) \subseteq D(F_n)$.
4. A direct path in i from the root to a terminal node, denoted $\langle n_1 e_1 ... n_d e_d n_{d+1} \rangle$, is known as a *decision path* and satisfies the following condition:
   - *Compactness:* $\bigcup_{m=1}^{d}(I(e_m) \cap I(e'_m)) = \emptyset$ for any two distinct decision paths $\langle n_1 e_1 ... n_d e_d n_{d+1} \rangle$ and $\langle n_1 e'_1 ... n'_d e'_d n'_{d+1} \rangle$ in i.

   No two nodes on a decision path have the same label.
5. The set of all a outgoing edges of a node n in i, denoted $E(n)$, satisfies the following two conditions:
   - *Consistency:* $I(e) \cap I(e') = \emptyset$ for any two distinct edges e and e'.
   - *Completeness:* $\bigcup_{m=1}^{a} I(e_m) = D(F_n)$.

A sample IPSDD representing the IPS security policy from Listing 1 is shown in Fig. 1. The IPSDD is over three fields representing source and destination IP addresses of a packet and the matched signature ID. The domain of the fields representing source and destination IP addresses is the $[0, 2^{32} - 1]$ interval. The domain of the field representing matched signature ID is the $[0, 32608]$ interval. The IPSDD consists of 15 nodes, seven of which, marked as examined fields, are non-terminal nodes, and the remaining eighth, marked with an "action" prefix, are terminal nodes. All edge sets are represented in a legible form. The A set consists of the following arrays of characters: *"deny-packet-inline"*, *"log-attacker-packets"*, *"none"*, *"produce-alert"*, and *"reset-tcp-connection"*, representing actions to be taken by the IPS.

The IPSDD itself can also be used as a packet examination engine, and it does not require any other algorithms to be implemented. In order to determine a decision path for a packet, the IPSDD performs a test from the root to the terminal node. On each node, the corresponding packet field is examined. The value of the field is searched in the outgoing edge sets of the node and the corresponding outgoing edge is selected. Once this is complete, the packet is moved to the next node indicated by the outgoing edge, and the path between these two nodes starts forming the decision path. On the last non-terminal node, the packet content is matched against the signatures whose IDs belong to the outgoing edge sets. The ID of the first signature that matches is used to determine the outgoing edge. Finally, the packet reaches the terminal node and the full decision path is determined. The label of the terminal node represents the actions to be taken by the IPSDD on the packet.

Let us consider a sample packet sourced by a host with an IP address of 149.156.1.2, destined to a host with an IP address of 10.128.3.4, and containing

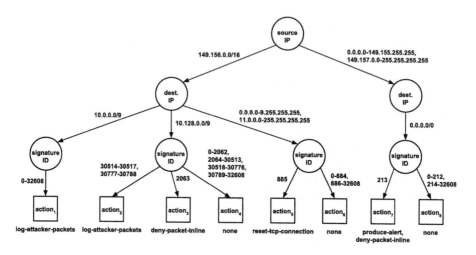

Fig. 1. The intrusion prevention system decision diagram

an SQL injection attempt being tested in the IPSDD. The packet field containing the source IP address is examined first. As the 149.156.1.2 value is found in the 149.156.0.0/16 set, the corresponding outgoing edge is selected. Next, the packet field containing the destination IP address is examined. The 10.128.3.4 value is found in the 10.128.0.0/9 set, and thus the corresponding outgoing edge is selected. Finally, packet content is examined, first against the signatures ranging between 30514–30517 and 30777–30788. As the packet content does not match any of the attack patterns defined in these signatures, it is later examined against the signature with the ID of 2063. This time there is a match and the corresponding outgoing edge is selected. The decision path terminates on the terminal node marked as *"log-attacker-packet, deny-packet-inline"*. As a result the IPS will starts logging all packets sourced in the host with the IP address of 149.156.1.2 and terminates the packet.

The IPSDD is universal and scalable: universal, since it can be used to represent all existing IPS security policies, and scalable, since it can be used to represent all future IPS security policies. This is due to its flexibility; the IPSDD is not tied to specific packet fields, but rather it can be used to represent any packet fields. Therefore, the IPSDD is a formal representation of IPS security policies. Additionally, as shown, the IPSDD fully eliminates the issue of redundant, conflicting and deficient security rules which are common in rule-based representations of IPS security policies. This is because the IPSDD satisfies the compactness, consistency and completeness conditions. Thus the IPSDD is an ideal open-source framework for IPS implementations.

3.3   IPSDD Generation and Decision Path Computation

The IPSDD generation algorithm is shown in the Algorithm 1 listing. It takes the rule-based IPS security policy as the input, and generates the IPSDD as the

---

Algorithm 1. IPSDD generation

Input: Rule-based IPS security policy
Output: IPSDD
Steps:

1. For each security rule from the rule-based IPS security policy, read the rule ID, actions and the remaining elements.
2. For each element, sort the security rules within the same value of the preceding element.
3. For each security rule, check whether elements of the preceding or following rule include the elements of the rule. If so, check whether the rules have different, non-conflicting decisions. Merge the rules if so, and repeat the process until no more rules can be merged.
4. For each security rule, check whether elements of the preceding or following rule include the elements of the rule. If so, check whether the rules have different, conflicting decisions. Remove the rule with the higher rule ID if so, and repeat the process until no more rules can be removed.
5. For each security rule, for each element j, check whether e of n_j whose $I(e)$ represents j exists. If not, create it and the corresponding n_{j+1}. Move to n_{j+1} indicated by e whose $I(e)$ represents j.
6. For each n_j from $(n_1,...,n_{d-1})$ in i check whether sum of all its $I(e)$ equals to $D(F_{n_j})$. If no, create e whose $I(e)$ equals to missing set and corresponding n_{j+1}. Repeat the above process until no more new e can be created.
7. For each n_d in i check whether the sum of all its $I(e)$ is equal to $D(F_{nd})$. If not, create e whose $I(e)$ is equal to the missing set and the corresponding n_{d+1} marked as *"none"*. The resulting structure is the IPSDD.

Algorithm 2. Decision path computation

Input: IPSDD, packet
Output: Decision path
Steps:

1. Read $(p_1,...,p_d)$ from the network packet.
2. For each p_j from $(p_1,...,p_{d-1})$, for each e of n_j of i sorted ascending by $card(I(e))$, check for the presence of p_j in $I(e)$ and move to n_{j+1} indicated by e if true.
3. For each e of n_d sorted ascending by $card(I(e))$, check whether p_d matches any element of $I(e)$ and move to n_{d+1} indicated by e if true. The resulting path is the decision path.

---

output. Point 3 ensures the compactness condition, point 4 ensures the consistency condition, and points 6 and 7 ensure the completeness condition. In turn, the decision path computation algorithm is shown in the Algorithm 2 listing. It takes the IPSDD and the packet as the input, and provides the decision path as the output.

4   IPSDD in SecaaS Solutions

The main motivation when designing the IPSDD was its applicability for SecaaS services. The authors found that tree-based structures are well suited to representing security policies of cloud-based security services in privacy-preserving solutions. However, detailed description of motivations behind the need to preserve the privacy of cloud-based security services is out of scope of this article, it can be found in [9,19]. The following section presents a sample privacy-preserving platform based on the IPSDD and the LHC for cloud-based IPS services. Directions for future work on applicability of the IPSDD for solutions of this type are also noted. It is shown that the IPSDD has huge potential and that the number of use cases for the IPSDD keeps growing.

4.1   IPSDD in LHC Framework

Although the LHC was originally designed as a privacy-preserving framework for cloud-based firewall services, with the introduction of the IPSDD it is also well suited for cloud-based IPS services. Such a framework uses the hybrid cloud model and implements the BFIPSDD (*Bloom Filter Intrusion Prevention System Decision Diagram*) in a public cloud, and the regular IPSDD in a private cloud. The IPSDD represents the client's IPS security policy, whereas the BFIPSDD is formed from the IPSDD by replacing its edge sets with BF (*Bloom Filters*). Because of the false positive rate of BF building the BFIPSDD, it can return multiple conflicting actions (i.e. *"none"* and *"deny-packet-inline"*) when examining network packets, resulting in an uncertainty regarding the desired actions to be taken. Furthermore, to further increase this uncertainty, the BFIPSDD is re-designed to always return multiple conflicting actions for packets for which preventive actions should be taken. Because of this forced uncertainty, the CSP (*Cloud Service Provider*) is deprived of most of the information regarding the IPS security policy which it can gather by traffic eavesdropping and analysis.

This concept is shown in Fig. 2. Unmalicious packets are represented there by plain envelopes, whereas malicious packets are represented by striped envelopes. All packets enter the public cloud first (step 1) where they are examined in the BFIPSDD (step 2). Those for which no actions are returned by the BFIPSDD are transmitted directly to the client's network via a trusted link, represented by the continuous line (step 3). In turn, those for which any action is returned are transmitted to the private cloud on the client's premises via an untrusted link, represented by the striped line (step 4), where an additional examination in the regular IPSDD takes place (step 5). Next, unmalicious packets are transmitted to the client's network via a trusted link (step 6) where they join unmalicious packet streams transmitted directly from the public cloud (step 7). As a result the private cloud is offloaded and the privacy of the IPS security policy is preserved.

4.2   Future Work

Solution presented above is not the only use case for the IPSDD in privacy-preserving solutions for cloud-based IPS services. The authors have already

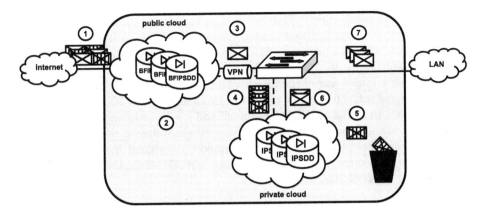

Fig. 2. Ladon hybrid cloud for intrusion prevention system services

started a research on a universal privacy-preserving framework for cloud-based security services of any type. This solution is based on a tree-based structure representing security policies of the cloud-based service and the hybrid cloud model. As in the LHC, the tree-based structure is implemented in the public cloud, but instead of regular decisions it returns masked decisions when examining network packets. The masked decisions are then transferred together with network packets to the private cloud where they are unmasked and processed accordingly. For a purpose of preserving privacy of cloud-based IPS services in this novel solution, the IPSDD is the best candidate.

5 Experimental Results

In order to demonstrate that the IPSDD is a more effective packet examination engine than the rule-based engine, the following simulations were conducted. Based on Algorithm 1, a program which transforms a rule-based IPS security policy into the IPSDD was implemented. This program will be referred to as the "generator" in the rest of the article. Furthermore, based on Algorithm 2, another program which computes the decision path for a given packet in the IPSDD was implemented. This second program will be referred to as the "IPSDD tester" in the rest of the article. Finally, one more program for a purpose of packet examination in the ACL, referred to as the "ACL tester" in the rest of the article, was implemented. All programs were written in Python. Existing solutions like Snort were intentionally avoided to ensure that the maximum possible reliability of the results is obtained. However, Snort code was used to perform the signature-matching operation itself both in the IPSDD tester and the ACL tester. The rule-based IPS security policy from Listing 1 was then transformed into the IPSDD using the generator.

Next, a set of 100 000 randomly generated packets was tested against both the rule-based IPS security policy from Listing 1 using the ACL tester and the resulting IPSDD using the IPSDD tester. Corresponding packet examination times were gathered, marked as t_r and t_i respectively in the rest of the article. The above tests were performed on 11 different sets, each with a different ratio of packets resulting in the "none" action, referred to as a "good packet ratio" and marked as g in the rest of the article. The good packet ratio ranged from 0 to 1 with steps of 0.1. The results are shown in Table 1. It also shows the rate of t_r to t_i, referred to as the "IPSDD efficiency" and marked as f in the rest of the article. They are grouped by rows depending on the value of the good packet ratio of the tested set. All tests were performed on a virtual machine running CentOS 6.5 with a single virtual Intel(R) Core(TM) i5-3320M CPU @ 2.60GHz processor and 4 GB of 1600 MHz memory.

Table 1. Experimental results

g	t_r [s]	t_i [s]	f
0	7007	140	50.05
0.1	6118	141	43.39
0.2	5466	133	41.10
0.3	4886	141	34.65
0.4	4672	173	27.01
0.5	4337	171	25.36
0.6	3200	173	18.50
0.7	2699	223	12.10
0.8	2002	213	9.40
0.9	1293	201	6.43
1	668	269	2.48

Graphs representing functions of packet examination time in the ACL tester, packet examination time in the IPSDD tester, and the IPSDD efficiency of the good packet ratio argument are shown in Figs. 3, 4 and 5 respectively. The good packet ratio is shown on the ordinate, whereas the packet examination times and the IPSDD efficiency are shown on the abscissa. The simulations clearly show that the IPSDD is a better performing packet examination engine than the rule-based engine. It can also be seen that the lower the value of the good packet ratio, the higher the value of the IPSDD efficiency.

Shorter packet examination times in the IPSDD tester are a result of a smaller number of pattern-matching operations being performed in the IPSDD compared to the ACL. This is because in the IPSDD each packet field, including the content, is examined only once while in the ACL they are examined again in each ACE. As pattern-matching operations are the most computationally-expensive operations in the whole packet examination process, the smaller the number of them, the better the performance. Similarly, high values of the good packet ratio

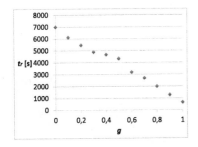

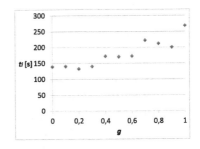

Fig. 3. Packet examination time in the ACL tester

Fig. 4. Packet examination time in the IPSDD tester

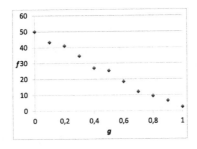

Fig. 5. IPSDD efficiency

have a positive impact on packet examination times in the ACL tester because during the packet examination process the engine often moves to the next ACE without a need to examine the content field. On the other hand they affect packet examination times in the IPSDD tester as decision paths associated with good packets rarely have one edge on the "signature ID" node.

6 Conclusions

This article introduces and presents the IPSDD as a new and formal representation of signature-based IPS security policies. The IPSDD is a decision tree structure which transforms the rule-based representation of the IPS security policies in a similar way to how the FDD transforms ACL. Additional extensions, specific to IPS security policies, are also introduced. The IPSDD is universal and scalable. It is shown that by ensuring the compactness, consistency and completeness conditions the IPSDD fully eliminates the issue of redundant, conflicting and deficient security rules, which are common in rule-based representations of IPS security policies.

The IPSDD can also be used for preserving confidentiality of cloud-based IPS security policies. A sample privacy-preserving solution based on the LHC framework is presented with directions for future work on this topic. Finally, by implementing the IPSDD and performing a simulation on a set of randomly generated packets, the authors show that the IPSDD is a better performing packet examination engine than the rule-based engine. It is also shown that the higher the value of the good packet ratio, the higher the value of the IPSDD efficiency.

The IPSDD changes the way IPS security policies are represented, configured and implemented. In return, it provides an IPS security policy with no redundant, conflicting or deficient security rules. Thanks to its tree-based structure the IPSDD can be used for preserving the confidentiality of cloud-based IPS security policies. The solution based on the LHC framework is the first solution of this type. Finally, the IPSDD is also fast compared to the rule-based engine.

References

1. Bahrololum, M., Khaleghi, M.: Anomaly intrusion detection system using Gaussian mixture model. In 3rd International Conference on Convergence and Hybrid Information Technology, pp. 1162–1167 (2008)
2. Asia-Pacific Security Appliance Market to Reach $2.6bn: IDC. Computer Business Review. http://www.cbronline.com/news/security/asia-pacific-security-appliance-market-to-reach-26bn-idc-231112. Accessed 15 March 2017
3. Brox, A.: Signature-based and anomaly-based intrusion detection: the practice and pitfalls. SC Media. http://www.scmagazine.com/signature-based-or-anomaly-based-intrusion-detection-the-practice-and-pitfalls/article/30471/. Accessed 15 Mar 2017
4. Stoianov, N., Uruena, M., Niemiec, M., Machnik, P., Maestro, G.: Security infrastructures: towards the INDECT system security. Multimedia Communi. Serv. Secur. **287**, 304–315 (2012)
5. Tzur-David, S.: Network intrusion prevention systems: signature-based and anomaly detection. Ph.D. thesis, The Hebrew University of Jerusalem (2011)
6. Wool, A.: Trends in firewall configuration errors: measuring the holes in Swiss cheese. IEEE Internet Comput. **14**, 58–65 (2010)
7. Wool, A.: A quantitive study of firewall configuration errors. Computer **37**, 62–67 (2004)
8. The Snort Project. https://www.snort.org/. Accessed 15 Mar 2016
9. Varadharajan, V., Tupakula, U.: Security as a service Model for Cloud Environment. IEEE Trans. Netw. Serv. Manag. **11**, 60–75 (2014)
10. Kurek, T., Niemiec, M., Lason, A.: Taking back control of privacy: a novel framework for preserving cloud-based firewall policy confidentiality. Int. J. Inf. Secur. **15**(3), 235–250 (2016)
11. Alsubhi, K., Bouabdallah, N., Boutaba, R.: Performance analysis in intrusion detection and prevention systems. In: IFIP/IEEE International Symposium on Integrated Network Management, pp. 369–376 (2011)
12. Alsubhi, K., Alhazmi, Y., Bouabdallah, N., Boutaba, R.: Rule mode selection intrusion detection and prevention systems. In: IEEE Global Telecommunications Conference, pp. 1–6 (2011)
13. Chen, Y., Yang, Y.: Policy management for network-based intrusion detection and prevention. In: Network Operations and Management Symposium, pp. 219–232 (2004)
14. Gouda, M.G., Liu, A.X.: Structured firewall design. Comput. Netw. Int. J. Comput. Telecommun. Netw. **51**, 1106–1120 (2007)

15. Akers, S.B.: Binary decision diagrams. IEEE Trans. Comput. **27**, 509–516 (1978)
16. Fulp, E.W., Tarsa, S.J.: Trie-based policy representations for network firewalls. In: IEEE Symposium on Computers and Communications, pp. 434–441 (2005)
17. Bryant, R.E.: Graph-based algorithms for boolean function manipulation. IEEE Trans. Comput. **100**, 677–691 (1986)
18. Quinlan, J.R.: Induction of decision trees. Mach. Learn. **1**, 81–106 (1986)
19. Li, L.: Write-only oblivious RAM-based privacy-preserved access of outsourced data. Int. J. Inf. Secur. **16**, 23–42 (2017)
20. Markey, J.: Using decision tree analysis for intrusion detection: a how-to guide. https://www.sans.org/reading-room/whitepapers/detection/decision-tree-analysis-intrusion-detection-how-to-guide-33678. Accessed 07 Sept 2017
21. Kurek, T., Lason, A., Niemiec, M.: First step towards preserving the privacy of cloud-based IDS security policies. Secur. Commun. Netw. **8**(18), 3481–3491 (2015)
22. Greensmith, J., Aickelin, U.: Firewalls, Intrusion Detection Systems and Anti-Virus Scanners. University of Nottingham, Nottingham (2004)
23. Paquet, C.: Network Security Using Cisco IOS IPS, pp. 437–488. Cisco Press, Indianapolis (2009)
24. Kruegel, C., Valeur, F., Vigna, G.: Computer security and intrusion detection. In: Kruegel, C., Valeur, F., Vigna, G. (eds.) Intrusion Detection and Correlation, pp. 10–28. Springer, Boston (2005). doi:10.1007/0-387-23399-7_2
25. Goyvaerts, J.: Words, lines, and special characters. In: Goyvaerts, J., Levithan, S. (eds.) Regular Expressions Cookbook, p. 291. O'Reilly, Sebastopol (2009)
26. Yang, Y.E., Prasanna, V.K.: Space-time tradeoff in regular expression matching with semi-deterministic finite automa. In: Proceedings IEEE INFOCOM, pp. 1853–1861 (2011)
27. Jalali, A., Ghamarian, A., Rensink, A.: Incremental pattern matching for regular expressions. In: Proceedings of the 11th International Workshop on Graph Transformation and Visual Modeling Techniques (2012)

Semantically Enhanced Navigation System Using Augmented Reality

Krzysztof Kutt[✉], Grzegorz J. Nalepa, and Dominik Burdzy

AGH University of Science and Technology,
Al. Mickiewicza 30, 30-059 Krakow, Poland
{kkutt,gjn}@agh.edu.pl

Abstract. We present a navigation system combining augmented reality with semantic annotations of POIs. The prototype was implemented using regular Android smartphone and Google Cardboard. For semantic annotations we use RDF, SPARQL and a triplestore on the server. We developed a semantic information system integrated with a basic augmented reality interface.

Keywords: Augmented reality · Google Cardboard · Navigation system · Semantic annotations · POI

1 Background and Motivation

Today we can observe that multimedia systems combining augmented reality (AuR) and virtual reality (VR) have a lot of momentum (see [1,5,14] for a research survey). They can support many tasks, from entertainment such as games [15], to real life applications, such as navigation systems [8,10], medical imaging systems [16], ambient assisted living [3], etc. There are also attempts to extend current solutions to new areas of interest, e.g. there are studies that try to combine VR games with physiological signals analysis [7,11]. While the visual aspect of VR and AuR systems has been greatly improved in last years, number of challenges persist [13]. Some important ones include optimal interfaces for VR systems, as well as knowledge processing regarding the environment.

In this paper we introduce a prototype navigation system combining augmented reality with semantic description of the environment, forming a simple metadata information system. For providing the augmented reality experience, we use the *Google Cardboard*[1] technology combined with the image from the camera of a mobile phone. The original part includes the layer of semantic annotations for Points Of Interest (POI) in the user environment. We use Semantic Web technologies [4], namely the RDF [6] for annotations and SPARQL for querying [12] with a selected triplestore solutions. The system allows for an enhanced experience in terrain navigation, and can be further developed in an intelligent assistant.

The paper is supported by the AGH UST Grant.

[1] See https://vr.google.com/cardboard.

A. Dziech and A. Czyżewski (Eds.): MCSS 2017, CCIS 785, pp. 62–72, 2017.
https://doi.org/10.1007/978-3-319-69911-0_5

The rest of the paper is organized as follows. In Sect. 2 we provide the requirements specification of the system. Then in Sect. 3 we discuss its architecture and implementation. We discuss the developed prototype in Sect. 4. The paper is summarized in Sect. 5.

2 System Specification

Our motivation was to create an augmented reality system for terrain navigation that would address two issues: (1) how to find the Point of Interest (POI) based on user requirements that is open on specified time, and (2) how to navigate the user to the selected POI in the intuitive way.

Semantic database was selected as a storage due to the ease of processing, support for incomplete data and ease of extension with new element types and new attributes. In order for a user to be able to simultaneously navigate the city and use the system, the tool should be built using the mobile platform. To provide navigation understandable to everyone, it was decided to use the augmented reality: live image is obtained from the device camera and is supplemented by navigation elements such as arrows pointing the direction of the route.

In such a tool, two system roles have been specified: (a) Administrator that manages the database structure, (b) User that searches for and adds new POIs.

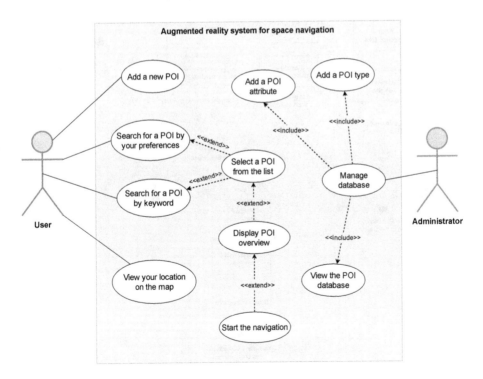

Fig. 1. Use Cases diagram for augmented reality system for space navigation.

In particular, the following use cases have been identified for these roles (see Fig. 1):

1. **View the POI database** – each user has a full POI database overview.
2. **Add a POI type** – an administrator can define the new object type, e.g. shop, post office or petrol station.
3. **Add a POI attribute** – an administrator can specify new object attribute, e.g. is_gas_available for petrol station.
4. **Add a new POI** – an user can define new POI by specifying the name, POI type and GPS coordinates. Other POI attributes are optional.
5. **Search for a POI by preferences** – an user can do a search by specifying the POI type, maximal distance to the destination and other optional attributes. Results are filtered using the specified time of departure.

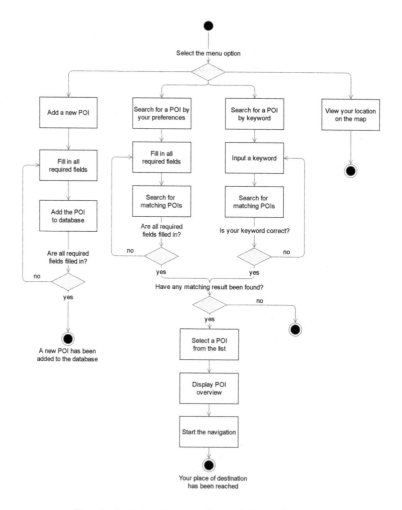

Fig. 2. Activity diagram for mobile application.

6. **Search for a POI by keyword** – an user can do a search using an arbitrary text phrase.
7. **Select a POI from the list** – an user can select a POI from the presented list of search results. Only basic information like name and GPS coordinates are displayed on the list.
8. **Display POI overview** – after POI selection, full POI description is presented.
9. **Start the navigation** – user puts the smartphone into the Google Cardboard and the augmented reality navigation starts.
10. **View your (current) location on the map**.

A general workflow for the main part of the system, the user mobile application, is summarized in Fig. 2.

3   Architecture and Implementation

Based on the specification an application was developed [2]. It is based on a client-server architecture. Server stores the data, both database schema and POIs information, and responds to requests from two types of clients. The first type of client is a web application that allows all users to browse the database, and administrators to easily maintain the server even without specific technical skills. Second type of client is a mobile application used by the system users. It communicates with the server using HTTP requests. A more comprehensive description of server and clients is provided in the following subsections.

3.1   Server and Web Client

Server was written using Java 8. Among other used technologies there are:

Spring[2] – an application framework for preparing application skeleton. Within the discussed system, mainly two sub-modules were used. Spring Boot was used for server configuration and startup without having to carry out a tedious deployment process. Spring Security was used for authentication. Sprint Test was used for preparing tests.
RDF4J[3] (formerly known as Sesame) – a framework for processing and analysing RDF data. It consists of a triplestore database and packages responsible for its maintenance. The triplestore is accessible through the SPARQL queries.
Apache Maven[4] – a tool for Java-based projects management.
Thymeleaf[5] – XML, XHTML and HTML5 templates engine. It provides an easy integration with Spring framework. It was used to create the web application pages.

---

[2] See: https://spring.io/.
[3] See: http://rdf4j.org/.
[4] See: http://maven.apache.org/.
[5] See: http://www.thymeleaf.org/.

Bootstrap[6] – HTML, CSS and JavaScript framework for developing responsive web interfaces and applications.

All server-related functionalities are packed using Model-View-Controller architectural pattern. There is also a Security module for authentication available (see Fig. 3).

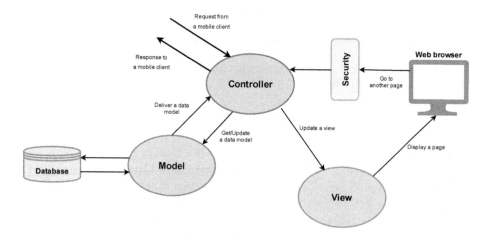

Fig. 3. Structure of the server.

Model is a triple representation of POIs inside the RDF4J triplestore (see Fig. 4). Such a database can easily be accessed through SPARQL queries.

View is responsible for presenting current database state to users and management forms to the administrator through the web application consisting of HTML pages.

Controller is actually a group of controllers responsible for processing queries from users based on REST API. Among them there are: *AndroidController* responsible for handling mobile client requests. *LoginController* used for processing login requests. *TripleController* whose job is to pass the list of triples to the view.

Security is a module responsible for users authentication and for guarding the user access levels. From a Security point of view, there are four system sections: *admin* for managing triplestore, *user* for browsing and searching the triplestore, *shared* consisting of information available for both of them and *guest* for not logged users that provides registration and login panels.

---

[6] See: http://getbootstrap.com/.

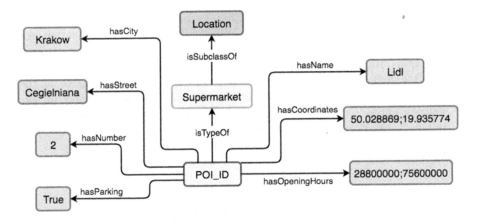

Fig. 4. Triple representation of typical POI information.

3.2 Mobile Client

Mobile application was developed for Android platform. The minimal supported Android version is API level 21 (Lollipop 5.0). Among the main technologies used in a mobile client there are:

Google Cardboard[7] – low-budget virtual reality glasses made up of a piece of cardboard, two plastic lenses, a magnet and a rubber band (see Fig. 5). The set is complemented by a smartphone that performs all computational tasks.

Google VR API[8] – set of libraries for programming applications that use Google Cardboard.

OpenGL ES[9] – subset of OpenGL libraries designed for creating 3D graphics on mobile devices.

Fig. 5. Google Cardboard VR glasses.

---

[7] See: https://vr.google.com/cardboard/.
[8] See: https://developers.google.com/vr/.
[9] OpenGL for Embedded Systems. See: https://www.khronos.org/opengles/.

Google Directions API[10] – a tool that returns a sequence of "steps" to reach given destination point. It uses HTTP requests for communication. All requests are prepared in the form: https://maps.googleapis.com/maps/api/directions/outputFormat?parameters, where `outputFormat` is either JSON or XML and `parameters` are all details of the request. Among them the most important are: *origin, destination* – the start and finish places for the journey, *mode* – mean of the transport (by car, by foot, by bicycle or by public transport), *key* – Google API key for authentication.

Mobile client consists of several interconnected modules (see Fig. 6):

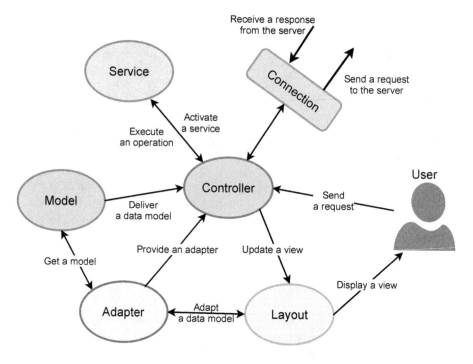

Fig. 6. Structure of the mobile client.

Layout defines graphical user interface for each of application activities.
Model in mobile client defines only the main concepts like POI. As full database is maintained on server and mobile client does not store the copy of a full database, data is sent or received to/from server immediately after user request.
Adapter is an intermediary that adjusts the data from the model to the current user view (eg. the number of displayed attributes).

---

[10] See: https://developers.google.com/maps/documentation/directions/.

Controller is a set of so-called activities, that are responsible for the whole interaction with user. Among them there are, e.g.: *MainActivity* with main menu of the application and *PoiActivity* that presents all POI-related information.

Connection module maintains the communication with server.

Service is responsible for communication with the Google Directions API and for update of map and direction-arrows within the mobile client.

Both server and mobile client were developed accordingly to the presented specification and then tested. Step-by-step system presentation is the matter of the following section.

4   System Presentation

System usage starts with administration tasks done with the simple Web Client (see Fig. 7a for menu, displayed on the left-hand side). Here new users can create accounts[11] and manage their details (password, e-mail) in section **Profile**. Administrators can also manage user roles ("Administrator" and "User"). Within the Client both administrators and users can view all POI-related triples that are stored in the database using **Triples Overview** option (see Fig. 7b). The remaining options are available for administrators to manage the database. **Types Overview** lists all current POI types (e.g. Shop, Petrol Station; see Fig. 7a) while **Attributes Overview** lists all optional object attributes (e.g. is_gas_available). Two more options are available to add new types and attributes, respectively **Add Type** and **Add Attribute**.

Main part of the system is the Mobile Client. It requires internet connection to download the POIs data from the Server and to update map and current direction arrows. The Client also requires GPS signal to provide a navigation. Within the Client, an user can see her or his current position on the map of the neighbourhood (**View Map** option in the main menu). User can also define the new POI information (**Add POI** option; see Fig. 7c). It requires specification of the POI name, selection of the POI type (e.g. Shop) and determination of GPS coordinates. The latter can be either entered by hand or gathered from the current user position. It is also possible to define the Opening Hours and other optional attributes, provided by the administrator in the Web Client.

Find POI and **Enter Target** options give the possibility to search for the POI. The first allows to search by the given keyword and the second one asks for more detailed user preferences. After selecting the **Enter Target** option, user can specify (see Fig. 7d): the type of the POI, when the POI should be opened and how far from current location (in kilometers) it should be placed. It is also possible to narrow search to specific optional attributes' values. Results of the search are presented in the form of a list with basic POI information

---

[11] These accounts are valid only for Web Client. They are not required to use the Mobile Client.

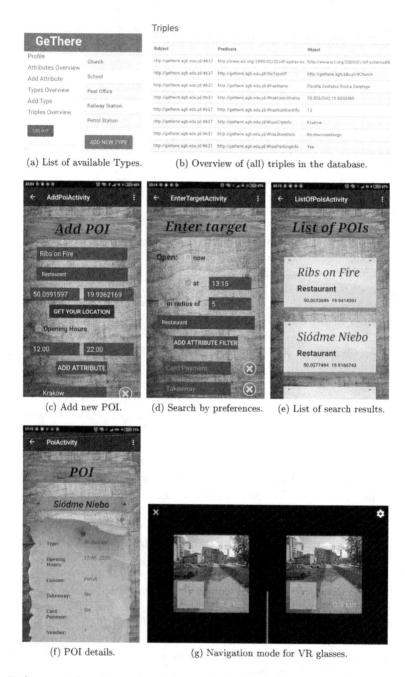

(a) List of available Types.   (b) Overview of (all) triples in the database.

(c) Add new POI.   (d) Search by preferences.   (e) List of search results.

(f) POI details.   (g) Navigation mode for VR glasses.

Fig. 7. Augmented reality system for space navigation presentation. Figures 7 a and b present the Web Client, Figs. 7 c–g show the Mobile Client.

(see Fig. 7e). A user can select one of them to see its details (see Fig. 7f) and to enter the navigation mode.

Navigation requires the user to put the smartphone inside the Google Cardboard device (see Fig. 5). In this mode two identical parts are displayed for two user eyes (through the lenses of the Cardboard) presenting live camera image with four pieces of information overlaid (see Fig. 7g): the nearest maneuver (e.g. left turn) represented by the arrow in the top left corner, distance to the maneuver in the top right corner, distance to the destination in the bottom right corner and a semi-transparent map of the nearest area in the bottom left corner. Distances and an arrow are updated every second by sending requests to the Google Directions API. The map is refreshed every three seconds.

5   Summary and Future Work

In the paper we described a prototype navigation system combining augmented reality with semantic annotations of POIs in the environment. The prototype was implemented using standard technologies such as regular Android smartphone and Google Cardboard. It is an example of semantic information system integrated with a basic augmented reality interface.

In the current version of application, all attributes could be used for every type of POI. What is more, all of them accept all possible UTF-8 encoded strings as a values. It is planned to provide the possibility to specify both the domain and the range of each attribute. Domain (list of POIs affected by this attribute) could be used to restrict the list of available attributes during adding new POI and searching for a POI. Only attributes connected with the selected POI type will be displayed. Specification of the attribute range (e.g. `xsd:string`. `xsd:decimal` or other XML Schema Datatypes [9]) will give the possibility to display more appropriate widgets for entering values (e.g. numerical keyboard instead of full keyboard for numbers). Also, Web Client capabilities should be enhanced to give the administrator a possibility to edit and delete types, attributes and POI-related triples. Finally, Mobile Client usability should be tested "in the wild" by many users and then appropriate corrections should be introduced. Especially more clear and less distracting layout is planned to introduce.

Practical integration with the natural environment of the user is considered. In the current version of the technology it is not easy, as Google's solution is not very comfortable. However, we are considering porting the application to another platform, possibly an augmented reality glasses such as Microsoft Hololens.

References

1. Bauer, J., Ebert, A.: Mobile devices for virtual reality interaction. A survey of techniques and metaphors. In: Brunnett, G., Coquillart, S., van Liere, R., Welch, G., Váša, L. (eds.) Virtual Realities. LNCS, vol. 8844, pp. 91–107. Springer, Cham (2015). doi:10.1007/978-3-319-17043-5_6

2. Burdzy, D.: System rzeczywistości poszerzonej do nawigacji przestrzennej. Master's thesis, AGH University of Science and Technology, supervisor: G. J. Nalepa (2017)

3. Hervás, R., Garcia-Lillo, A., Bravo, J.: Mobile augmented reality based on the semantic web applied to ambient assisted living. In: Bravo, J., Hervás, R., Villarreal, V. (eds.) IWAAL 2011. LNCS, vol. 6693, pp. 17–24. Springer, Heidelberg (2011). doi:10.1007/978-3-642-21303-8_3

4. Hitzler, P., Krötzsch, M., Rudolph, S.: Foundations of Semantic Web Technologies. Chapman & Hall/CRC, Boca Raton (2009)

5. Kipper, G., Rampolla, J.: Augmented Reality: An Emerging Technologies Guide to AR. Elsevier, London (2012)

6. Lassila, O., Swick, R.R.: Resource description framework (RDF) model and syntax specification. Technical report, World Wide Web Consortium. W3C Recommendation (1999). http://www.w3.org/TR/REC-rdf-syntax

7. Li, Y., Elmaghraby, A.S., El-Baz, A., Sokhadze, E.M.: Using physiological signal analysis to design affective VR games. In: 2015 IEEE International Symposium on Signal Processing and Information Technology (ISSPIT), pp. 57–62, December 2015

8. Menozzi, A., Clipp, B., Wenger, E., Heinly, J., Dunn, E., Towles, H., Frahm, J.M., Welch, G.: Development of vision-aided navigation for a wearable outdoor augmented reality system. In: Position, Location and Navigation Symposium-PLANS 2014, 2014 IEEE/ION, pp. 460–472. IEEE (2014)

9. Peterson, D., Gao, S., Malhotra, A., Sperberg-McQueen, C.M., Thompson, H.S.: W3C XML Schema Definition language (XSD) 1.1 part 2: Datatypes. W3C recommendation, W3C, April 2012. https://www.w3.org/TR/xmlschema11-2/

10. Rehman, U., Cao, S.: Augmented-reality-based indoor navigation: a comparative analysis of handheld devices versus google glass. IEEE Trans. Hum. Mach. Syst. **47**(1), 140–151 (2017)

11. Rodríguez, A., Rey, B., Clemente, M., Wrzesien, M., Alcañiz, M.: Assessing brain activations associated with emotional regulation during virtual reality mood induction procedures. Expert Syst. Appl. **42**(3), 1699–1709 (2015)

12. Seaborne, A., Prud'hommeaux, E.: SPARQL query language for RDF. W3C recommendation, W3C, January 2008. http://www.w3.org/TR/2008/REC-rdf-sparql-query-20080115/

13. Sharma, P.: Challenges with virtual reality on mobile devices. In: Special Interest Group on Computer Graphics and Interactive Techniques Conference, SIGGRAPH 2015 (2015). Article 57

14. Van Krevelen, D., Poelman, R.: A survey of augmented reality technologies, applications and limitations. Int. J. Virtual Reality **9**(2), 1 (2010)

15. Wang, Y.S., Chen, C.M., Hong, C.M., Tsai, Y.N.: Interactive augmented reality game for enhancing library instruction in elementary schools. In: 2013 IEEE 37th Annual Computer Software and Applications Conference Workshops (COMPSACW), pp. 391–396, July 2013

16. Zheng, G., Liao, H., Jannin, P., Cattin, P., Lee, S.-L. (eds.): MIAR 2016. LNCS, vol. 9805. Springer, Cham (2016). doi:10.1007/978-3-319-43775-0

Application of Local Features for Calibration of a Pair of CCTV Cameras

Adam Lach and Michał Grega[✉]

AGH University of Science and Technology,
al. Mickiewicza 30, 30-059 Kraków, Poland
grega@kt.agh.edu.pl

Abstract. The paper presents a new approach to the problem of calibration of a pair of CCTV cameras – a wide angle camera and Pan-Tilt-Zoom (PTZ) camera. The proposed solution allows for accurate control of the PTZ camera using point of interest selected in the coordinate system of the wide angle camera. In the paper we describe the local feature based calibration algorithm, camera control algorithm. We present results of the tests conducted with a real-life a setup of two high end CCTV cameras overseeing a $3000\,m^2$ parking lot. We have achieved an average $1{,}24°$ accuracy of calibration that translates to approximately $1.7\,m$ at $80\,m$ of observation distance. The proposed solution is designed in such a way, that after a one-time, heavy-computing calibration the camera control procedure is instantaneous and thus very well suited for operation with advanced object detection algorithms.

Keywords: SIFT · SURF · CCTV · PTZ · Camera calibration

1 Introduction

Closed Circuit Television Systems (CCTV) are getting increasingly popular, and they are being deployed at many offices, housing estates and in most public spaces. In 2016 UK Surveillance Camera Commissioner Tony Porter claimed, that there are six million CCTV cameras are currently in operation in the United Kingdom alone [6]. It is not only the number of deployments world wide that matters, but also progress in technical solutions and drop in prices. IP systems have now replaced analogue ones and Pan-Tilt-Zoom (PTZ) cameras are entering the consumer market. In general the CCTV cameras can be divided into stationary, fixed focal length cameras (we refer to those as "wide angle" for the purpose of this paper) and Pan-Tilt-Zoom cameras with two degrees of freedom (pan and tilt) and mechanically adjusted focal length. We refer to latter as "PTZ cameras".

While PTZ cameras offer much more in terms of functionality – they have on serious drawback. When operated, either manually or automatically in order to zoom into the object of interest, the view of the whole scene is lost hindering the situational awareness of the operator. In this paper we propose a solution to this problem by using a pair of calibrated CCTV cameras - a wide angle and a

© Springer International Publishing AG 2017
A. Dziech and A. Czyżewski (Eds.): MCSS 2017, CCIS 785, pp. 73–85, 2017.
https://doi.org/10.1007/978-3-319-69911-0_6

PTZ. By "calibrated" we mean that the pair operates in a coherent coordinate system in the plane of the camera sensor.

In this paper we propose a fully automated, accurate algorithm for calibration and control of a pair consisting of a PTZ and wide angle camera. We discuss the construction of the algorithm and present the results of the calibration using a setup consisting of high-end CCTV cameras in real environment.

Our solution has several significant features that differ it from competing solutions and make it well suited for application. Our algorithm is easy to deploy as the calibration procedure is fully automated and requires no user input. We have no requirements on precision of mount of both cameras, apart from that it is supposed to be fixed. While the calibration process is time consuming, the resulting calibration data allows the system to be used in real time and no additional computations are needed during the system operation. The proposed solution can be applied for wide range of security related applications, such as dangerous object detection as proposed in [8] or traffic security like proposed by Baran et al. in [2].

The remainder of this paper is structured as follows. In Sect. 2 we present the problem of camera calibration. In Sect. 3 related work is described. It is followed by Sect. 4 in which we present the principles of operation of our solution. Results are presented in Sect. 5 and the paper is concluded in Sect. 6.

2   Problem Statement and Hardware Setup

The goal of the research was to create a system that is capable of unifying (what we call - calibrating) the coordinate systems of a PTZ and wide angle camera overlooking the same scene. Practically, we wanted to be able to select a point in an image of the wide angle camera (denoted as (x, y)) and direct the PTZ camera so that the middle of the PTZ image (denoted as (x_{PTZ}, y_{PTZ}) would point at the same point we have selected in the wide angle camera image. Moreover, the problem is complicated by the fact, that at any given moment of time the PTZ camera may be at any given state of pan and tilt angles and any given level of zoom. Formally the problem can be defined as a function (1). We will explain later on why both $pan_{PTZ}/tilt_{PTZ}$ angles and x_{PTZ}, y_{PTZ} are required.

$$f(x, y) = (pan_{PTZ}, tilt_{PTZ}, x_{PTZ}, y_{PTZ}) \qquad (1)$$

In general the operation of the system was conducted in three steps as depicted in Fig. 1. First, the pair of the cameras has to be calibrated in order to obtain the calibration data stored in the result matrix. This step has to be performed only once. Based on the calibration data from the result matrix the (x, y) coordinates from the wide angle camera image are translated into a set of four data $(pan_{PTZ}, tilt_{PTZ}, x_{PTZ}, y_{PTZ})$ which are used in order to control the PTZ camera.

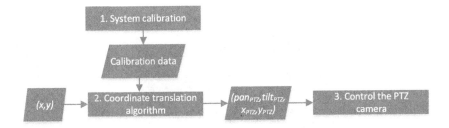

Fig. 1. Algorithm for camera calibration and operation.

Test setup consisted of two professional CCTV cameras. AXIS P1357 is a 5M pixel IP camera with a fixed mount and a Tamron 2.8–8 mm F1.2 lens fixed at 2.8 mm focal length. AXIS Q6115-E is a 2M pixel IP camera with a Pan/Tilt mount. The camera was capable of panning in 360° and tilting in the range of +20° to −90°. What is important – the mechanical construction of the camera offers very fast operation in both pan (700°/s) and tilt (500°/s) axes. The camera was equipped with a 4.4–132 mm F1.4-4.6 lens with auto-focus and auto-iris.

The cameras were fixed to an external wall of the building in a distance of approximately 50 cm between the lenses. No special attention was put to symmetrical installation of the cameras. The cameras overlooked a parking lot that is roughly 65 m long, with the furthest observed point at 80 m from the camera (Fig. 2). Both cameras were controlled with use of the manufacturer provided API called VAPIX from a server. The cameras and the server were connected using Gigabit Ethernet to minimize delays.

3   Related Work

The problem of calibration of multi camera systems was addressed in the 80' by multiple researchers when the concept of 3D capture using a stereo rig became more popular along with miniaturization of the camera systems. A good overview of methods along with a well formalized approach is provided by Tsai in [13].

One of solutions of geometry-based calibration is proposed by Scotti et al. in [11]. Authors propose to combine an omni directional camera with a PTZ camera mounted on a single axis, which significantly simplifies the calibration procedure. The system is limited by distortions caused by optics of the omni directional camera at the peripherals of its image. While our solution has limited coverage of the scene (limited to the scene observed by the wide angle camera) we do not impose any limitation on the method of mounting of the cameras.

A very common approach to calibration is proposed by Davies and Chen in [4]. In this work the authors calibrate a set of PTZ cameras using an external marker. In this case a red LED is used as a marker. This makes the calibration

Fig. 2. Overview of the monitored area (source: Google Maps 2017)

procedure more robust, but requires significant effort in order to carry the marker in the scene. It is also not practical in huge scenes, such as covered by our system (over $3000\,m^2$).

A very similar problem is solved by Senior et al. The authors in their initial work [9] have proposed to manually create a look-up table that would match regions of interest in the field of view of the wide camera to the corresponding areas that may be focused on by the PTZ camera. In the extension of their work [12] the authors have proposed to use epiplanar geometry in order to calibrate the PTZ camera to the wide angle camera. As features authors use object detection and object tracks as observed from both cameras. The drawback of this solution is that the PTZ camera has to be able to observe the same area as the wide angle camera during the calibration - and thus have the similar (or smaller) minimal focal length - which was not the case for our setup.

Liao and Cho [10] propose a trigonometry based solution that computes provides equations used for camera control. Their method requires a low number of characteristic points but its accuracy is lower than spatial-based methods. Liao and Cho's work provides also a through classification of camera calibration methods.

Szwoch et al. in [1] propose a calibration method that is based on manual selection of the calibration points and the previously mentioned Tsai [13] method for calculation of the camera parameters. When compared to the method proposed in our paper, this method has the drawback of not being fully automated at the callibration stage. The authors in [1] have also provided a method for tracking of moving objects using their calibrated set of cameras.

4   Proposed Solution

In this section the proposed calibration and camera control algorithms are described. The calibration algorithm is a fully automated procedure. In order to make the section more comprehensive its description was split into three conceptional phases:

- Data collection
- Rating and sorting
- Calibration computation

During the data collection phase the server was used for camera control and image storage. During the data collection one frame from wide angle camera and a set of frames from PTZ camera were downloaded. We refer to the frame from the wide angle camera as the "wide frame" and to the frames from the PTZ camera as the "PTZ Frames". PTZ camera's focal length was set to the shortest possible and the angles used for PRZ frames capture were computed according to the formulas (2) and (3).

$$tilt_{PTZ} = MINtilt_{PTZ} + n * \frac{MAXtilt_{PTZ} - MINtilt_{PTZ}}{VERT\_DENS} \tag{2}$$

$$pan_{PTZ} = MINpan_{PTZ} + m * \frac{MAXpan_{PTZ} - MINpan_{PTZ}}{HOR\_DENS * cos(tilt_{PTZ})} \tag{3}$$

Where $VERT\_DENS, HOR\_DENS$ are configuration parameters defining the density of the PTZ frames. Larger values result in higher calibration quality but at a cost of a longer computation time due to higher number of input PTZ frames. $MAXtilt_{PTZ}, MINtilt_{PTZ}, MAXpan_{PTZ}, MINpan_{PTZ}$ are PTZ camera parameters defining range of tilt and pan angles and are defined by the camera specification. n, m are pairs of natural numbers. We save both PTZ frames and corresponding $tilt_{PTZ}$, pan_{PTZ} angles.

When the visual data is collected the algorithm starts the rating and sorting phase. The goal of this phase is to find the best frames for further use in the calibration computation phase. For this purpose we have defined the fitness function (6) and an algorithm used for its computation, as depicted in Fig. 3.

First, we detect local features for both PTZ and wide frame using the SURF algorithm [3]. In the second step we match the features using simple brute-force algorithm by matching the feature set of the wide frame witch each of the features sets of the PTZ frames. Next, each pair of matched features is filtered with two level filter: first level is using matching distance, as a second level is used RANSAC filter [5]. At this point $matchesSize$ and $meanDistance$ parameters can be calculated. $matchesSize$ is a number of pairs which pass the filtering stage of the algorithm and the $meanDistance$ is an arithmetic mean of matching distances of pairs.

The next step is calculation of the homography, that is of a perspective transformation between PTZ and wide frames. In our case the homography is a

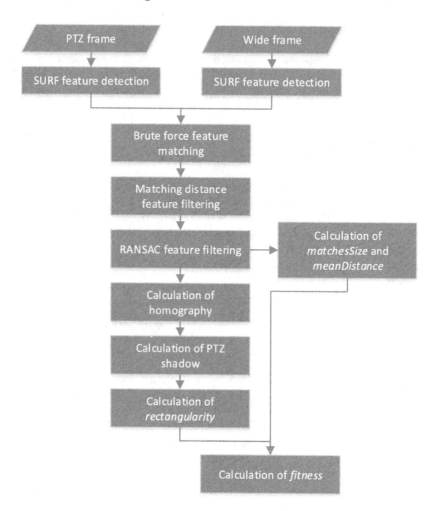

Fig. 3. Block diagram of a fitness function calculation. Fitness function value is used for sorting and filtering frames.

3 by 3 matrix (denoted as H) as presented in formula (4). It allows us to convert from the coordinates in the PTZ camera to the coordinates in the wide camera and vice versa.

$$\begin{bmatrix} x \\ y \\ 1 \end{bmatrix} = H \cdot \begin{bmatrix} x_{PTZ} \\ y_{PTZ} \\ 1 \end{bmatrix} = \begin{bmatrix} h_{00} & h_{01} & h_{02} \\ h_{10} & h_{11} & h_{12} \\ h_{20} & h_{21} & h_{22} \end{bmatrix} \begin{bmatrix} x_{PTZ} \\ y_{PTZ} \\ 1 \end{bmatrix} \qquad (4)$$

Homography is calculated using the method provided by the openCV image processing library. This transformation is used to translate the coordinates of the PTZ frame into a related quadrilateral on wide frame. We refer to this quadrilateral a "shadow" of the PTZ frame on the wide frame.

For this shadow the *rectangularity* parameter is computed using formula (5)

$$rectangularity = Area_{quadrilateral}/Area_{rectangle} \qquad (5)$$

In formula (5) $Area_{quadrilateral}$ is a two-dimensional geometric area of the quadrilateral and $Area_{rectangle}$ is the area of the rectangle described on the four points found using the homography relation. The *fitness* value can be calculated

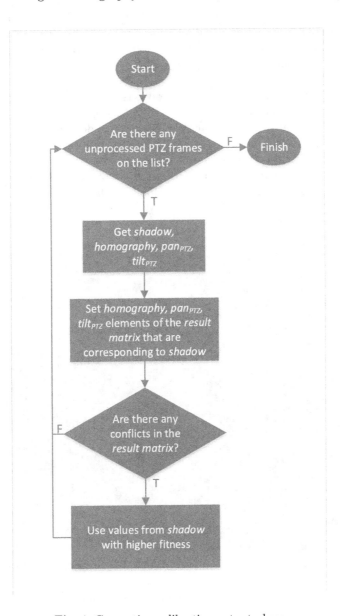

Fig. 4. Computing calibration output phase

using formula (6). It is computed for each of the PTZ frames separately. Finally, the list of all PTZ frames was sorted in the descending order using the *fitness* value.

$$fitness = \frac{matchesSize * rectangularity}{meanDistance} \tag{6}$$

With sorted list of PTZ frames the calibration computation phase is performed as shown in Fig. 4. During this phase the final calibration data is computed. This data is stored as two-dimensional matrix with dimensions equal to the size of the wide frame in pixels. The elements of this matrix are a tuple consisting of a homography and a $pan_{PTZ}, tilt_{PTZ}$ pair. We refer to this matrix as "result matrix".

The homography is collected from previous phase and inverted to obtain the transformation from wide frame into PTZ frame. $pan_{PTZ}, tilt_{PTZ}$ are corresponding to actual PTZ frame angles. This step is done for each PTZ frame. When two PTZ frames have an intersection – the transformation from better fitted PTZ frame will be used in result matrix.

Results can be interpreted as set of shadows on wide frame. Where each shadow is corresponding into the same Homography and $pan_{PTZ}, tilt_{PTZ}$ as shown in Fig. 5.

Fig. 5. Set of shadows on wide frame

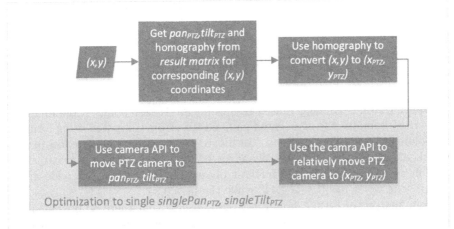

Fig. 6. Camera control procedure

Result matrix allows to control the PTZ camera using the coordinates from the wide camera. The control procedure is depicted in Fig. 6. First, we obtain the homography and the $pan_{PTZ}, tilt_{PTZ}$ from the result matrix for the corresponding x, y pair. In the second step using the built in camera API we move the PTZ camera to the $pan_{PTZ}, tilt_{PTZ}$ position. Finally, we use the homography to transform point x, y into x_{PTZ}, y_{PTZ} and use the relative camera API in order to point the center of the PTZ image into the desired x_{PTZ}, y_{PTZ} point at the scene.

In the process of optimization of the algorithm we have added function (7) that merges the two-stage process of panning to $pan_{PTZ}, tilt_{PTZ}$ and relatively moving to x_{PTZ}, y_{PTZ} into a single camera movement.

$$f(panPTZ, tiltPTZ, x_{PTZ}, y_{PTZ}) = (singlePanPTZ, singleTiltPTZ) \quad (7)$$

5   Results

In this section results of calibration tests will be presented. The tests were performed in good weather conditions in the area presented on Fig. 2. First we have selected 37 characteristic points, evenly distributed in the image from the wide camera. For each of this test points we have collected a pair of pan and tilt angles $pan_{ideal}, tilt_{ideal}$ that are the ground truth used for assessment of the accuracy of the algorithm.

For comparison between the ground truth and the data obtained through the calibration and the camera control procedures we have introduced two dimensional distance error function defined in (8).

$$twoDimensional = \sqrt{(pan_{ideal} - singlePan_{PTZ})^2 - (tilt_{ideal} - singleTilt_{PTZ})^2}$$
(8)

Table 1 contains the aggregated results for all 37 test points. Column "distance error" contains the aggregated pan and tilt errors computed using formula (8). Columns "pan difference" and "tilt difference" contain the differences in pan and tilt angles respectively. Average error of 1,24° corresponds approximately to 1,7 m at 80 m, which is the furthest observable point from our wide angle camera. The worst result was 4,44° while the best 0,24°.

From analysis of Figs. 7, 8 and 9 we can observe that there no obvious relations between error and position of test points. Some increase of of error near the edge in horizontal domain may be observed. This deterioration is too small to judge if it is a general problem of algorithm or it is related to the optical characteristics of the system.

Table 1. Calibration results

	Distance error	Pan difference	Tilt difference
Arithmetic mean [°]	1,24	0,86	0,75
Median [°]	0,97	0,56	0,51
Max [°]	4,44	3,84	2,23
Min [°]	0,18	0,02	0,03

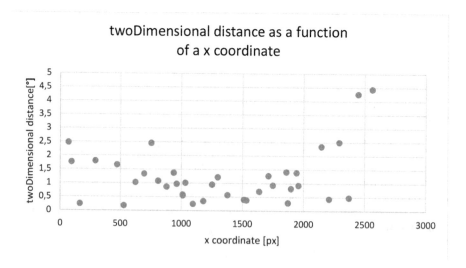

Fig. 7. Two-dimensional error as a function of x coordinate

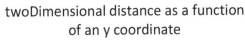

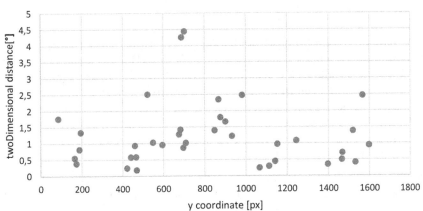

Fig. 8. Two-dimensional error as a function of y coordinate

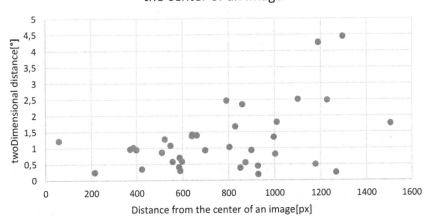

Fig. 9. Two-dimensional error as a function of distance to the center of the scene

It is worth to mention that the camera control procedure is instantaneous, as it does not require any complex computations. It is an important feature of our solution, as it allows the system to be used on low power machines. It also does not produce any significant overhead when used in conjunction with other image processing algorithms. It comes at a cost of lengthy calibration process which takes approximately 5 h of computing time on a desktop class computer.

6 Summary

In this paper we have proposed and tested a calibration algorithm that unifies the coordinate system of a wide angle and PTZ CCTV cameras. Our camera control algorithm allows for accurate control of a PTZ camera by selecting a point of interest from the wide angle camera image. The test we have conducted show high accuracy of our solution with average error of 1,24° that corresponds to 1,7 m in our deployment. Our approach is also very time effective, as the calibration result has a form of a look-up table, thus the camera control algorithm introduces little to no delay to the system.

Our solution has many practical applications. It can speed up and improve the performance of supervised CCTV systems, in which the operator will not loose the situational awareness while zooming into a detail of the scene. In the automated CCTV systems our solution, when combined with fast mechanics of the PTZ camera, allows for more effective object detection – such as e.g. dangerous tool detection (which is also a subject of our research in [7] or [8]).

In further work we plan to develop a visual demonstrator of our system, that will allow for manual control of the PTZ camera by selecting regions of interest in the image from the wide camera. We are also working on calibration of the zoom feature of the PTZ camera, which will allow not only to pan and tilt the camera into the object of interest but also to zoom in or out as needed.

Acknowledgment. This work was supported by the Polish National Center for Research and Development under the LIDER Grant (No. LIDER/354/L-6/14/NCBR/2015).

References

1. Spatial calibration of a dual ptzfixed camera system for tracking moving objects in video. J. Imaging Sci. Technol. 57(2) (2013)
2. Baran, R., Ruść, T., Rychlik, M.: A smart camera for traffic surveillance. In: Dziech, A., Czyżewski, A. (eds.) MCSS 2014. CCIS, vol. 429, pp. 1–15. Springer, Cham (2014). doi:10.1007/978-3-319-07569-3_1
3. Bay, H., Tuytelaars, T., Van Gool, L.: SURF: speeded up robust features. In: Leonardis, A., Bischof, H., Pinz, A. (eds.) ECCV 2006. LNCS, vol. 3951, pp. 404–417. Springer, Heidelberg (2006). doi:10.1007/11744023_32
4. Davis, J., Chen, X.: Calibrating pan-tilt cameras in wide-area surveillance networks. In: Proceedings of the Ninth IEEE International Conference on Computer Vision - ICCV 2003, vol. 4, pp. 144–150 (2003). http://dl.acm.org/citation.cfm?id=946247.946652
5. Fischler, M.A., Bolles, R.C.: Random sample consensus: a paradigm for model fitting with applications to image analysis and automated cartography. Commun. ACM **24**(6), 381–395 (1981). doi:10.1145/358669.358692

6. Greenwood, C.: One CCTV camera for every 10 people: Report says there are now six million across the UK.. but many of them are useless. Daily Mail (2016)
7. Grega, M., Lach, S., Sieradzki, R.: Automated recognition of firearms in surveillance video. In: 2013 IEEE International Multi-Disciplinary Conference on Cognitive Methods in Situation Awareness and Decision Support (CogSIMA), pp. 45–50, Feb 2013
8. Grega, M., Matiolański, A., Guzik, P., Leszczuk, M.: Automated detection of firearms and knives in a CCTV image. Sensors 16(1), 47 (2016)
9. Hampapur, A., Brown, L., Connell, J., Pankanti, S., Senior, A., Tian, Y.: Smart surveillance: applications, technologies and implications. In: Fourth International Conference on Information, Communications and Signal Processing 2003 and the Proceedings of the 2003 Joint Fourth Pacific Rim Conference on Multimedia, vol. 2, pp. 1133–1138, December 2003
10. Liao, H.C., Cho, Y.C.: A new calibration method and its application for the cooperation of wide-angle and pan-tilt-zoom cameras. Inf. Technol. J. 7(8), 1096–1105 (2008)
11. Scotti, G., Marcenaro, L., Coelho, C., Selvaggi, F., Regazzoni, C.S.: Dual camera intelligent sensor for high definition 360 degrees surveillance. IEEE Proc. - Vis. Image. Sig. Process. 152(2), 250–257 (2005)
12. Senior, A.W., Hampapur, A., Lu, M.: Acquiring multi-scale images by pan-tilt-zoom control and automatic multi-camera calibration. In: 2005 Seventh IEEE Workshops on Application of Computer Vision, WACV/MOTIONS 2005 vol. 1, pp. 433–438, January 2005
13. Tsai, R.: A versatile camera calibration technique for high-accuracy 3d machine vision metrology using off-the-shelf tv cameras and lenses. IEEE J. Robot. Autom. 3(4), 323–344 (1987)

Video Summarization Framework for Newscasts and Reports – Work in Progress

Mikołaj Leszczuk[1]($^\boxtimes$), Michał Grega[1], Arian Koźbiał[1], Jarosław Gliwski[1], Krzysztof Wasieczko[1], and Kamel Smaïli[2]

[1] AGH University of Science and Technology, al. Mickiewicza 30,
30-059 Kraków, Poland
leszczuk@kt.agh.edu.pl
[2] University of Lorraine, 54506 Vandoeuvre-lès-Nancy Cedex, France
Kamel.Smaili@loria.fr

Abstract. This paper presents a framework for summarization for newscasts and reports, that is a part of an ongoing research towards multilingual opinion analysis system conducted under the CHIST-ERA project "Access Multilingual Information opinionS" (AMIS). We present the results of qualitative analysis of newscast and reports published in the Internet by leading English, French and Arabic TV channels. We show the method used for creation of a database that contains 300 h of such content on controversial topics. Finally, we show the design and operation of our summarization framework. The framework is designed in such a way, that it allows for easy experimentation with different approaches to video summarization. The description is followed by a presentation of high- and low-level metadata extraction algorithms that include detection of the anchorperson, recognition of day and night shots and extraction of low-level video quality indicators.

Keywords: Opinion mining · Metadata extraction · Video summarization · Sentiment analysis · Anchorperson detection

1 Introduction

Language is the most common barrier in the access to newscasts and reports in foreign languages. Therefore, the following challenge appears: how a user can access the information and opinions in unknown languages? Moreover, due to cultural and political differences, it is very often necessary to compare the information in on the same subject in different languages.

We define the process of understanding as the assimilation of the main ideas carried by recorded video. The best way to help and speed up understanding is summarizing the information. In our research we focus on summarization of newscasts and reports, extraction of the opinion (also referred to as "opinion mining") and comparison of those opinions between newscasts presented in different languages.

© Springer International Publishing AG 2017
A. Dziech and A. Czyżewski (Eds.): MCSS 2017, CCIS 785, pp. 86–97, 2017.
https://doi.org/10.1007/978-3-319-69911-0_7

Therefore, our research focuses on the most relevant information, summarizing it, and presenting to the user. This goal can be achieved by embedding its video summarization technology into an either pipeline (video-only) or parallel (audio-visual) newscasts and reports processing system.

In this paper, we present an element of our ongoing research – a framework designed for summarization for newscasts and reports. First, we have analyzed a few dozens of video sequences and have categorized them into three basic categories. This has allowed us to design the summarization framework. The description of the framework is extended with the description of three example metadata extraction modules that have been developed so far. Approach to the summarization of video presented in this paper is simplistic, however being a work in progress it provides a solid foundation for further expansion in the direction of a fully functional and effective summarization system.

In the related research most of video summarization processes commonly starts with Shot Boundary Detection (SBD) [3]. As far as generic video modality is concerned, the first notable milestone work in this area was presented by Zhang [10] (and its follow-up [11]). Authors propose an integrated and content-based solution for video parsing, retrieval and browsing. Nevertheless, specific video modalities require tailored solutions. An example of a video summarization algorithm, designed for specific video modality – video-bronchoscopy, has been provided in [4]. in this paper, we are, however, more interested in another video modality – newscasts and reports. Here, some important works include those by Maybury et al. [5], and a more recent publication by Gao et al.: [1].

The remainder of this paper is structured as follows. Section 2 describes analysis of video sequences. Section 3 proposes our video summarization framework, including its exemplary modules. In Sect. 4 we describe future research directions. Finally, the paper is concluded in Sect. 5.

2   Analysis of the Video Sequences

In this section, we show the result of the qualitative analysis of the videos and initial division into three categories. We also propose a strategy for video summarization and a proposed approach for automated categorization of the video sequences.

We have selected a random number (between 5 and 10) videos per each considered news channel. Each video was analyzed to propose a summary strategy. We have tried to limit the number of scenarios, but if no existing scenario was applicable – a new scenario was created. For each video, we have also provided a brief description of the video content. While the project is supposed to deal with English (EN), French (FR) and Arabic (AR) content, we have limited this report to EN content only. We have, however, browsed through FR and AR content and assume that the strategies proposed in this document will extrapolate. In total, we have analyzed 43 sequences from Euronews, France 24, BBC, Russia Today and Al Jazeera channels.

We propose three general categories. Following paragraphs briefly describe these categories along with the proposed summarization strategies.

A – This content type covers a typical news coverage. For such type of videos the initial spoken part provides introduction and brief overview of the content of the video. Usually there are multiple "talking heads", it may be worth to extract the spoken text and analyze for valuable information. Examples of such videos are studio-started news coverage which shifts to shots or report from outside the studio. The best summarization strategy for this type of videos requires extraction of the first segment of speech and further extraction of interesting scenes. Such interesting scenes may be extracted using different features and selection of those features is a subject of our ongoing research. Initial experiments show that while spatial and temporal activity as a feature yields promising results, more elaborate techniques such as speaker identification may be required.

B – This type of content covers all types of discussions or interviews. The discussion or interviews can be done in the TV studio or via a video conferencing link. Examples of such videos are panels and discussions with one or many experts. In this scenario, the video does not contain any interesting visual information, while most of the information is conveyed via speech. For such video type the only feasible summarization is to extract spoken text and further spoken text analysis.

C – In this scenario there is no spoken text – only video with ambient noise and sounds. For such videos parts cut out using spatio-temporal analysis seem to be the best strategy. Examples of such videos are CCTV recordings or video recordings from a war zone.

The breakdown of occurrence of individual categories is presented in Table 1.

Table 1. Summary types

Type	Count
A	27
B	14
C	2

To be able to apply a summarization strategy to a given video first it must be categorized to one of the three (A, B or C) categories.

To categorize the videos, we propose to use (at least) the following tools:

- Spatial and Temporal Activity Detection – this algorithm is capable of detection the amount of activity within video sequence. This may help to distinguish between sequences that contain more dynamic content (B type videos are expected to contain less activity that A and possibly C).
- "Talking head" detection – this algorithm allows to detect sequences which contain a single talking speaker. The percentage of video that contains "talking head" may allow to further distinguish videos of type B from A and C.

- Shot Boundary Detection – this algorithm allows to detect the boundaries between the individual shots. The number of shots in the video may allow to distinguish C type videos from A and B types.
- Automated Speech Recognition – this algorithm allows to process the spoken text. For video type identification, the amount of spoken text may prove to be useful discriminator.
- Speaker Identification – this algorithm allows to label distinct speakers. The number of speaking persons in a video may be useful discriminator.

3   Video Summarization Framework

In this section we provide the description of the summarization framework (it is depicted in Fig. 1. It consists of three key elements: the video database, the metadata extraction algorithms with the metadata database and the summarization algorithm. The principle of the operation is as following.

First, for each video in the database a set of metadata is extracted. This metadata can be of high variety and level. For example, we extract the information on shot boundary, shot length, number of actors per frame and per shot, identify the actors in shots, we also recognize if a shot is taken during the day or during the night, detect if the shot contains an anchorperson (so called "talking head") etc. This metadata extraction is very time consuming but has to be performed only once per video.

Afterwards an interchangable module of summarization algorithms is applied. Well defined inputs and outputs of the summarization algorithms allow us to experiment with different summarization strategies starting from the most simplistic approach to more complex ones.

The summarization algorithm produces a summarization recepie. This is a file with a defined structure, that contains information on the start and finish frame numbers of the fragments of the source video and their order required to produce a summary. It is used by the summarization module in order to create a summarized video.

In the further part of this chapter we will provide information on the Video Database we have created and the exemplary metadata extraction algorithms.

3.1   Video Database

For the purpose of further research we have created a large corpus of newscasts and reports. This process is depicted in Fig. 1. In order to gather the videos we have first identified a list of controversial Twitter hash tags, such as #animalrights or #syria. Than we have extracted all twits from the Twitter service that were identified with this hashtag for a given period of time. Further on we have filtered the twits – only the twits containing valid YouTube links were passed to the next stage in which the videos were downloaded and stored into the video database (Fig. 2).

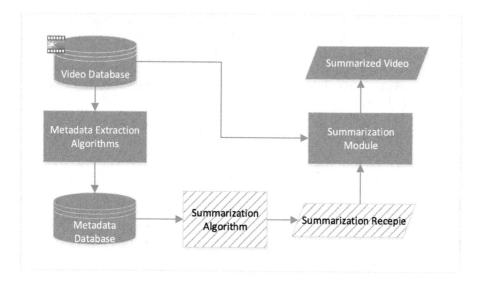

Fig. 1. Video Summarization Framework work-flow

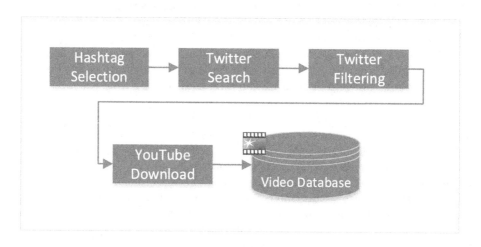

Fig. 2. Wokflow for Video Database creation

In total we have downloaded 310 h of video from 19 TV stations in 3 languages (English, French and Arabic). The total number of 5423 videos that vary from 1 to 64 min in length. We have downloaded all available image formats. Table 2 presents the breakdown of the downloaded content into languages and hash tags of interest.

Table 2. AMIS video summary – number of video sequences per language

Hashtag	Arabic		English		France		Total	
	Downloaded videos	Time in hours of downloaded videos	Downloaded videos	Time in hours of downloaded videos	Downloaded videos	Time in hours of downloaded videos	Downloaded videos	Time in hours of downloaded videos
#animalrights	17	0.52	162	5.36	193	8.66	372	14.54
#deathpenalty	113	5.89	110	3.43	381	15.69	604	25.01
#extremeright	43	2	156	5.65	172	6.28	371	13.93
#fcbarcelona	91	6.56	13	0.42	13	0.31	117	7.29
#homosexualmarriage	81	6.83	97	5.09	37	2.47	215	14.39
#occupiedterritories	165	18.11	49	1.28	132	5.05	346	24.44
#realmadrid	357	16.3	24	1.43	32	2.18	413	19.91
#syria	419	38.59	237	13.78	542	31.08	1198	83.45
#trump	178	11.04	874	48.73	463	24.14	1515	83.91
#womenright	39	3.95	152	15.53	81	4.41	272	23.89
Total	1503	109.79	1874	100.71	2046	100.26		

3.2 Metadata Extraction Algorithms

Detection of "Talking Head" Shots. The goal of this algorithm is to detect whether a shot contains a "talking head" – that is a single talking person that is the main focus point of the scene.

The analysis of a shot is performed in a frame-by-frame manner (as depicted in Fig. 3). Thus, we work not on videos, but on single images. Partly, the algorithm flow is imposed by the implementation of the methods available in the well-known OpenCV library.

First the frame is converted to gray-scale. There are a few reasons why gray-scale is desirable in video processing. First, we reduce the computational load while retaining most of the relevant information. In the single luminance channel pixels are represented by 256 intensity levels, from black to white. Second, edge detection (which is a part of our algorithm) is easier when only one parameter of desired region is analyzed.

The next step is to carry out the histogram equalization. This action affects the picture contrast, as it expands the range of intensity levels and improves pixel's value representation in whole bitmap.

After this initial processing the frame is a good input to face detection algorithm. It is the basic criterion for acceptance as a useful frame in finding "talking head" shots, because when there is no face on frame, the frame can be rejected before progressing to the next stage of our cascade classifier. Face detection is conducted using the well known Viola and Jones method as implemented in the OpenCV library [9]. For every frame we store the information on the detected number of faces.

After rejecting frames without any features, further analysis is focused on the face region. Each face region has a bounding box, which attributes (x-coordinate, y-coordinate, width and height) allow us to assess the size of the face in relation

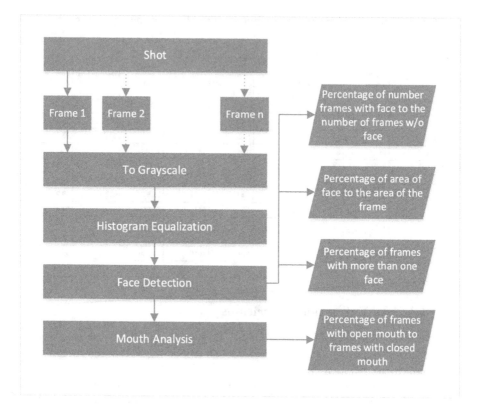

Fig. 3. Frame analysis for "Talking Head" detection

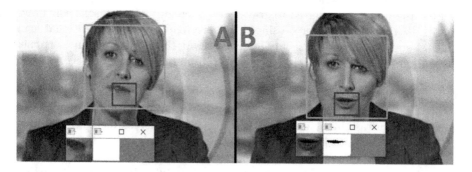

Fig. 4. Detection of opened and closed mouth

to the size of the frame. Based on the training data set we are also able to focus on mouth area.

When the area of lips defined, the mean value of region's pixel matrix is calculated. This value will be helpful to adjust threshold parameters, because of wide range of luminance in different images.

The final step of video shot processing is counting a number of all pixels in the mouth area. After that, we are checking how many black pixels are in this area, as all operations described in preceding paragraphs helped to obtain status about person's lips. This operation extracts information if person on frame has open or closed mouth, as depicted in Fig. 4. Mouth area can be a shifted on some frames due to the position of the reporter's head. The algorithm compensates for this.

During the entire application cycle the parameters and information about each frame is saved to be used in the cascade classifier. After processing the shot, application passes parameters to a classifier. The operation principle of the cascade classifier is depicted in Fig. 5.

The input values of the classifier are as following: percentage of frames without face, dominant percentage of face area compared to the entire image, percentage of frames with more than one face on screen and percentage value of frames where presenter has open mouth.

First level of classifier to check if there are not too many frames without any face detected. Based on training material we accepted safe upper limit of 20%. Rating above this value shows clearly that this video shot does not include the anchor person. Every result below 20% is treated as Haar cascade inaccuracy, because sometimes elements of background can have facial features and they match examples from included XML file, so OpenCV classifies this result as face detection.

The next step is more complex than the previous one. It contains two conditions linked with a logical "and". First thing checked by the classifier is the mean value of face area compared to entire video resolution. This part assumes that there is a face on the frame, but the face can be, for example, just a part of a background or a person walking down the street. Face area should be at least 3% of the whole scene size for that condition to be "true".

The second condition on this classifier level, linked to the previous one with logical AND operation is based on the number of faces detected in the scene. If more than 10% of frames in video shot have more than one face, it should be rejected. Now we can see that these two conditions on this level make sense only when they are combined, because they allow us to accurately assess if the shot should be sent to the last step of classifier.

During the last stage of the classifier the information about mouth is analyzed. If the ratio of frames with mouth open to mouth closed is above 20%, the algorithm marks the shot as a "talking head". Value below 20% denotes, that this is a recording with an anchor person in front of camera, which is not speaking (for example listening to people seating in TV studio).

Detection of Day and Night Shots. Another module that has been developed is Detection of Day and Night Shots. In this module analysis is also performed on single pictures, not videos. The module uses OpenCV methods to acquire and analyze information from the pictures.

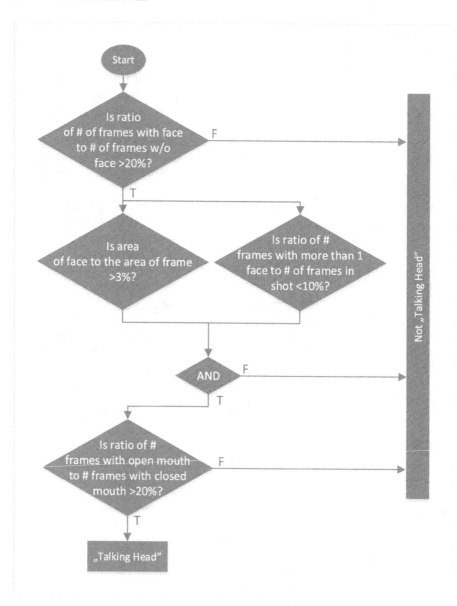

Fig. 5. Cascade classifier for "Talking Head" detection

In the first step, Python's script loads images from the given path and computes value of every pixel's luminance from the RGB components. The program subsequently calculates the mean value from all computed pixel's luminance values. That variable is the mean value of picture's luminance.

We have experimentally determined a threshold value which provides the maximum efficiency. Images with mean value of luminance not exceeding threshold value classify as night shots, and images exceeding threshold are day shots. In the end the script returns adequate information about the picture.

As the above-mentioned, simplistic approach based on luminance thresholding have not provided satisfactory results, the more advance approach has been proposed and presented in the following paragraph.

We have created a neural network to test the efficiency of the solution. In our neural network, there are 10 neurons in the hidden layer. A feed-forward neural network applies a series of functions to the data. The input data were 4 parameters which were acquired from the picture: R component, G component, B component and luminance. In the output, we can obtain 2 possible responses: 1 or 0, which means the picture was made in the day or in the night. Program was tested on a different set of pictures, amount on over 2000 photos. The efficiency in each case exceeded 90%.

Video Quality Indicators. Video Quality Indicators, which have been integrated within our Video Summarization Framework are a part of an already developed, broader framework for the integrated video quality assessment [6].

The software package to measure quality indicators, operate in a difficult No-Reference (NR) model. This software package is the realization of a previously developed concept of monitoring the quality of vision, by Key Performance Indicators (KPI). The idea proposed here goes by the name: Monitoring Of Audio Visual quality by Key Performance Indicators (MOAVI). MOAVI artifacts (or KPIs) are divided into four categories, depending on their origin: a category of capturing, processing, transmission and display. The MOAVI based application can isolate and improve incident investigation, aid algorithm configuration, extend the periods to monitor and ensure better prediction of Quality of Experience (QoE).

Video Quality Indicators are a versatile measurement system. Aiming to allow easier evaluation and debugging of the software, we decided to design it in a modular manner. This basically means that each of the metrics may be easily detached or attached to the whole topology. Utilizing such a strategy makes it possible to comfortably and efficiently modify the functionality of the package. In this way, the final shape of the application may be precisely carved to fit the desired use-case scenario.

The software consists of 15 visual metrics, which together form KPIs that could be used to model predicted quality of experience, as seen from the perspective of the end-user. The following set of metrics was developed:

1. Exposure [4],
2. Freezing,
3. Interlacing [2],
4. Spatial activity [8],
5. Temporal activity [8],
6. Letter-boxing,

7. Pillar-boxing,
8. Blockiness [8],
9. Noise [2],
10. Slicing
11. Block-loss
12. Blur [6,8],
13. Contrast,
14. Flickering [8],
15. Blackout.

The paper [7] gives a more comprehensive insight into the presented system. Furthermore, we show there the results of crowd-sourcing experiments used to estimate subjective threshold values for quality indicators.

4   Further Work

The basis of our research is that a high quality summarization provides the viewer with both valuable information and attractive visual content. For that purpose we plan to allow for desynchronization of audio and visual tracks in order to merge the most attractive content with the relevant and meaningful audio track.

The summarization framework provides us with a solid base for further development of the summarization algorithms. On one hand we will expand the metadata database with additional information – mostly audio based. In this field our efforts focus on providing automated transcription of the videos in English, French and Arabic.

Apart from expanding the metadata database we are working on developing summarization algorithms. Automated operation of the framework allows us to easily experiment with many different summarization strategies and approaches, instantly providing us with summarized videos based on developed algorithms.

The third direction of our research focuses on methods of assessment of the quality of the summarizations. We would like to develop a coherent methodology for judging of different summarization algorithms.

5   Conclusions

In this paper, we presented a video summarization framework for newscasts and reports. It is based on an analysis of several video sequences of this modality. The description of the framework was extended with the description of the video database and three exemplary modules that have been developed so far.

Acknowledgment. Research work funded by the National Science Centre, Poland, conferred on the basis of the decision number DEC-2015/16/Z/ST7/00559.

References

1. Gao, X., Tang, X.: Unsupervised video-shot segmentation and model-free anchorperson detection for news video story parsing. IEEE Trans. Circuits Syst. Video Technol. **12**(9), 765–776 (2002)
2. Janowski, L., Papir, Z.: Modeling subjective tests of quality of experience with a generalized linear model. In: International Workshop on Quality of Multimedia Experience, QoMEx 2009, pp. 35–40, July 2009
3. Leszczuk, M., Papir, Z.: Accuracy vs. speed trade-off in detecting of shots in video content for abstracting digital video libraries. In: Boavida, F., Monteiro, E., Orvalho, J. (eds.) IDMS 2002. LNCS, vol. 2515, pp. 176–189. Springer, Heidelberg (2002). doi:10.1007/3-540-36166-9_16
4. Leszczuk, M.I., Duplaga, M.: Algorithm for video summarization of bronchoscopy procedures. BioMed. Eng. OnLine **10**(1), 110 (2011). http://dx.doi.org/10.1186/1475-925X-10-110
5. Maybury, M.T., Merlino, A.E.: Multimedia summaries of broadcast news. In: Proceedings of the Intelligent Information Systems, IIS 1997, pp. 442–449, December 1997
6. Mu, M., Romaniak, P., Mauthe, A., Leszczuk, M., Janowski, L., Cerqueira, E.: Framework for the integrated video quality assessment. Multimedia Tools Appl. **61**(3), 787–817 (2012). http://dx.doi.org/10.1007/s11042-011-0946-3
7. Nawała, J., Leszczuk, M., Zajdel, M., Baran, R.: Software package for measurement of quality indicators working in no-reference model. Multimedia Tools Appl., 1–17 (2016). http://dx.doi.org/10.1007/s11042-016-4195-3
8. Romaniak, P., Janowski, L., Leszczuk, M., Papir, Z.: Perceptual quality assessment for h.264/avc compression. In: 2012 IEEE Consumer Communications and Networking Conference (CCNC), pp. 597–602, January 2012
9. Viola, P., Jones, M.: Rapid object detection using a boosted cascade of simple features. In: Proceedings of the 2001 IEEE Computer Society Conference on Computer Vision and Pattern Recognition, CVPR 2001, vol. 1, pp. I-511–I-518 (2001)
10. Zhang, H.J., Low, C.Y., Smoliar, S.W., Wu, J.H.: Video parsing, retrieval and browsing: An integrated and content-based solution. In: Proceedings of the Third ACM International Conference on Multimedia, MULTIMEDIA 1995, pp. 15–24. ACM, New York (1995). http://doi.acm.org/10.1145/217279.215068
11. Zhang, H.J., Wu, J., Zhong, D., Smoliar, S.W.: An integrated system for content-based video retrieval and browsing. Pattern Recogn. **30**(4), 643–658 (1997). http://www.sciencedirect.com/science/article/pii/S0031320396001094

A Method of Object Re-identiciation Applicable to Multicamera Surveillance Systems

Karol Lisowski[(✉)] and Andrzej Czyżewski

Gdansk University of Technology, G. Narutowicza 11/12, 80-233 Gdansk, Poland
{lisowski,andcz}@sound.eti.pg.gda.pl

Abstract. The paper addresses some challenges pertaining to the methods for tracking of objects in multi-camera systems. The tracking methods related to a single Field of Vision (FOV) are quite different from inter-camera tracking, especially in case of non-overlapping FOVs. In this case, the processing is directed to determine the probability of a particular object's identity seen in a pair of cameras in the presence of places non-observed by any camera, thus an object can disappear in one observed region and then re-appear in another one. A methodology for evaluation of the introduced re-identification method is presented in the paper. Problems related to the preparation of the ground-truth database and to the impact of a single-camera tracking on the efficiency of the re-identification algorithm are discussed.

Keywords: Re-identification · Multi-camera · Surveillance

1 Introduction

A continuous increment is seen in the number of CCTV cameras included in video surveillance systems. Meanwhile, the development of technology related to the acquisition of video data resulted in a larger video image resolution. Owing to the aforementioned reasons an automated analysis is necessary, on one hand, and it becomes feasible on the other. The video processing is essential because of human perception limitations and the need to focus on a multitude of cameras for a long time. The circumstances are particularly adverse from the point of view of operators of multi-camera surveillance systems. Automated processing of video data allows for a detection and for a tracking of objects as well as for interpreting of various events entailed by moving objects in a given camera's FOV (Field of View). Multi-camera tracking is applied in order to support the operator in analysing video images from many cameras which can be distributed over a certain area. The key method of multi-camera tracking is called re-identification. The paper presents briefly the proposed re-identification method with a focus on the approach for an assessment of results based on the prepared ground-truth database. The main challenge in evaluation of re-identification methods is related to the dependency on the results obtained from the algorithms for analysis of video data on a single camera image. Therefore, in order to evaluate the re-identification properly, a possible incorrectness of these

© Springer International Publishing AG 2017
A. Dziech and A. Czyżewski (Eds.): MCSS 2017, CCIS 785, pp. 98–109, 2017.
https://doi.org/10.1007/978-3-319-69911-0_8

algorithms has to be taken into account. The content is organised in the following way. In Sect. 2 works related to the topic of the paper are mentioned. Section 3 contains a description of methodology for evaluation of re-identification method. Subsequent Sect. 4 is devoted to presentation of experiments and results. The paper is concluded by some general remarks contained in Sect. 5.

2   Related Works

In order to obtain input data for re-identification method, the video data from each single source have to be processed. This analysis consists of a few steps, as follows:

- background subtraction;
- object detection and tracking;
- event detection.

Background subtraction methods are related to distinguishing between stable region of video image and regions (called also as blobs) which differ from the background. Various method and approaches (i.e. utilization of the Gaussian Mixture Model [21] or the codebook algorithm [13]) are described in the literature [4,22].

Having the blobs found within a video image, moving objects can be detected and tracked. In case of methods described in this paper modified Kalman filters were used [10]. As a result of this step of video analysis, trajectories of moving object can be obtained. Also these methods are widely presented in the literature [5].

The event detection algorithms are mostly based on trajectories of tracked objects. In order to detect an event in video data, some rules describing this event are necessary. Types of events can refer to the crossing barrier, entering certain area or moving towards a given direction, etc. In the literature, methods for detecting various types of events are provided [9].

Multi-camera video analysis utilizes information related to time and location of appearing or disappearing tracked object, as well as appearance of it. Many approaches were presented in the literature [8,20]. In order to cope with challenges related to using of non-overlapping cameras where changes of illumination can occur, visual descriptors that are independent of these fluctuations were proposed [2,3,11,12,14]. Moreover, methods for obtaining and for the usage of spatio-temporal dependencies were also developed. They are using various approaches like: particle filters [14], Bayesian networks [11], Markov chains [12], probability dispersion function [3] etc.

3   Used Method

As an input for the re-identification method the so-called observations are needed. The single observation contains tree types of information:

- descriptors of object's visual features;
- location of the observed object;
- time of the observation.

In order to compare and to match a pair of the observations, a measure of fitness has to be considered. A role of such a measure can be fulfilled with a probability of identity of the object represented by the pair of observations. It can be, in turn, formulated as the following Eq. 1:

$$P_i(O_A, O_B) = w_v \cdot P_v(O_A, O_B) + w_t \cdot P_t(O_A, O_B) + w_b \cdot P_b(O_A, O_B) \qquad (1)$$

where O_A, O_B is a pair of observed object, P_v, P_t and P_b are probabilities of identity for the given object that is based on visual features, spatio-temporal dependencies and object behaviour patterns, respectively. Thus, w_v, w_t, w_b are weights of importance of particular probabilities ($w_v + w_t + w_b = 1$).

3.1 Spatio-Temporal Dependencies Model

In re-identification methods besides using the video data, information is related to spatio-temporal dependencies between cameras' FOVs and patterns of object movement through a whole observed area. The previous authors' efforts were focused on methods of obtaining this kind of information. The spatial dependencies of camera network can be easily gathered from a building or a city plan, but obtaining of temporal ones requires certain statistical data related to times of transitions between cameras. In order to describe these dependencies, a time of transition has to be modeled with the probability density function. Using Expectation-Maximization (EM) algorithm the probability of transition time is modeled with Gaussian Mixture Model (more precisely three gaussians were used). Thus, temporal dependencies are described by the following formula (as in Eq. 3):

$$p(t_{trans}) = \sum_{i=1}^{i=M} w_i \cdot N(t|\mu_i, \sigma_i) \qquad (2)$$

$$\sum_{i=1}^{i=M} w_i = 1$$

where: $p(t_{trans})$ express the probability of given time of transition t_{trans} between the particular pair of cameras; $N(t|\mu_i, \sigma_i)$ determines the value of normal distribution for the given time of transition; the parameters of the distribution are described with the mean value μ_i(mean transition time related to gaussian i) and standard deviation σ_i; w_i is the weight assigned to the particular gaussian; M is the number of gaussians in the GMM.

3.2 Behaviour Pattern Modelling

Moreover, basing on statistical data related to object movement through observed area the patterns of objects behavior are modeled and utilized in re-identification method. The approach proposed by the authors is based on the idea of Pawlak's flow graphs and rough set theory. Using terms of rough set theory a transition between pairs of cameras can be described with a rule (IF conditions, THEN decision). The rule is combined with two types of attributes conditions and decision. In case of multi-camera system the condition is appearance of the object in the given location and the decision is that the same object will also appear in the particular neighbor location. If it happens, the new location becomes a condition for the consecutive rules (generated until the object leaves the observed area). All rules can be organized into a graph which contains a knowledge about patterns of objects movements (called also a flow graph). In the flow graph, vertices are described with attributes and edges refer to rules. Each rule is described with tree parameters, namely: strength, certainty and coverage [18] (see Eqs. 3–6). These terms belong also to the rough set terminology. Therefore, the input statistical data necessary for building a flow graph is a set of objects' paths through the observed area. A single path is a sequence of locations (called also as steps) visited by the object.

$$\sigma\left(x_i, y_j\right) = \frac{\varphi\left(x_i, y_j\right)}{\varphi\left(G\right)} \tag{3}$$

where $\sigma(x_i, y_j)$ express the strength of rule and describes the rate of objects passing from location x in step i of the path to location y in step j; the number of objects passing from x_i to y_j is denoted as $\varphi(x_i, y_j)$, and the total number of paths in the input data is denoted as $\varphi(G)$. Similarly, in Eq. 2, $\varphi(x_i)$ is the number of objects that passed the node x_i.

$$\sigma\left(x_i\right) = \frac{\varphi\left(x_i\right)}{\varphi\left(G\right)} \tag{4}$$

where similarly as in Eq. 3 $\varphi(x_i)$ is the number of objects that passed location x in the step i. Having defined formulae Eqs. 3 and 4 next parameters of rule can be defined. Hence, the first of them is the certainty (cer):

$$cer\left(x_i, y_j\right) = \frac{\sigma\left(x_i, y_j\right)}{\sigma\left(x_i\right)} \tag{5}$$

where value of $cer(x_i, y_j)$ estimates the probability that the object which left location x in step i of the its path will appear in location y in step j. The last rule parameter is coverage which is defined as it is formulated in Eq. 6.

$$cov\left(x_i, y_j\right) = \frac{\sigma\left(x_i, y_j\right)}{\sigma\left(y_j\right)} \tag{6}$$

where $cov(x_i, y_j)$ determines estimation of probability that an object which appears in location y in step j of the path was seen before in location x in step i of the path.

3.3   Visual Features

Hence, as visual features description a SURF (Speeded Up Robust Features) descriptor was used [1], because this method allows not only for the detection of characteristic points in the image but also for easy matching of points from a pair of images. These characteristic points obtained from a video image are stored as descriptors of object's visual features in the observation. The implementation descriptor SURF and matcher FLANN (Fast Library for Approximate Nearest Neighbors) [17] from OpenCV library were used in the experiments. A ratio between matched characteristic points and detected points provides a measure of fitness of appearance (see Eq. 7).

$$P_v(O_A, O_B) = \frac{matchNum(O_A, O_B)}{detectNum(O_A)} \tag{7}$$

where $P_v(.)$ is probability of visual identity of objects from observations O_A, O_B, the function $detectNum(O_A)$ returns a number of detected characteristic points in observation O_A, and $matchNum(O_A, O_B)$ returns a number of matched characteristic points between the pair of observations (O_A, O_B).

3.4 Using of Spatio-Temporal Dependencies and Bahaviour Pattern Model

The spatio-temporal dependencies are represented with a directed graph in which vertices refer to regions observed with cameras, edges present the possibility of transition from one to another camera, and weights on edges are described with probabilities of transition time (in Eq. 1 noted as P_t). Probability of the transition time is estimated with Eq. 3. This type of a graph can be called a topology graph. Details related to the description, obtaining and using spatio-temporal dependencies are contained in the previous authors' publications [6,7,15].

In case of behaviour patterns used in the re-identification method they are also contained in a graph. Creation of this graph is based on the idea of Pawlak's flow graphs and on the rough set theory [18,19]. The flow graph is a directed graph in which the vertices refer to consecutive regions observed by cameras, whereas weights on the edges describe the probability that an object that just disappeared in the given camera will appear in the another (neighbouring) one. Actually, in order to determine the probability P_b from Eq. 1, the certainty parameter is used (See Eq. 5). Details about using of Pawlak's flow graphs in the re-identification are also described in the previous authors' works [6,7,15].

3.5 Decision Making

The re-identification method is based on making the decision informing if a pair of observations is related to the single real object. For each pair of observations the probability of object identity can be determined and pairs with the highest probability are chosen as those presenting the transition between cameras of the real object. It is obvious that pairs of observations which are physically impossible or are too distant in time are filtered out at the beginning of the algorithm and they are not taken into account in the next step of the re-identification (See Fig. 1). The consecutive phase is obtaining the three summands of Eq. 1.

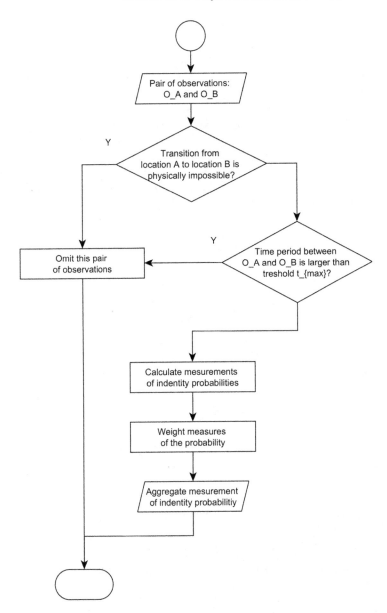

Fig. 1. Flowchart of obtaining measurement of the probability of object identity

In the mentioned authors' works the ways of obtaining them and of using them are presented. The topology graph and the flow graph both need initialization with statistical data from the past, in order to obtain probability distributions of transition times between cameras and patterns of objects movement on the whole observed area.

4   Experiments and Results

Hitherto, pilot tests of the system were performed. They were carried out, in order to prove the whole concept. Before the experiments were made, the topology and the flow graph had to be built up as a part of the initialization of the algorithm. These graphs are presented in Fig. 2. Employing the equations presented in Sect. 3.1 the parameters of GMMs for the particular transitions are shown in Table 1. Moreover, the values of bahaviour pattern model is presented in Table 2 (the symbols are consistent with Sect. 3.2).

The first part of the experiments was a creation of the ground truth base with correctly detected transitions of objects through the whole observed area. Next, re-identification method was performed on these pairs of observations, in order

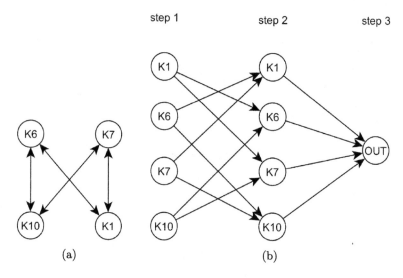

Fig. 2. Graphs used for estimation of probabilities P_t and P_b (See Eq. 1): (a) topology graph; (b) flow graph - vertex labeled as 'OUT' refer to the event when an object is leaving the observed area

Table 1. Parameters of GMM for topology graph used for the experiments (time is expressed in seconds)

Transition		w_1	μ_1	σ_1	w_2	μ_2	σ_2	w_3	μ_3	σ_3
from	to									
K1	K6	0.599706	55.6548	16.4292	0.166952	81.9792	12.2291	0.233343	67.5843	6.9635
K1	K7	0.501205	80.5872	3.1122	0.298830	73.9965	0.6657	0.199966	1.0034	89.0002
K6	K1	0.162216	69.3590	0.8711	0.166667	81.6667	1.5556	0.671117	56.1650	1.5556
K6	K10	0.281250	79.1111	2.9877	0.281250	79.1111	2.9877	0.437500	67.5714	2.1020
K7	K1	0.312233	82.3893	13.9951	0.322821	90.3258	6.7113	0.364946	85.2627	3.1618
K7	K10	0.357164	122.5990	18.6577	0.354433	96.3335	15.3770	0.288403	103.0196	2.5185
K10	K6	0.219122	78.9915	1.0032	0.345710	84.3249	1.5292	0.435169	91.8811	19.4572
K10	K7	0.342896	115.8483	24.7113	0.493019	100.1222	5.0633	0.164085	132.5366	6.2494

Table 2. Values of certainty (according to Eq. 5) for the flow graph presented in Fig. 2b

Transition		$cer(x_1, y_2)$
from (x_1)	to (y_2)	
K1	K6	0.7059
K1	K7	0.2941
K6	K1	0.3600
K6	K10	0.6400
K7	K1	0.3913
K7	K10	0.6087
K10	K6	0.4286
K10	K7	0.5714

(a) Camera K6

(b) Camera K7

(c) Camera K10

(d) Camera K1

Fig. 3. FOVs of cameras with marked hot areas (regions in which events of object appearing are detected) marked.

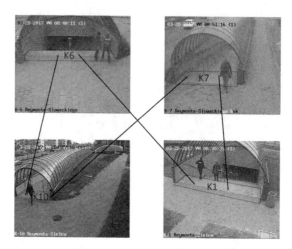

Fig. 4. FOVs of cameras and possible transitions between them (called also as topology of camera network)

to test how efficient is the proposed method in case of utterly correct tracking and detection for each single camera. For the experiments camera was placed near the exits of an underpass. In this case there is a certainty that an object which enters the underpass in a given camera will appear within the another camera while exiting the underpass (see Fig. 3). In connection with above, the topology graph is quite simple (see Fig. 4).

During the preparation of data necessary for initialization of the topology graph and the flow graph two hours of video data were analysed manually. In this period 76 object passed through the observed area and their timestamps and locations were determined. The next step was the preparation of the ground truth base. First, other two hours fragments of video data from the cameras had to be analysed, in order to obtain location and timestamps of events related to entering or exiting of the underpass. During this period 81 objects were observed. After that an automatic analysis was performed for each single camera, in order to remove those observed object which were detected incorrectly or those which were not detected. Moreover, timestamps were corrected according to time of detected events (entering or exiting of the underpass). As result of this step 62 of real object remained in the ground truth base for the testing of the re-identification.

According to Eq. 1 particular weights were modified, in order to determine the best values of weights in reference to efficiency. The results are presented in Table 3.

First, the two weights (related to visual appearance and temporary dependencies) were taken into account with different values (expressed with w'_v and w'_t, respectively), as it is represented with the first row of Table 3 in which the weight related to behaviour patterns was omitted that means $w'_b = 0$. The sum of all weights has to be equal to one, therefore adding the third weight implicates

Table 3. Number of correct re-identifications in dependence on the weights. In ground-truth base are 62 object transitions to detect.

w'_b	w'_v								
	0.000	0.125	0.250	0.375	0.500	0.625	0.750	0.875	1.000
	w'_t								
	1.000	0.875	0.750	0.625	0.500	0.375	0.250	0.125	0.000
0.000	15	23	30	34	35	31	19	12	7
0.125	11	17	22	29	36	18	12	6	5
0.250	5	10	18	21	27	9	3	2	1
0.375	1	4	12	20	18	7	1	0	0
0.500	0	1	3	7	8	1	0	0	0
0.625	0	0	1	3	2	0	0	0	0
0.750	0	0	0	0	0	0	0	0	0
0.875	0	0	0	0	0	0	0	0	0
1.000	0	0	0	0	0	0	0	0	0

a small modification in the calculation of the values of weights which is described with Eq. 8:

$$w_x = \frac{w'_x}{w'_v + w'_t + w'_b} \tag{8}$$

where $w'_x = w'_v, w'_t, w'_b$ and w_x is a value of the weight x after modification. It is to notice that if a single weight w'_x is equal to zero the values of the rest of weights are exactly like those given in the table (See Table 3). In case of using only two types of measures of the probability of identity (that are related to visual features and topology graph) the best result was obtained for the following weights $w'_v = 0.5$ and $w_t = 0.5$. Addition of the third probability measure related to behaviour patterns causes a slight improvement for the following values $w'_v = 0.5$, $w'_t = 0.5$, $w'_v = 0.125$.

Comparison with Other Re-identification Methods. In the literature many methods of re-identification can be found, but it is quite hard to compare them, because of different methodologies of experiments and efficiency measures. In this paper the accuracy is used to evaluate proposed method. Thus the best obtained accuracy is equal to $36/62 = 58.06\%$. Because, the proposed method allows for a fork in the path of object when it disappeared from the FoV of cameras not all re-identification method found in the literature can be taken into account in this comparison. The two approaches are very similar to the proposed one:

- the method using constrained dominant sets clustering technique [23] obtained accuracy 59.6%;
- the approach using segmentation of the cameras' FoVs based on the object activity and Cross Canonical Correlation Analysis (as method for discovery of temporal dependency between regions within and between cameras) [16] obtained accuracy 45%.

5 Conclusions

In order to evaluate the re-identification algorithm the impact of has to be minimized. Modification of the weights also has an impact on the re-identification. The optimal weights values can be different for various types of cameras and for spatio-temporal dependencies. Thus, initialization process is needed before applying the proposed method in a new cameras setup. It also can be related to the simple topology of the camera network. Future works are focused on using different descriptor of visual features and on the determination of their employment for the re-identification method.

Acknowledgements. This work has been partially funded by the Polish National Science Centre within the grant belonging to the program "Preludium" No. 277900 entitled: Methods for design of the camera network topology aimed to re-identification and tracking objects on the basis of behavior modelling with the flow graph.

References

1. Bay, H., Tuytelaars, T., Van Gool, L.: SURF: speeded up robust features. In: Leonardis, A., Bischof, H., Pinz, A. (eds.) ECCV 2006. LNCS, vol. 3951, pp. 404–417. Springer, Heidelberg (2006). doi:10.1007/11744023_32
2. Cheng, Y., Huang, C., Fu, L.: Multiple people visual tracking in a multi-camera system for cluttered environments. In: 2006 IEEE/RSJ International Conference on Intelligent Robots and Systems, pp. 675–680, October 2006
3. Colombo, A., Orwell, J., Velastin, S.: Colour constancy techniques for re-recognition of pedestrians from multiple surveillance cameras. In: Workshop on Multi-camera and Multi-modal Sensor Fusion Algorithms and Applications, pp. 1–13 (2008)
4. Czyżewski, A., Szwoch, G., Dalka, P., Szczuko, P., Ciarkowski, A., Ellwart, D., Merta, T., Łopatka, K., Kulasek, Ł., Wolski, J.: Multi-stage video analysis framework. In: Weiyao, L. (ed.) Video Surveillance, Chap. 9, pp. 145–171. Intech (2011). http://dx.doi.org/10.5772/16088
5. Czyżewski, A., Dalka, P.: Moving object detection and tracking for the purpose of multimodal surveillance system in urban areas. In: Tsihrintzis, G., Virvou, M., Howlett, R., Jain, L. (eds.) New Directions in Intelligent Interactive Multimedia. SCI, vol. 142, pp. 75–84. Springer, Heidelberg (2008). doi:10.1007/978-3-540-68127-4_8
6. Czyżewski, A., Lisowski, K.: Adaptive method of adjusting flowgraph for route reconstruction in video surveillance systems. Fundam. Inf. **127**(1–4), 561–576 (2013). http://dx.doi.org/10.3233/FI-2013-927
7. Czyzewski, A., Lisowski, K.: Employing flowgraphs for forward route reconstruction in video surveillance system. J. Intell. Inf. Syst. **43**(3), 521–535 (2014). http://dx.doi.org/10.1007/s10844-013-0253-8
8. Dalka, P., Ellwart, D., Szwoch, G., Lisowski, K., Szczuko, P., Czyżewski, A.: Selection of visual descriptors for the purpose of multi-camera object re-identification. In: Stańczyk, U., Jain, L.C. (eds.) Feature Selection for Data and Pattern Recognition. SCI, vol. 584, pp. 263–303. Springer, Heidelberg (2015). doi:10.1007/978-3-662-45620-0_12

9. Dalka, P., Szwoch, G., Ciarkowski, A.: Distributed framework for visual event detection in parking lot area. In: Dziech, A., Czyżewski, A. (eds.) MCSS 2011. CCIS, vol. 149, pp. 37–45. Springer, Heidelberg (2011). doi:10.1007/978-3-642-21512-4_5

10. Dalka, P., Szwoch, G., Szczuko, P., Czyzewski, A.: Video content analysis in the urban area telemonitoring system. In: Tsihrintzis, G.A., Jain, L.C. (eds.) Multimedia Services in Intelligent Environments, pp. 241–261. Springer, Heidelberg (2010). doi:10.1007/978-3-642-13396-1_11

11. Javed, O.: Appearance modeling for tracking in multiple non-overlapping cameras. In: IEEE International Conference on Computer Vision and Pattern Recognition, pp. 26–33 (2005)

12. Kim, H., Romberg, J., Wolf, W.: Multi-camera tracking on a graph using Markov Chain Monte Carlo. In: Third ACM/IEEE International Conference on Distributed Smart Cameras, ICDSC 2009, pp. 1–8, August 2009

13. Kim, K., Chalidabhongse, T.H., Harwood, D., Davis, L.: Real-time foreground-background segmentation using codebook model. Real Time Imaging 11(3), 172–185 (2005). http://dx.doi.org/10.1016/j.rti.2004.12.004

14. Lev-Tov, A., Moses, Y.: Path recovery of a disappearing target in a large network of cameras. In: Proceedings of the Fourth ACM/IEEE International Conference on Distributed Smart Cameras, ICDSC 2010, pp. 57–64. ACM, New York (2010). http://doi.acm.org/10.1145/1865987.1865997

15. Lisowski, K., Czyzewski, A.: Complexity analysis of the Pawlak's flowgraph extension for re-identification in multi-camera surveillance system. Multimedia Tools Appl. 75, 1–17 (2015). http://dx.doi.org/10.1007/s11042-015-2652-z

16. Loy, C.C., Xiang, T., Gong, S.: Time-delayed correlation analysis for multi-camera activity understanding. International J. Comput. Vis. 90(1), 106–129 (2010). https://doi.org/10.1007/s11263-010-0347-5

17. Muja, M., Lowe, D.G.: Scalable nearest neighbor algorithms for high dimensional data. IEEE Trans. Pattern Anal. Mach. Intell. 36, 2227–2240 (2014)

18. Pawlak, Z.: Rough sets and flow graphs. In: Ślęzak, D., Wang, G., Szczuka, M., Düntsch, I., Yao, Y. (eds.) RSFDGrC 2005. LNCS (LNAI), vol. 3641, pp. 1–11. Springer, Heidelberg (2005). doi:10.1007/11548669_1

19. Pawlak, Z.: Flow graphs and data mining. In: Peters, J.F., Skowron, A. (eds.) Transactions on Rough Sets III. LNCS, vol. 3400, pp. 1–36. Springer, Heidelberg (2005). doi:10.1007/11427834_1

20. Radke, R.J.: A survey of distributed computer vision algorithms. In: Nakashima, H., Aghajan, H., Augusto, J.C. (eds.) Handbook of Ambient Intelligence and Smart Environments, pp. 35–55. Springer, Boston (2010). doi:10.1007/978-0-387-93808-0_2

21. Stauffer, C., Grimson, W.E.L.: Adaptive background mixture models for real-time tracking. In: CVPR, pp. 2246–2252. IEEE Computer Society (1999)

22. Szwoch, G.: Performance evaluation of the parallel codebook algorithm for background subtraction in video stream. In: Dziech, A., Czyżewski, A. (eds.) MCSS 2011. CCIS, vol. 149, pp. 149–157. Springer, Heidelberg (2011). doi:10.1007/978-3-642-21512-4_18

23. Tesfaye, Y., Mequanint, E., Prati, A., Pelillo, M., Shah, M.: Multi-target tracking in multiple non-overlapping cameras using constrained dominant sets, June 2017

Traffic Noise Analysis Applied to Automatic Vehicle Counting and Classification

Karolina Marciniuk[1](✉), Bożena Kostek[1], and Andrzej Czyżewski[2]

[1] Laboratory of Audio Acoustics, Faculty of ETI, Gdańsk University of Technology,
Narutowicza 11/12, 80-233 Gdańsk, Poland
karmarci@pg.edu.pl, bokostek@audioacoustics.org
[2] Multimedia Systems Department, Faculty of ETI,
Gdańsk University of Technology, Narutowicza 11/12, 80-233 Gdańsk, Poland
andcz@multimed.org

Abstract. Problems related to determining traffic noise characteristics are discussed in the context of automatic dynamic noise analysis based on noise level measurements and traffic prediction models. The obtained analytical results provide the second goal of the study, namely automatic vehicle counting and classification. Several traffic prediction models are presented and compared to the results of in-situ noise level measurements. Synchronized audio recordings were made to determine Sound Quality parameters describing the nature of acquired sound signals. Video recordings and information about the traffic structure using commercially available automatic vehicle detection methods were also collected in order to create ground truth data used for the experiments.

Keywords: Traffic noise · Audio parametrization · Automatic dynamic noise map creation · Automatic traffic counting and vehicle recognition

1 Introduction

The European Directive No. 2002/49/EC on the assessment and management of environmental noise (the Environmental Noise Directive – END) appeared in 2002 [14,15], however the integrated environment noise management notion was introduced more than a decade earlier [24], which eventually evolved into dynamic noise maps concept [6,23,26,28,37,39,43]. It should be noted that several noise prediction models appear through the years [30], that served dynamic noise map (DNM) creating. Noise maps (NMs) in most cases are prepared by numerical calculations, with their accuracy depending on quality of the input data (traffic flow), considering also the complexity of the building geometry and terrain elevation [11,26,42]. The basic technique, however, that underlies DNM prediction models is reverse engineering [8,25,36,38].

Environmental noise pollution is defined as noise caused by road, rail or airport traffic, industry, construction works, as well as by some other outdoor activities. The adverse effects of noise are also originated from the known fact that they are related to a long list of potential health problems, both physical and

© Springer International Publishing AG 2017
A. Dziech and A. Czyżewski (Eds.): MCSS 2017, CCIS 785, pp. 110–123, 2017.
https://doi.org/10.1007/978-3-319-69911-0_9

psychological ones [14,29,35]. However, the noise maps according to European Commission guidelines are to be updated every five years. This causes numerous discrepancies between the NMs and DNMs, the latter ones being a valuable source for noise pollution, as well as traffic prediction, used for modeling and eventually creating anti-noise means. Recently, new approaches to the assessment of noise pollution appeared, either online noise measurement systems based on a distributed network of sensors [3,10] or involving general public-based mobile phones serving as noise sensors that enable citizens to measure their personal exposure to noise in their everyday environment. The latter approach results in geo-localized measurements and a collective noise map creation [5,23]. It is worth noting that both: online and collective noise map may contribute to the creation of a more realistic dynamic noise map.

In the paper, issues related to traffic monitoring are discussed in the context of automatic dynamic noise analysis based on noise level measurements and traffic prediction models. The obtained analytical results serve the second goal of the study performed, namely automatic vehicle counting and recognition, as well as road pavement conditions determination related to weather changes. Section 2 presents several traffic prediction models that are subsequently compared to in-situ noise level measurements. Standard traffic management systems are also presented. Next section refers to the conducted experiments with audio-video recordings for the purpose of serving as the ground truth data source for automatic traffic counting and vehicle recognition. Audio recordings are segmented into individual events, they are labeled accordingly to the gathered image content, and then they are parameterized. Finally, the parameter vectors are submitted to Neural Networks for classification. Also, Sound Quality metrics are recalled and discussed in the context of information that may be useful in the traffic structure discerning.

2   Noise Pollution Management

As was already mentioned, due to noise pollution the regulation proposed by the authorities of the Member Sates of the European Union and by the Council of Europe (the Directive 2002/49/EC [15]), all cities with above the 250 thousand residents are obliged to prepare Noise Map in the period of every 5 years. Some of the cities authorities implemented a mesh of live tracking noise monitoring sensors, including wearable and portable sensors, as well as smartphones as Smart City solutions (e.g. Dublin, Glasgow, Gdańsk, Turin, etc.) [2] or the so-called Array of Things (e.g. Chicago) [2].

The Noise Map serves as a document of the acoustic climate in a given area. Typically, it contains both: text with tables of results, charts and necessary descriptors, and the graphical representation of calculated noise levels. Thanks to the presentation of sound pressure level contours, it is easy to identify areas at risk of noise pollution. Nevertheless, road traffic noise has the largest influence on acoustic urban environment compared to other sources such as rail or aircraft noise [7].

Road noise may be defined as a sum of a few individual but connected sources. The main three elements that generate noise are as follows: engine with exhaust system, friction noise from tire component, and aerodynamic noise. All of them play a different role as a function of speed, and vehicle type [22]. For the express road (that is a subject of this study) the main noise sources are related to tire/road coupling [33].

2.1   Noise Prediction Models

The most popular noise models are related to the outcomes of the European project Harmonoise, NMPB, ISO 9612-2 [31]. Even though, the Harmonoise model was intended to provide a basis for a new standard European model, whereas it was NMBP, the French model, that was recommended by European Union in directive 2002/49/EC for countries that did not develop their national models. It should be noted, that the NMBP method is similar to the ray tracing model, its accuracy depending on the number of paths formed between the source and the receiver, and on the number of the emitted sound reflections set. The method takes into consideration the standard meteorological conditions. Contrarily, a method implemented in the Harmonoise directive considers the point-to-point propagation, therefore linear sources should be segmented for the analysis [34].

The French model was used for the ex-situ calculation is presented in the study. A design of a small area of the closed road was prepared in CadnaA(4.4) software [12].

2.2   Sound Quality Studies Applied to Automotive Industry

In automotive industry sound quality is important in the context of:

- Vehicles interior noise - associated with driving comfort [20].
- Automotive onboard multimedia devices audio quality [1,19].
- Exterior noise - related to driving safety, law requirements and used for recognition [9].

As a part of this study we focus on the exterior noise, as the European Union imposes precise requirements on acceptable levels of noise generated by the vehicle [32]. For now it is set between 72–80 dB(A) depending on the weight and horsepower of a vehicle. However, of a great importance are also Sound Quality metrics, as they are related to the psycho-acoustical models of human hearing system [16]. For example, the way sound amplitude is perceived in critical bands is described by the Loudness metric with unit "sone" (Eq. 1) or with additional metric - Loudness Level. It is an important parameter for signals with non-stationary characteristics such as traffic noise. Loudness Level is represented in "phon" unit. The specific curves of equal-loudness can be found in Zwicker and Fastl book [16] (Chap. 8, Fig. 8.1). Sharpness is information about the amount of the energy concentrated in higher frequency bands. Roughness and Fluctuation

(Eqs. 4–5) can deliver information on the traffic structure - vehicle types and noise related to engine functioning. For example, as results from the following analysis, the diesel engines tend to have more irregularities in the lower part of 1.5 kHz frequency band [9]:

$$N = \int_0^{24Bark} N' dz \quad \text{sone} \tag{1}$$

where N' are values of specific loudness in sone per Bark.

$$S = c \cdot \frac{\int_0^{24Bark} N' g'(z) \cdot z \cdot dz}{\int_0^{24Bark} N' dz} \quad \text{acum} \tag{2}$$

where c is proportional constant, z is a band order and $g'(z)$ is the weighting function for frequency above 16 bark (Zwicker and Fastl [16]) that:

$$\begin{cases} z < 14, \rightarrow g'(z) = 1 \\ z < 14, \rightarrow g'(z) = 0.00012 \cdot z^4 - 0.0056 \cdot z^3 + 0.1 \cdot z^2 - 0.81 \cdot z + 3.51 \end{cases} \tag{3}$$

$$R = cal \cdot \int_0^{24Bark} f_{mod} \cdot \Delta L \cdot dz \quad \text{asper} \tag{4}$$

where cal is a callibration factor, f_{mod} is the frequency of modulation and ΔL is the perceived masking depth [16].

$$F = \frac{0.008 \cdot \int_0^{24Bark} \Delta L \cdot dz}{\left(\frac{f_{mod}}{4\,Hz}\right) + \left(\frac{4\,Hz}{f_{mod}}\right)} \quad \text{vacil} \tag{5}$$

4 Hz is a modulation frequency where maximum values are being found.

2.3   Vehicle Detection Systems

The very first Intelligent Transportation System (ITS) constructed was a sound detector invented by Charles Adler Jr. in 1928 [4]. The invention was a traffic signal light actuated by sound of a car horn. Another invention was a vehicle counter that detected sound of cars passing-by a metal object at the ground (similar to counting cars at the bridge from sound dilatation passing). Nowadays, we can distinguish two groups of ITS sensors - passive and active ones. The first ones do not need any additional probe signal. Typically, they are the off-roadway non intrusive sensors, such as: video or acoustic detectors. Their role is to observe an environment and to extract information from the processed signals. The active system task is to detect additional signals (such infra-red or radar detectors) in order to get information from the returning signal. Other examples of active systems are intrusive ones, such as: inductive loop detectors and magnetometers. In Table 1 typical ITS systems are presented with their most significant capabilities.

Table 1. Typical ITS systems and their features (according to [21], Chap. 1, pp. 8–10)

Sensor	Feature			
	Count	Speed	Classification	Price
Inductive loop	Yes	Yes	Yes	Low
Passive infrared	Yes	Yes	No	Low to moderate
Microwave radar	Yes	Yes	No	Low to moderate
Video image processor	Yes	Yes	Yes	Moderate to high
Acoustic array	Yes	Yes	No	Moderate
Ultrasonic	Yes	No	No	Low to moderate

3   Experiments

In the first step of the research, a series of measurements was performed. They were conducted near a busy road in the city of Gdansk in several sessions (Fig. 1). The tested area was chosen with regard to the project assumptions and requirements. Firstly, a road should be a straight line in at least 1 Km distance. Measurement stations were placed away from the urbanized area, i.e. close to the typical high speed national road. For the first case scenario an easy option was chosen - all vehicles were driving in one direction.

The main purpose of this research was an examination of usefulness of noise-based measurements as the traffic monitoring technique. For that purpose the used equipment was DSA-50 Sonopan - the digital sound analyzer. The measured values were time-averaged sound levels with A weighting (L_{Aeq}), maximum RMS S-time-weighted sound level (L_{ASmx}) and maximum peak sound level (L_{ZMPk}) refreshed every single second.

At the same time audio recording was performed in 24-bit resolution and for 96 kHz sampling ratio using the Behringer B-5 condenser omni-directional microphone and an additional ZOOM SGH-6 shotgun microphone (Super-Cardioid Polar Pattern). For the ground truth the EasyCOUNT traffic flow the analyzer was used (courtesy of the General Direction of National Road and Highways in Gdańsk). It constitutes a mobile radar traffic measurement station that is able to classify vehicles into five categories based on their length [13].

The measurement error for vehicle counts is less than 1% in this case and for the vehicle classification it is equal to 5% (according to the technical note). For the speed measurements the error value was less than 3 km/h for speeds being lower than 100 km/h. The road analyzed was a two-lane street, so that the obtained result may differ from the real in-situ conditions due to the obscuring effect of the vehicles. For the synchronization purposes an additional information related to video image was recorded, specifically in order to check the reliability of the automatic vehicle counting performed by the EasyCOUNT application and to deliver move detailed information about the vehicles such as technical class (not the length division) and speed.

Fig. 1. Set up for the measurements conducted near the road

3.1 Measurement Scenario

The equipment was placed 4 m away from the road edge at 1.5 m height. The distance between the Zoom microphone and the Sonopan device was 0.5 m. The working scenario of the EasyCOUNT vehicle detector forced the equipment placement being situated close to the road sign, two meters away from the measurement point (Fig. 1). It should be noted, that this may have an influence on the vehicle counting results.

3.2 Results

Thanks to the EasyCOUNT sensor employment we were able to gather information on the current traffic intensity and its structure. We checked out the error ratio during the first two minutes of the experiment with video recordings performed in the background. Based on that observation, we were able to add correction for traffic ratio during the observation hour. Obtained numbers were used in CadnaA for noise map calculation. As was mentioned before, the geometrical and the technical aspects of the road with their statistic information are translated into corresponding noise level analyzed in frequency bands [31]. In the case of Armii Krajowej Av. (the name of a street in Gdańsk) the value in octave bands are presented in Table 2. The number of cars registered during the measurement slot was 1868 and 2.3% of them were classified as heavy tracks (class 4 and 5 in 5+1 classification method), two of them were motorcycles. The noise map obtained is presented in Fig. 2. Results of calculations were contained along with the results of the performed measurements in Table 3.

Sound Level Comparison. Sound Quality metrics (SQ) were calculated for two sound sources employing the PULSE Reflex software. Loudness values were compared with the Sonopan Digital Sound Analyzer. The FFT Autospectrum

Table 2. Main source - Armii Krajowej Av. and theoretical model based on the traffic measurements from EasyCOUNT

Street	Power L_p [dB] for frequency octave bands					
	125	259	500	1000	2000	4000
Armii Krajowej	45.7	49.8	52.9	55.9	52.7	47.3

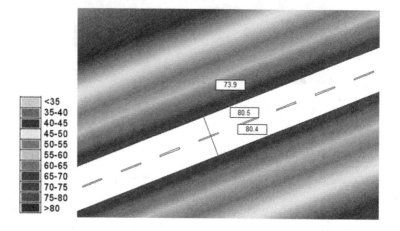

Fig. 2. Noise map obtained for the experiment area

Table 3. Obtained sound levels using chosen equipment and software

Measurement method	Sound level [dB]
Digital sound analyzer DSA-50 Sonopan	72.1
SQ Loudness - PULSE Reflex shotgun mic.	78.2
SQ Loudness - PULSE Reflex B-5 mic.	81.9
CadnaA - CTRN Road Noise Model	76.7
CadnaA - NBPS Road Noise Model	73.9

was also calculated. The comparison between the equipment used and the calculation method are presented in Table 2 and in Fig. 3. Recording from B-5 microphone (omni directional) was significantly different from the sound meter measurements. The microphone whit shot-gun characteristic acted like a soundgate, recording mainly the sound in the corner of the detection. Significant road events took place during the observation as follows:

- Ambulance pass-by was registered twice (Fig. 4a),
- Significant increases in sound levels were noted for older vehicles, even in comparison to faster-moving vehicles (Fig. 4b),
- Slowly driving cars (less than 30 km/h) tend to cause a significant increase in the sound level for the band 6–8 kHz (Fig. 4c).

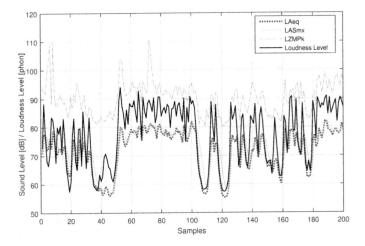

Fig. 3. Sound level obtained from the measurement with Sonopan device and information extracted from an audio recorder using SQ metrics (Shoot-gun microphone)

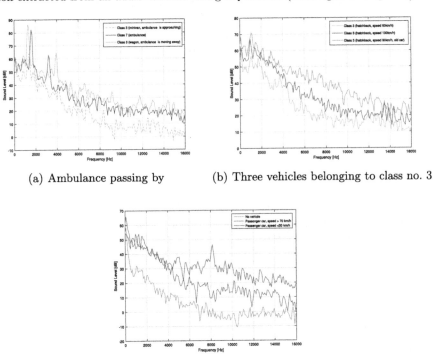

(a) Ambulance passing by   (b) Three vehicles belonging to class no. 3

(c) Slow car vs fast moving

Fig. 4. FFT spectrum for selected road events (with frame length equal to 500 ms, 75% overlapping and 80 Hz frequency resolution)

Sound Quality parameters in 1 Hz sampling rate were compared with the vehicle presence in time vector (EasyCOUNT and video recordings). Besides Loudness, and Loudness Level metrics (according to DIN 45631 an Zwicker), it was found that Sharpness (Zwicker) metric also allows for vehicle detection. The results of the SQ-based analysis are to be shown in the next Section.

Automatic Counting. An algorithm for detecting a vehicle activity in a road was developed by the authors. Similarly to a typical Voice Activity Detection (VAD) algorithm, vectors with data were split into sequences/frames. In absence of a vehicle, Loudness Levels were approximately 60 dB, for a single pass-by of passenger car - about 85 dB (signal from shot-gun microphone). For vehicle columns the level rises above 90 dB. The event detection threshold depends on the parameter being tested and was a combination of the mean and the standard deviation taking also into account the road class. Correctness metrics were calculated based on the comparison of the total number of detected events and the number of vehicles in the tested sample recording. The results are shown in Table 4. Precision (p) is a metric of positive prediction values shown as the ratio between true positives to the sum of all positive decisions in a system (Eq. 6). Recall (r) (or sensitivity) is a true positive ratio described by Eq. 7. F-Score is the weighted harmonic mean of precision and recall. The most common representation of the F-Score measure is presented in Eq. 8.

$$p = \frac{TP}{TP + FP} \tag{6}$$

$$r = \frac{TP}{TP + FN} \tag{7}$$

$$F = \frac{2 \cdot p \cdot r}{(p + r)} \tag{8}$$

The General Direction of National Roads and Highways (GDDKiA, [40]) in their specification for testing detection and classification systems requires determination of detection level by the formula 9:

$$d = \frac{(N - \epsilon_m - \epsilon_f)}{N} \tag{9}$$

Table 4. Proposed vehicle detection algorithm evaluation for 106 vehicles

Parameter	Detection evaluation metrics				
	F-score	Precision	Sensitivity	Detection ratio	Detected
L_{ZMPk}	0.563	0.615	0.516	84.3%	100
L_{Aeq}	0.648	0.648	0.648	100%	100
Loudness Level	0.857	0.792	0.934	82.1%	125
Sharpness	0.704	0.764	0.642	91.5%	115

where: N is the actual number of vehicles at the detection area, ϵ_m is the number of skipped vehicles, and ϵ_f is the number of the false positives.

From the economic point of view, it is very important to keep traffic within the designed parameters. High vehicle volume reinforces overall noise levels, pavement destruction, what may lead to high safety risk [41].

Using Sonopan device-based L_{ZMPk} values as a vehicle detection in time results in substantial number of False Positive and False Negative readings, the calculated number of cars was, however, close to their correct value. The detection was delayed by one frame (1S/s). In dynamic traffic management we are more interested in volume per some observation time (typical 3–5 min, maximum 15 min interval [17]) than a specific time stamp the vehicle presents, so information from the city noise monitoring station can provide valuable information for ITS.

Automatic Vehicle Type Classification. Volume of vehicles per hour is not the only information that is needed from traffic observation. The structure of the traffic flow has also a significant influence on safety and noise levels [8]. When based on sound level only, one can observe that a single lorry can be as loud as two or more car passing by at the same time. The only difference between them can be the nature of the sound [22].

Given the data obtained during the measurements, the frequency analysis was performed, i.e. audio parameters were extracted to create a feature vector. Mean and standard deviation of the three most significant parameters within the most common vehicle classes are presented in Table 5. Vehicles were divided according to the Table 1 in the journal of statutes from 2014 position 1727 (*pl. Dz.U. 2014 poz. 1727*). Vehicle type 3 means passenger car, 4 is a bus, and group 6 are heavy trucks. This type of classification were used for feature more specific classification base of car body type (wagon, hatchback, sedan etc.). In automatic vehicle detection classification system 5+1 and 8+1 is used (i.e.: other vehicles$_1$/motorbike$_2$/car$_3$/van$_4$/car with trailer$_5$/lorry$_6$/lorry with trailer$_7$/articulated lorry$_8$/bus$_9$). Besides Sharpness and Roughness, the energy distribution in 1/3 octave bands was analyzed. The results are presented in a graph in Fig. 5. Differences between vehicle classes are noticeable in the lower band, as well as at frequencies above 4 kHz.

Table 5. Sound Quality metric for different vehicle types

	Loudness Level [phon]		Sharpness [acum]		Roughness [asper]	
	Mean	*StD*	*Mean*	*StD*	*Mean*	*StD*
Silence	65.907	5.245	1.251	0.173	1.968	0.225
Passengers (class 3)	89.604	2.375	1.651	0.133	1.758	0.208
Buses (class 4)	90.512	1.519	1.630	0.044	1.865	0.074
Lorries (class 6)	92.470	1.241	1.677	0.151	1.675	0.189

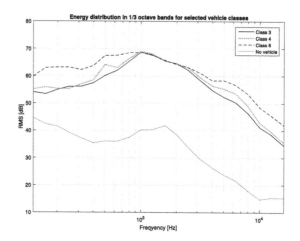

Fig. 5. Sound level for group of vehicles within the class. 3 - passenger car, 4 - bus, 6 - lorry

4   Conclusions

Short term sound levels measurements can reflect an approximate traffic volume [27], but without additional information about the nature of sound, the classification can easily result in false positives because of other noise components presence. Feature extraction or spectrum analysis can provide important information for detection and classification effectiveness improvement. Traffic recordings were registered in an area where no additional noise sources exist (this area is located far away from industrial facilities and/or human/animal activities), therefore it is possible that the algorithm may work less efficiently for traffic detection in more urbanized areas. Calibration phase can correct results, but still the main goal of the project is to build up a traffic data acquisition station for a typical high speed road outside the city center. Further research is needed to improve efficiency of detection of a vehicle presence and to investigate in the real time the environmental sounds influencing the effectiveness of classification at different roads with similar traffic conditions.

Acknowledgments. Research was subsidized by the Polish National Centre for Research and Development and the General Directorate of Public Roads and Motorways within the grant No. OT4- 4B/AGH-PG-WSTKT.

References

1. Automotive audio quality. JAES **53**(6), 542–548 (2005)
2. Array of things project. https://arrayofthings.github.io/. Accessed July 2017
3. Acoustic mapping and noise monitoring portal of Gdańsk city. http://mapaakustyczna.gdansk.gda.pl/GdanskMakus/

4. Archives Center, National Museum of American History, Charles Adler, Jg. Collection, ca. 1920–1980. http://amhistory.si.edu/archives/d8351.htm. Accessed July 2017

5. Athanasiadis, I.N., Mitkas, P.A., Rizzoli, A.E., Gómez, J.M. (eds.): Information Technologies in Environmental Engineering. Environmental Science and Engineering. Springer, Heidelberg (2009). doi:10.1007/978-3-540-88351-7_16

6. Beca, I.M., Holonec, L., Hoda, G., Clitan, A.: Analysing noise levels in urban area during the evening period. ProEnvironment **9**, 95–98 (2016). http://journals.usamvcluj.ro/index.php/promediu. Accessed July 2017

7. Botteldooren, D., Dekoninck, L., Gillis, D.: The influence of traffic noise on appreciation of the living quality of a neighborhood. Int. J. Environ. Res. Public Health **8**(3), 777–798 (2011). doi:10.3390/ijerph8030777

8. Berengier, M.: Noise classification methods for urban road surfaces: "Backing Board" method: LCPC contribution, report F.R1, silence project (2012). http://www.silence-ip.org/site/fileadmin/SP_F/SILENCE_F.R1_140108_LCPC.pdf. Accessed July 2017

9. Cerrato, G.: Automotive sound quality powertrain, road and wind noise. Sound & Vibration, April 2009. http://www.sandv.com/downloads/0904cerr.pdf. Accessed July 2017

10. Czyżewski, A., Kotus, J., Szczodrak, M.: Online urban acoustic noise monitoring system. Noise Control Eng. J. **60**(1), 69–84 (2012)

11. Czyżewski, A., Marciniuk, K., Kostek, B.: Dynamic road traffic density estimation employing noise mapping with the use of grid supercomputing. In: Proceedings of Acoustical Society of America 2016 Meeting, 2478337, Salt Lake City, USA, 23 May –27 August 2016 (2016). doi:10.1121/1.4949894

12. DataKustikCadnaA: State-of-the-art noise prediction software. http://www.datakustik.com/fileadmin/user_upload/PDF/2012/CadnaA_at_a_glance_english.pdf. Accessed July 2017

13. EasyCOUNT technical note. http://www.cat-traffic.pl/wp-content/uploads/EasyCOUNT.pdf. Accessed July 2017

14. EEA (European Environment Agency): Technical report, No. 11, good practice guide on noise exposure and potential health effects, Copenhagen (2010). ISSN 1725-2237

15. European Directive 2002/49/EC, European Parliament and Council of 25/06/2002 Relating to the Assessment and Management of Environmental Noise (2002)

16. Fastl, H., Zwicker, E.: Psychoacoustics: Facts and Models. Springer Science and Business Media, Heidelberg (2007)

17. Gaca, S., Suchorzewski, W., Tracz, M.: Inżynieria ruchu drogowego. Teoria i praktyka, Wydawnictwo Komunikacji i Łączności MKŁ (2014)

18. FONOMOC - The main network for noise monitoring, working group noise EUROCITIES. https://workinggroupnoise.com/fonomoc/. Accessed July 2017

19. Herrera, C.G., Donoso-Garcia, P.F., Medeiros, E.B.: Intelligibility in low-cost automotive audio systems. J. Audio Eng. Soc. **64**(5), 320–331 (2016). https://doi.org/10.17743/jaes.2016.0010

20. Kaplanis, N., Bech, S., Tervo, S., Pätynen, J., Lokki, T., Waterschoot, T., Jensen, S.H.: A rapid sensory analysis method for perceptual assessment of automotive audio. J. Audio Eng. Soc. **65**(1/2), 130–146 (2017). https://doi.org/10.17743/jaes.2016.0056

21. Klein, L.A., Mills, M.K., Gibson, D.R.P.: Traffic Detector Handbook, 3rd edn., vol. I. FHWA-HRT-06-108, October 2006

22. Kurowski, A., Marciniuk, K., Kostek, B.: Separability assessment of selected types of vehicle-associated noise. In: proceedings of 10th International Conference on Multimedia and Network Information Systems, vol. 506, No. 10, pp. 113–121, Wrocław, Polska, 14–16 September 2016 (2016). doi:10.1007/978-3-319-43982-2_10

23. Maisonneuve, N., Stevens, M., Niessen, M.E., Steels, L.: NoiseTube: measuring and mapping noise pollution with mobile phones. In: Proceedings of Information Technologies in Environmental Engineering (ITEE 2009), Proceedings of the 4th International ICSC Symposium (2009)

24. Manvell, D.: Managing urban noise in cities – an integrated approach to mapping, monitoring, evaluation and improvement. In: Proceedings of Internoise (1999)

25. Manvell, D., et al.: Reverse engineering: guidelines and practical issues of combining noise measurements and calculations. In: Proceedings of Internoise 2007 (2007)

26. Marciniuk, K., Kostek, B.: Creating a numerical model of noise conditions based on the analysis of traffic volume changes in cities with low and medium structure. Arch. Acoust. **40**(3), 438–439 (2015)

27. Marciniuk, K., Szczodrak, M., Kostek, B.: Analysis of noise assessment of selected areas in Gdańsk. Arch. Acoust. **40**(4), 621–625 (2015). doi:10.1515/aoa-2015-0062

28. Marciniuk, K., Szczodrak, M., Kostek, B.: Performance of noise map service working in cloud computing environment. Arch. Acoust. **41**(2), 297–302 (2016). doi:10.1515/aoa-2016-0029

29. Notbohm, G., Gartner, C., Schwarze, S.: Psycho-physiological responses to the perception of vehicle pass-by noises. Institute of Social and Occupational Medicine, Heinrich-Heine-University of Duesseldorf, QWU

30. Quartieri, J., Mastorakis, N.E., Iannone, G., Guarnaccia, C., D'Ambrosio, S., Troisi, A., Lenza, T.L.L.: A review of traffic noise predictive models. In: Proceedings of Recent Advances in Applied and Theoretical Mechanics, 5th WSEAS International Conference on Applied and Theoretical Mechanics (MECHANICS 2009), Puerto De La Cruz, Tenerife, Canary Islands, Spain, 14–16 December, pp. 72–80 (2009)

31. Probst, F., Probst, W., Huber, B.: Comparison of noise calculation methods. In: Proceedings of Inter Noise 2011, Osaka, Japan, 4–7 September (2011)

32. Regulation (EU) No 540/2014 of the European Parliament and of the Council of 16 April 2014 on the sound level of motor vehicles and of replacement silencing systems, and amending Directive 2007/46/EC and repealing Directive 70/157/EEC. Official Journal of the European Union, L 158/131 (2014)

33. Sandberg, U., Żurek, B.Ś., Ejsmont, J.A., Ronowski, G.: Tyre/road noise reduction of poroelastic road surface tested in a laboratory. In: Proceedings of Acoustics 2013–Victor Harbor, 17–20 November 2013, Victor Harbor, Australia (2013)

34. Salomons, E., Van Maercke, D., Defrance, J., De Roo, F.: The Harmonoise sound propagation model. Acta Acust. United Acust. **97**, 62–74 (2011)

35. Sørensen, M.: Road traffic noise and stroke: a prospective cohort study. Eur. Heart J. **32**, 737–744 (2010). http://cordis.europa.eu/news/rcn/33064_en.pdf

36. Stapelfeldt, H., Vukadin, P., Manvell, D.: Reverse Engineering Improving noise prediction in industrial noise impact studies. In: Proceedings of EuroNoise 2009 (2009)

37. Stapelfeldt, H., Ponzo: Validation and calibration in noise mapping – the Madrid study. In: Proceedings of IOA Autumn Conference (2005)

38. Stapelfeldt, H., Manvell, D.: Using dynamic noise mapping for pro-active environment noise management. In: Proceedings of Inter-Noise 2011 (2011)

39. Szczodrak, M., Czyżewski, A., Kotus, J., Kostek, B.: Frequently updated noise threat maps created with use of supercomputing grid. Noise Mapp. **1**(1), 32–39 (2014)
40. Test stanowiska ważenia pojazdów w ruchu sprawdzaj acy poziom detekcji, identyfikacji i klasyfikacji pojazdów. https://www.gddkia.gov.pl/pl/d/d9801c129323a6857b5e79b96e52cc88
41. Valuch, M., Pepucha, L., Pitoňák, M., Fraňo, P.: Surface pavement characteristics and accident rate. In: Proceedings of the 10th International Conference "Reliability and Statistics in Transportation and Communication" (RelStat 2010), 20–23 October 2010, Riga, Latvia, pp. 71-78 (2010). ISBN 978-9984-818-34-4 Transport and Telecommunication Institute, Lomonosova 1, LV-1019, Riga, Latvia
42. Wetlesen, T.: Cloud computing for noise monitoring. In: INTER-NOISE and NOISE-CON Congress and Conference Proceedings. Institute of Noise Control Engineering, pp. 2987-2982 (2013)
43. Wu, R., Zhang, B., Hu, W., Liu, L., Yang, J.: Application of noise mapping in environmental noise management in Hangzhou, China. In: Proceedings of EuroNoise, Maastricht, 31 May–3 June (2015)

Multicast Steganography
Using Routing Protocols

Miralem Mehic[1](✉), Miroslav Voznak[1], and Peppino Fazio[2]

[1] Department of Telecommunications, VSB-Technical University of Ostrava,
17. listopadu 15, 70800 Ostrava-poruba, Czech Republic
{miralem.mehic,miroslav.voznak}@vsb.cz
[2] Department DIMES, University of Calabria, Via P. Bucci 41/C,
870 36 Arcavacata di Rende, Italy
p.fazio@dimes.unical.it

Abstract. The strengthening of security solutions for computer networks increases the interests in new methods for the transfer of hidden information. In this paper, we considered the use of routing protocols for transmission of steganographic messages. We evaluated such approach using proactive and reactive routing protocols by analyzing the amount of sent data, the number of generated routing packets, the average size of routing packets, and the packet delivery ratio using the NS-3 simulator. Simulations included random network topologies with a various number of nodes and mobility settings. The obtained results showed that reactive routing protocols exchange a large amount of routing packets which can be suitable for steganographic purposes due to network flooding mechanism.

Keywords: Steganography · Information hiding · Ad-hoc networks · Routing protocols

1 Introduction

Covert channels are used for information transmission even though they are neither designed nor intended to transfer information at all [1] while steganography is a method of hiding data inside of existing channels of communications so no one except participants is able to detect it [2,3]. Hidden communication can significantly affect the level of security and reputation that certain system represents. Viewed from the client's side, it is reasonable to doubt the safety and quality of a system which has weak points that can be used for the undetected leak of confidential data. Hence, hidden communication channels are of great interest for security agencies seeking to reduce information leaks and increase security standards. In previous period, a various covert channels and steganographic methods have been reported such as utilization of unused packet header fields [4–6], encoding information in the traffic behavior [7–10], encoding information in encrypted silent VoIP packets [11] or even exploiting anomalies in the network to mask hidden data flow [3,12,13].

© Springer International Publishing AG 2017
A. Dziech and A. Czyżewski (Eds.): MCSS 2017, CCIS 785, pp. 124–135, 2017.
https://doi.org/10.1007/978-3-319-69911-0_10

In general, the hidden communication method seeks to meet the following criteria to maximize its efficiency and reduce the probability of detection [7,12]:

- To select an information carrier with a large network flow to hide the stream of hidden data and minimize detection,
- To choose a popular information carrier such that the selected carrier would not attract attention of network detection tools,
- To encode small fragments of hidden/stego message per packet to reduce probability of detection. Packets should be sent with a higher frequency since encoding a small amount of hidden data per packet reduces the probability of detecting the entire stego message.

The basis of every modern network are devices that have the ability to manage and control network traffic. One of the fundamental network devices is a router that connects at least two networks and has traffic directing functions. Routing devices implement routing protocols that are of crucial importance for determining the availability of network nodes and network states. Given the irreplaceable role and presence of routing protocols in communication networks, this paper addresses the usage of routing protocols for transmission of hidden information to multiple receivers which is defined as multicast steganography [14]. Such steganography requires sending of the same stego message to all previously defined receivers and it can be implemented only on multicast communication to reduce the cost and the possibility of detection compared to multiple unicast steganography. To meet the requirements listed above, we look for those scenarios and routing protocols that generate the most routing packets. Taking into account the dominant use of the OSPF routing protocol in conventional wired IP networks, we analyze the amount, frequency and the dynamics of exchange of routing packets using popular routing protocols from mobile ad-hoc networks (MANETs). The main motivation is to analyze various routing protocols with the goal of finding those settings that provide the best basis for stenographic use. Assuming that senders of hidden data have full control over the routing protocol, in this paper we assume that the entire payload of the routing packet can be encrypted and used for steganographic purposes.

This paper is organized as follows: Sect. 2 discusses proactive and reactive routing protocols. The simulation setup is presented in Sect. 3 while in Sect. 4 we provide an evaluation of obtained result and discuss the broader aspects of our approach. Section 5 concludes this study and outlines the future work.

2   Routing Protocols

Routing protocols can be broadly classified into proactive and reactive routing protocols. In a reactive protocol, routing paths are searched only when needed, mainly by flooding the network, where the discovery procedure terminates when either a route has been found, or no route is available after all route permutations have been checked [15,16]. Conversely, the proactive protocols continuously evaluate routes to all reachable nodes and attempt to maintain consistent, up-to-date routing information, by exchanging periodically its routing tables or exchanging network topology information [17,18].

MANETs are designed for fast and simple communication in situations where pre-installed infrastructure is not available (such as search and rescue operations in the case of natural disasters, earthquakes, fires, battlefield scenarios and etc.). Communication takes place on a hop-by-hop basis and mobile nodes are typically powered by batteries placing special attention to energy-aware solutions. The nodes connect themselves in a decentralized, self-organizing manner with no authority in charge of managing and controlling the network. The main characteristic of MANETs is the unpredictable mobility of nodes, which can often lead to unstable routing paths [19].

2.1 Proactive Routing Protocols

Destination-Sequenced Distance-Vector Routing (DSDV) is the most popular proactive routing protocol which is based on the distributed Bellman-Ford algorithm. In DSDV, each node maintains two tables. The permanent routing table holds the list of all possible destinations within the network, the address of next hop and the total number of hops to reach that destination. Each node is in charge to periodically broadcast its routing table to its neighbor nodes by using periodic update packets based on periodic route update interval which is set to 15 s by default. After receiving the update packet, the neighbor node updates its routing table by incrementing the number of hops by one and forwards the packet further in the network. The process is repeated until all the nodes receive a copy of the updated packet with a corresponding value. To avoid the formation of routing loops, entries in the routing table are marked with a sequence number. In addition to regular periodic updates, DSDV uses triggered updates when the network topology suddenly changes. The main purpose of these updates is to advertise the information that has changed since the last periodic update. However, if a periodic and triggered update occurs in a short period of time, the values are merged and only the periodic update is performed. To limit the propagation of unstable information, the transmission of triggered updates is delayed using settling time which is recorded in the second DSDV table for each destination node. By default, the settling time is set to 5 s [18,20]. DSDV uses the same type of messages for periodic and triggered updates.

Optimized Link State Routing Protocol (OLSR) is the proactive link-state routing protocol which uses Hello and Topology Control (TC) routing messages to discover and disseminate link-state information throughout the network. OLSR reduces the control traffic overhead by using Multipoint Relays (MPR), which is the key idea behind OLSR. The MPR node is a node's one-hop neighbor which has been chosen to forward packets. Instead of pure flooding of the network, packets are forwarded by node's MPRs. This delimits the network overhead, thus being more efficient than pure link state routing protocols. By default, OLSR sends Hello messages each 2 s while TC messages are exchanged each 5 s. The holding time is usually three times the Hello message period. Therefore, a link breakage is detected after 6 s in the worst case [21–23]. OLSR uses four types of messages:

- Hello messages are sent periodically to all of the node's neighbors and it contains information about the node's neighbors, the nodes it has chosen as MPRs (i.e., the MPRSelector set), and a list of list of neighbors whom bidirectional links have not yet been confirmed.
- Multiple Interface Declaration (MID) - used to declare the presence of multiple interfaces on a node. The MID message is flooded throughout the network by the MPRs.
- Topology Control (TC) - used to perform the task of topology declaration (advertisement of link states).
- Host Network Association (HNA) - are flood messages that contain the list of associated networks and/or hosts.

Open Shortest Path First (OSPF) is a widely deployed link-state routing protocol in wired IP networks which maintains a link-state database describing the network topology. It uses periodic Link State Announcement (LSA) to exchange routing information. From the link-state database, each router constructs a tree of shortest paths with itself as the root. By default, OSPF floods LSA update information each 30 min and it exchanges Hello packets to establish and maintain a neighbor relationship on each 10 s. If a node does not receive a Hello message from a neighbor within a fixed amount of time, OSPF modifies its topology database to indicate that the neighbor is unavailable. The "dead interval" specifies the time interval that OSPF waits before declaring the neighbor node to be unavailable. By default, this interval is set to four times the default hello interval, which is 40 s in case of point-to-point networks [24,25]. The IETF has thus proposed three different MANET extensions to the OSPF protocol, allowing heterogeneous networks encompassing both wired and wireless routers [25]. However, since those versions are not implemented in the simulation environment, we used OSPFv2 [26]. OSPF distinguishes eight LSA messages [27]:

- Router LSA
- Network LSA
- Summary LSA
- Summary ASBR LSA
- External LSA
- Multicast LSA
- NSSA External LSA
- External attributes LSA for BGP

2.2   Reactive Routing Protocols

Ad hoc On-Demand Distance Vector (AODV) is an on-demand variation of distance vector reactive routing protocol which determines a route to a destination only when a route is required. Each node maintains a table with information referring to the first neighbor to contact to reach the destination. The obtained route is maintained as long as it is needed by the source and sequence numbers are used to ensure the freshness of routes. When a route for the desired destination is not available or when a routing table entry expires after a predetermined period, the route discovery is flooded through the network [28,29]. AODV is based on RFC 3561 and it uses four types of messages:

- Route Request (RREQ) is flooded throughout the network to find the route for the desired destination,
- Route Reply (RREP) is used to indicate that the node has a valid route to the destination. RREP is unicasts reply message which is sent back to the source,
- Route Reply Acknowledgment (RREP-ACK) - The receiver of the RREP is expected to return a RREP-ACK message,
- Route Error (RERR) used to inform precursor nodes to find some other route when the used route to the destination breaks.

3   Simulation Setup

To measure the amount and frequency of generated routing data, we simulated networks with random topologies consisting of 10, 20 and 30 nodes. We measured the amount of routing traffic in static networks as well as in networks with the arbitrary mobility of network nodes. The simulation was performed using the NS-3 Simulator of version 3.26 [30] to deploy DSDV, OLSR and AODV while NS-3-DCE of version 1.9 was used to deploy OSPF routing protocol [31].

Table 1. Parameter values of the simulation

Parameter	Value	Parameter	Value
Simulation area	$500 \times 500\,m^2$	Energy Detection Threshold	−61.8
Number of NetDevices per node	1	Cca Model Threshold	−64.8
Wifi Phy mode	OfdmRate 12 Mbps	Data Traffic Type	UDP
RtsCtsThreshold	1492	Data Traffic Rate	1 Mbps
TxPowerStart	33	Mobility Model	Random WayPoint
TxPowerEnd	33	Routing Protocols	DSDV, AODV, OLSR, OSPF
TxPowerLevels	1	Node Speed	0, 10, 20, 30 m/s
TxGain	0	Total Simulation Time	150 s
RxGain	0		

We used the BRITE topology generator to generate random topologies since it is supported under NS-3 and the source code is freely available [32]. NS-3 and NS-3-DCE were set to share the same seed file for generation of random values. Such setup has enabled the use of the same random topology with the identical configuration values in NS-3 and NS-3-DCE. Table 1 lists the simulation parameters including parameters of WiFi NetDevices which were set to provide a maximal coverage area of $250\,m^2$ and enable multi-hop communication. Parameters not given here are default parameters of the NS-3 and NS-3-DCE simulator.

4   Simulation Results

Tables 2, 3, 4 and 5 list the number of packets, amount of data, average packet size in bytes, and packet delivery ratio (PDR) which is calculated as the ratio of received and sent data packets for DSDV, OLSR, OSPF and AODV respectively. Figure 1 shows the distribution of the traffic generated by routing protocols in a network consisting of 30 nodes moving at a speed of 30 m/s. As shown in Fig. 1, distribution of DSDV packets is almost regular with the period of 15 s since DSDV calculates average settling time for each hop [33] to prevent the advertisement of unstable routes. It is known that DSDV has high routing overhead [34] as listed in Table 2. DSDV periodically exchanges whole routing tables resulting in the increase of routing packets with the increase in the number of nodes. In cases of increased mobility of nodes and considering that WiFi interface is used, the number of routing packets decreases since one WiFi transmission

Table 2. Number of packets, amount of data, average packet size (bytes) and packet delivery ratio for DSDV.

Nodes/Mobility	10 nodes	20 nodes	30 nodes
0 m/s	10 k	51 k	117 k
	1010 kB	5049 kB	11 MB
	96,87	98,30	97,06
	0.991994	1	0.999894
10 m/s	8564	46 k	120 k
	818 kB	4519 kB	11 MB
	95,59	96,30	96,43
	0.927654	0.999973	0.702928
20 m/s	8010	46 k	122 k
	768 kB	4476 kB	11 MB
	95,99	96,59	95,34
	0.909886	0.938772	0.568583
30 m/s	7639	47 k	120 k
	730 kB	4578 kB	11 MB
	95,63	96,30	96,12
	0.840599	0.842541	0.451738

Table 3. Number of packets, amount of data, average packet size (bytes) and packet delivery ratio for OLSR.

Nodes/Mobility	10 nodes	20 nodes	30 nodes
0 m/s	7800	31 k	70 k
	1209 kB	7296 kB	21 MB
	155,08	234,05	313,02
	1	0.991701	0.993271
10 m/s	6406	24 k	54 k
	925 kB	5021 kB	14 MB
	144,41	201,84	259,30
	0.927521	0.991701	0.821847
20 m/s	6359	24 k	53 k
	894 kB	4901 kB	13 MB
	140,74	196,67	252,41
	0.916137	0.953241	0.584036
30 m/s	5976	24 k	54 k
	837 kB	4771 kB	13 MB
	140,06	194,46	249,58
	0.840599	0.846052	0.477964

Table 4. Number of packets, amount of data, average packet size (bytes) and packet delivery ratio for OSPF.

Nodes/Mobility	10 nodes	20 nodes	30 nodes
0 m/s	5039	53 k	114 k
	639 kB	10 MB	24 MB
	126,83	189,26	212,78
	1	0.955954	0.686012
10 m/s	5736	37 k	141 k
	780 kB	7308 kB	35 MB
	136,10	193,36	249,37
	0.795595	0.999947	0.689151
20 m/s	5736	51 k	95 k
	780 kB	10 MB	18 MB
	136,10	203,55	187,88
	0.795595	0.970423	0.679974
30 m/s	7544	51 k	95 k
	1212 kB	10 MB	18 MB
	160,77	203,55	187,88
	0.687448	0.970423	0.679974

is sufficient to deliver data to a greater number of mobile nodes. The average size of packets does not change considerably while it is interesting to notice that PDR decreases with increased mobility of nodes.

Table 5. Number of packets, amount of data, average packet size (bytes) and packet delivery ratio for AODV.

Nodes/Mobility	10 nodes	20 nodes	30 nodes
0 m/s	15 k	56 k	80 k
	1274 kB	4702 kB	6747 kB
	83,90	83,94	84,02
	1	0.999947	1
10 m/s	11 k	40 k	102 k
	953 kB	3434 kB	8575 kB
	83,95	83,99	83,30
	0.865601	0.999973	0.912333
20 m/s	11 k	41 k	102 k
	951 kB	3502 kB	8534 kB
	83,72	83,81	83,24
	0.92909	0.999867	0.707689
30 m/s	10 k	40 k	158 k
	883 kB	3427 kB	13 MB
	83,75	83,70	82,27
	0.904833	0.999628	0.677102

The small value of Hello and dead interval allows OLSR to react quickly to the changes in a network topology. OLSR floods Hello and TC packets each 2 and 4 s, respectively, which results in almost constant propagation of the routing packets as shown in Fig. 1. But still, the flooding based on MPR reduces the total number of packets sent. Also, OLSR provides better results in terms of PDR compared to DSDV.

By default, OSPF exchanges Hello messages every 10 s while OSPF Route advertisement packets are exchanged most often. In our simulation with 30 nodes moving at 30 m/s, 9.7% packets were Hello messages, OSPF Database Description packets took 18% while OSPF Route advertisement (LS Update, LS Acknowledge) took 72.3% of the total number of exchanged packets.

AODV floods the network with route request and Hello messages which result with the largest number of packets sent. According to RFC 3561, AODV needs to update Active Route Life of the route which is used for packet forwarding to be no less than the current time plus ACTIVE_ROUTE_TIMEOUT which is set to 3 s by default. Therefore, forwarding node is in charge to extend the validity of route toward destination regardless of whether that route is feasible at all. The lifetime for an active route is updated each time the route is used regardless of whether the destination is a single node or a subnet. If a link break is detected, an AODV RERR message is sent to the source informing each intermediate node to invalidate routes to the unreachable destination. Further, when the source receives the RERR, it invalidates the route and reinitiates route discovery [28].

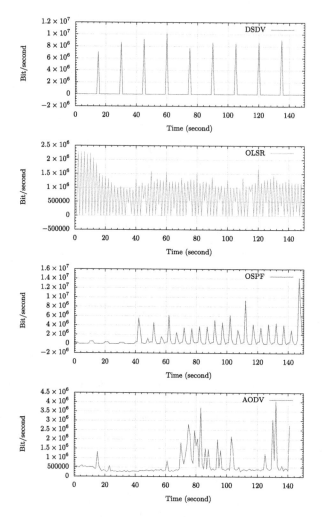

Fig. 1. Comparison of traffic generated by routing protocols; Mobility 30 m/s; 30 nodes;

Evidently, AODV generates the largest number of packets which results in a high PDR value. But since most AODV packets only contain route requests or route information (small packet payload), in networks with slow mobility the total amount of routing data is not significantly high. With increased mobility in a network with a small number of nodes, the amount of routing packets decreases since the number of intermediate nodes in the route decreases due to mobility. In a network with a greater number of nodes, the number of nodes that forward flooding route request packets increases which increase the overall amount of routing packets.

4.1   Discussion

From the obtained results, we notice that reactive routing protocols such as AODV can be convenient for steganographic purposes due to large amount of routing data. AODV floods entire network until a route to a destination is found which allows usage of routing packets to transfer stego messages to multiple receivers [4–6]. In addition, AODV generates feedback messages (RREP or RREP-ACK) that can be used to confirm receipt of stego message.

Unlike AODV, proactive routing protocols mainly use static update period time to keep routes up-to-date. OLSR reduces the control traffic overhead using MPR nodes to filter received routing packets and control the flooding which can filter and prevent the distribution of stego messages.

DSDV uses sequence numbers to ensure freshness of provided information and avoid routing loops. Routes with higher sequence number are preferred since it is likely that they provide most accurate information. The sequence number from each node is independently chosen and it is incremented each time when the update is performed: the sequence number of the regular periodic update is an even number while an urgent update for an expired route to its neighbors is marked with an odd sequence number. To limit the propagation of unstable information, the transmission of triggered updates is delayed using settling time. Therefore, instead of instant propagation of triggered DSDV route update, the node can decide to ignore instant propagation and to send its entire routing table within periodic update interval. When updating the DSDV table the node can select those data from received packets that will provide the best description of the current network status. Also, it means that DSDV performs the selection of received packets which as viewed from the steganographic point of view is not desirable because the stego message can be discarded.

OSPF implements the flooding of LSA update packet one hop further from its origin where several LSAs may be included in a single packet. Upon receiving the LSA, the node needs to compare the LSA to the contents of its present database. If the received LSA is more recent, the receiving node will forward the LSA on all interfaces except the one on which the LSA was received. To make the flooding of LSA more reliable, flooded advertisements are explicitly acknowledged which differentiates OSPF from other proactive protocols [35].

5   Conclusions

Multicast steganography attempts to deliver secret messages simultaneously to multiple receivers using the same cover object. The main part of this paper deals with the network simulations of random network topologies with a various number of nodes and mobility settings. The obtained data showed that reactive routing protocols exchange a large amount of routing packets which can be used to transfer of stego message due to network flooding mechanism and the fact that the packets are not filtered before being forwarded further to the network.

Proactive routing protocols have limited steganographic application due to filtering of data on nodes prior forwarding and use of control mechanisms to prevent pure flooding which may interrupt the flow of stego messages.

The main contribution of this paper is an analysis of routing protocols from the multicast steganographic point of view. Our future work will focus on the practical application of routing protocols for the transfer of hidden data.

Acknowledgments. The research received a financial support from the SGS grant No. SP2017/174, VSB - Technical University of Ostrava, Czech Republic.

References

1. Lampson, B.W.: A note on the confinement problem. Commun. ACM **16**(10), 613–615 (1973)
2. Artz, D.: Digital steganography: hiding data within data. IEEE Internet Comput. **5**(3), 75–80 (2001)
3. Mehic, M., Slachta, J., Voznak, M.: Hiding data in SIP session. In: 2015 38th International Conference on Telecommunications and Signal Processing (TSP), pp. 1–5. IEEE, July 2015
4. Mazurczyk, W., Smolarczyk, M., Szczypiorski, K.: Retransmission steganography applied. In: 2010 International Conference on Multimedia Information Networking and Security, pp. 846–850 (2010)
5. Mehić, M., Mikulec, M., Voznak, M., Kapicak, L.: Creating covert channel using SIP. In: Dziech, A., Czyżewski, A. (eds.) MCSS 2014. CCIS, vol. 429, pp. 182–192. Springer, Cham (2014). doi:10.1007/978-3-319-07569-3_15
6. Mileva, A., Panajotov, B.: Covert channels in TCP/IP protocol stack-extended version. Cent. Eur. J. Comput. Sci. **2**, 45–66 (2014)
7. Berk, V., Giani, A., Cybenko, G.: Detection of Covert Channel Encoding in Network Packet Delays. Technical report TR536 Darthmouth College (2005)
8. Mazurczyk, W., Lubacz, J.: LACK-a VoIP steganographic method. Telecommun. Syst. **45**, 153–163 (2010)
9. Yargicoglu, A.U., Ilk, H.G.: Hidden data transmission in MELP coded speech signal using quantization index modulation. In: 2007 IEEE 15th Signal Processing and Communications Applications, pp. 1–4. IEEE, June 2007
10. Mazurczyk, W., Smolarczyk, M.M.M., Szczypiorski, K.: Hiding information in retransmissions. arXiv preprint arXiv:0905.0363 (2009)
11. Mazurczyk, W., Karas, M., Szczypiorski, K.: SkyDe: a Skype-based Steganographic Method. p. 7, January 2013
12. Mehic, M., Voznak, M., Safarik, J., Partila, P., Mikulec, M.: Using DNS amplification DDoS attack for hiding data. In: SPIE Sensing Technology+ Applications, pp. 9120 91200R. International Society for Optics and Photonics, May 2014
13. Voznak, M., Zbranek, I., Mehic, M., Komosny, D., Toral-Cruz, H., Lin, J.C.W.: Covert channel in RTP payload using a pointer in sip header. Komunikacie **18**(1), 40–47 (2016)
14. Kamesh, S.P.N.: Security enhancement of authenticated RFID generation. Int. J. Appl. Eng. Res. **9**(22), 5968–5974 (2014)
15. Perkins, C., Belding-Royer, E., Das, S.: Ad-hoc On-Demand Distance Vector Routing (2003)
16. Fazio, P., De Rango, F., Sottile, C.: An on demand interference aware routing protocol for VANETS. J. Netw. **7**, 1728–1738 (2012)

17. Perkins, C.E., Bhagwat, P.: Highly dynamic destination-sequenced distance-vector routing (DSDV) for mobile computers. ACM SIGCOMM Comput. Commun. Rev. **24**(4), 234–244 (1994)
18. Mehic, M., Fazio, P., Voznak, M., Partila, P., Komosny, D., Tovarek, J., Chmelikova, Z.: On using multiple routing metrics with destination sequenced distance vector protocol for multihop wireless ad hoc networks, p. 98480F. International Society for Optics and Photonics, May 2016
19. Sarkar, K.S., Basavaraju, T., Puttamadappa, C.: Ad Hoc Mobile Wireless Networks, vol. 1. Auerbach Publications (2007). https://doi.org/10.1201/9781420062229
20. Das, S.R., Castaneda, R., Yan, J.: Simulation based performance evaluation of routing protocols for mobile ad hoc networks. Mob. Netw. Appl. **5**(3), 179–189 (2000)
21. Ilyas, M.: The Handbook of Ad Hoc Wireless Networks. Electrical Engineering Handbook, vol. 20021643. CRC Press (2002). https://doi.org/10.1201/9781420040401
22. Conti, M., Giordano, S.: Multihop ad hoc networking: the theory. IEEE Commun. Mag. **45**(4), 78–86 (2007)
23. Barbeau, M., Kranakis, E.: Principles of Ad Hoc Networking. Wiley, Chichester (2007). doi:10.1002/9780470512494
24. Szigeti, T., Hattingh, C.: End-to-End QoS Network Design, 1st edn. Networking Technology Series. Cisco Press (2005). 734 pages
25. Apostolopoulos, G., Guerin, R., Kamat, S.: Implementation and performance measurements of QoS routing extensions to OSPF. In: IEEE INFOCOM 1999 Conference on Computer Communications Proceedings, Eighteenth Annual Joint Conference of the IEEE Computer and Communications Societies. The Future is Now (Cat. No.99CH36320). vol. 2, pp. 680–688. IEEE (1999)
26. Moy, J.T.: OSPF version 2. Internet Req. Comment RFC **1247**, 1–124 (1991)
27. Parkhurst, W.R.: Cisco OSPF Command and Configuration Handbook, 1st edn. Pearson Education (2002). 528 pages
28. Chakeres, I., Belding-Royer, E.: AODV routing protocol implementation design. In: 24th International Conference on Distributed Computing Systems Workshops, 2004 Proceedings, pp. 698–703. IEEE (2004)
29. Barakovic, S., Barakovic, J.: Comparative Performance Evaluation of Mobile Ad Hoc Routing Protocols. In: Proceedings of the 33rd International Convention MIPRO 2010, pp. 518–523 (2010)
30. Henderson, T.R., Riley, G.F.: Network Simulations with the ns-3 Simulator. In: Proceedings of SIGCOMM, p. 527 (2006)
31. Riley, G.F., Henderson, T.R.: The ns-3 network simulator. In: Wehrle, K., Güneş, M., Gross, J. (eds.) Modeling and Tools for Network Simulation, pp. 15–34. Springer, Heidelberg (2010). doi:10.1007/978-3-642-12331-3_2
32. Medina, A., Lakhina, A., Matta, I., Byers, J.: BRITE: an approach to universal topology generation. In: MASCOTS 2001 Proceedings Ninth International Symposium on Modeling, Analysis and Simulation of Computer and Telecommunication Systems, pp. 346–353. IEEE Computer Society (2001)
33. He, G.: Destination-sequenced distance vector (DSDV) protocol, pp. 1–9. Networking Laboratory, Helsinki University of Technology (2002)
34. Liu, F.: Routing in Multi Hop Wireless Infrastructures. Master thesis, University of Twente, Master Thesis (2004)
35. Moy, J.T.: OSPF: Anatomy of an Internet Routing Protocol. Addison-Wesley Professional, Reading (1998)

QSIP: A Quantum Key Distribution Signaling Protocol

Miralem Mehic[1]([⊠]), Almir Maric[2], and Miroslav Voznak[1]

[1] Department of Telecommunications, VSB-Technical University of Ostrava,
17. listopadu 15, 70800 Ostrava-Poruba, Czech Republic
{miralem.mehic,miroslav.voznak}@vsb.cz
[2] Faculty of Electrical Engineering, University of Sarajevo, Zmaja od Bosne bb,
Kampus Univerziteta, 71000 Sarajevo, Bosnia and Herzegovina
almir.maric@etf.unsa.ba

Abstract. The rapid development of quantum equipment has led to increased interest in the application of Quantum Key Distribution (QKD) in everyday life. One of the questions is the establishment of a QKD session, namely the procedure for negotiating session parameters that is solved using a signaling protocol. In this paper, we analyze the existing signaling protocols and their limited application in a QKD network. We present a new QKD signaling protocol (QSIP) that aims to establish a session, modify the parameters of the established session and tear down the session. Additionally, QSIP is expanded to carry values that can be used to calculate average delay and perceive the state of the public channel of QKD link.

Keywords: Quantum Key Distribution (QKD) · Signaling · Networks

1 Introduction

One of the central issues in cryptography is a secure distribution of key between geographically distant users, known as secret key agreement problem [1]. The current solutions in most applications are based on the usage of public key infrastructure (PKI) which relies on assumptions about the computation power of eavesdropper and computational complexity of mathematical problems. As results, these solutions fall within the scope of theoretically breakable computational security and with the increase of computational power such solutions are under threat [2]. Quantum information theory suggests the possibility of solving secret key agreement problem by using an information-secure quantum key distribution, known as QKD [3]. Based on the laws of physics, QKD provides a secure way of establishing symmetrical binary keys between two geographically distant users without relying on the hardness of mathematical problems. In contrast to public-key cryptography, the combination of QKD with suitable message authentication scheme such as Wegman-Carter [4] has been proven to be secure without intractability hypotheses [5,6].

© Springer International Publishing AG 2017
A. Dziech and A. Czyżewski (Eds.): MCSS 2017, CCIS 785, pp. 136–147, 2017.
https://doi.org/10.1007/978-3-319-69911-0_11

Due to a noticeable progress in the development of quantum equipment [7–12], quantum technology has grown significantly and is rapidly approaching to the level of high maturity. The next natural step in the evolution of quantum systems is to study their performances and convergence with the applications used in everyday life. QKD networks differ from the traditional communication network in several aspects. The main difference is reflected in the implementation of a QKD link which employs two distinct communication channels: the quantum channel, which is used for transmission of raw key material encoded in certain photon properties, and the public channel, which is used for a verification of the exchanged key material and transmission of encrypted data. To provide information theoretically secure (ITS) communication on the public channel, the key tends to be applied with a One-Time Pad (OTP) cipher, which requires the length of the key to be the same as the length of the message that is to be encrypted. For current QKD systems, the stable key rate is restricted to a few tens or hundreds of kbps depending on the distance [13–15]. Therefore, in practice, a special attention is paid to reduce the consumption of scarce key material [16,17].

With an increased interest in the application of quantum cryptography in everyday life, there is a growing need for effective signaling and routing solutions in QKD networks. In this article, we evaluate well-known signaling protocols for usage in QKD network and we propose a new signalization protocol for QKD network which is responsible for establishment, modification and tear down of QKD session. We address the question of the establishment of QKD session and encapsulation of QKD packets using QKD header. This paper is organized as follows: Sect. 2 describes the purpose of signaling in a QKD network including state of the art. Section 3 describes the design principles of a new QKD signaling protocol, while Sect. 4 describes practical encapsulation of network packets in a QKD system. Section 5 concludes this study and outlines the future work.

2   Signaling in a QKD Network

Signaling is usually the most complex component in a network since it needs to support complex network services and perform rapid negotiations for setting up of the session with minimal signaling overhead. Examples include reserving resources to provide quality of service (QoS) guarantees, configuring firewall pinholes and network address translator (NAT) bindings, and diagnosing path status. In addition, a signaling solution should be extensible to support new service into the existing network. A signaling protocol is a type of protocol used to exchange information between nodes to establish, maintain, renegotiate and tear down a network connection.

The main aim of QKD is to provide end-to-end ITS communication [17, 18], and as such, it seeks to encrypt existing network communication without generating additional traffic that would increase the consumption of scarce key material. Therefore, signaling in a QKD network boils down to an exchange of information on supported cryptographic algorithms along the selected path and in practice, it is usually implemented on the data-link network layer, as discussed in the Sect. 4.

Depending on the transfer information method, signaling protocols can be classified into in-band and out-of-band. The former includes protocols that carry control information along with data packets while the latter refers to the approach that uses explicit control packets for transmission of control information.

2.1 RSVP

The most popular representative of out-of-band signaling is Resource reSerVation Protocol (RSVP) which is introduced to provide per-flow reservation of network resources in advance [19]. When the source node wants to establish a connection with the destination node, it first sends a PATH message which includes the specification of the traffic characteristics such as the average bit rate and burst size. Each intermediate node forwards the PATH message toward the path that is determined by a routing protocol while upon receiving the PATH message, the destination node responses with a RESV message which includes the resource requirements for the flow. When an intermediate note receives the RECV message from the destination node, it checks whether the required resources can be met. If yes, it allocates the resources for the flow, stores the flow state information and forwards the RESV message to the source node. Otherwise, the resource request is rejected and an error message is generated.

Although used in some projects [20,21], in our opinion RSVP is not an adequate solution for QKD network due to following:

- Considering the mutual interdependence of the public and quantum channel of QKD link [22], RSVP should be extended to reserve resources on both channels. But, since QKD networks are usually realized as overlay networks [16,17,23], reservation of resources in the underlying network is usually not feasible. Therefore, reservation of resources on the quantum channel without controlling the public channel does not pose any gain.
- Since RSVP is an out-of-band protocol, its packets contend for network resources with the data packets and consume a substantial amount of scarce key material.
- RSVP was designed when node mobility was in its infancy and therefore does not support mobile nodes [24,25]. For QKD networks with dynamic topology and link capacities, the overheads of connection maintenance usually outweigh the initial cost of establishing the connection.

2.2 INSIGNIA

Given the requirement to minimize the consumption of scarce key material, we analyze the usage of in-band signaling protocols where signaling commands are carried along with the data and operating close to packet transmission speeds.

As such, in-band signaling protocols are well suited for dynamic network behaviors [26] such as Mobile Ad-hoc Networks (MANETs) for which INSIGNIA was designed solely for. Similarly to RSVP, INSIGNIA is based on the per-flow end-to-end reservation of network resources [27,28].

The signaling data is transmitted using the OPTION field of IP header which is referred to as INSIGNIA option. The flow state information is managed in a soft-state manner, that is, the flow state information is refreshed periodically. In coordination with the admission control module, INSIGNIA allocates network resources (bandwidth) to the flow if requirements can be satisfied. Otherwise, the flow is degraded to best-effort service but without generating rejection or error messages. The intermediate nodes receiving packets with degraded values do not reallocate resources or refresh the flow reservation state. Instead, flow reservation state automatically times out and resources are afterward deallocated. Soft-state timers are continually refreshed and flow reservations are maintained as long as packets associated with a flow are received.

Unlike RSVP reservation model which is receiver-initiated, INSIGNIA sets flow reservation values from sender to receiver. A source node continues to send packets with the reservation request values until the destination node completes the reservation setup by informing the source node about the status using a reporting mechanism. Report values are sent back toward the source node but not necessarily along the reserve path. After receiving report values, the source node adjusts its settings and the reservation is considered successful [27].

3   Design Principles of QKD Signaling Protocol

Motivated by the efficient application of in-band signaling protocols in MANETs [27,29,30], we propose the in-band QKD Signaling Protocol (QSIP). The main goal of QSIP is to exchange information about cryptographic algorithms used in the session without relying on resource reservation. Additionally, QSIP should allow changes of session parameters and termination of the session after the completion of the data transfer.

In general, a QKD protocol which establishes a new key material consists of six successive stages: secret key exchange, extraction of the raw key (sifting), error rate estimation, reconciliation, privacy amplification and authentication [31,32]. Only the first stage is performed over a quantum channel while all other stages are performed over a public channel resulting in the communication which is referred as QKD post-processing. Since some of packets exchanged in QKD post-processing are authenticated, we propose extension of these packets with signaling data which provides an elegant way to tackle the problem of distribution of signaling information without introducing additional traffic overhead.

3.1   A Session Identifier

In RSVP, a data flow is identified as a unidirectional sequence of packets using a 5-tuple flow identifier: IP source address, IP destination address, protocol, source port, and destination port. Unlike RSVP, QSIP is based on a session identifier which is generated as a cryptographically random number used to probabilistically uniquely identify a signaling session.

Towards relaxing the common assumption that all nodes along the path in the QKD network must be fully trusted [17,33–35], the multipath transmission has been discovered as a necessary and sufficient alternative [36,37]. Taking into account dynamics of the change in the state of the QKD links due to the relatively low charging rate and the request for multipath communication, QSIP separates a session identifier from a flow identifier. A session can be mapped to a specific flow, but it allows a creation of more flexible flow-session relations such as multihoming and IPv4/v6 traversal. Therefore, the session does not strictly bound to IP addresses and it can involve multiple network flows, allowing simple usage of QSIP for establishing multicast/broadcast communications.

3.2   QSIP Protocol Basics

The QSIP format is made up of a number of text lines and formatted as <type>=<value>, where <type> defines a unique session parameter and the <value> provides a specific value for that parameter. QSIP defines two messages:

1. The *QUERY* message is used to initiate a session. It carries information about the encryption and authentication schemes preferred by the sender as well as other supported schemes. QSIP has no direct influence on the route selection from the source to the destination. The QoS routing protocol is in charge for calculation of routing metrics, evaluation of path states and the route selection based on calculated values. Therefore, the QSIP QUERY message is transmitted along with data packet and aims at examining the availability of preferred encryption and authentication schemes on hops along the already selected route. For instance, the sender defines preferred and supported encryption and authentication schemes using values as follows:

   $e = encryption$. This describes the supported encryption algorithms separated using semicolon where the first value indicates the preferred option. In example: $e = AES1024;OTP;IDEA128$

   $a = authentication$. This describes the supported authentication schemes separated using semicolon where the first value indicates the preferred option. In example: $a = VMAC;KRAWCZYK;BIERBRAUER$

2. The *ACK* message is used to respond to a session query. Upon receiving the incoming message at the intermediate node, a check of the available crypto algorithms and authentication schemes is performed. Details about the unsupported algorithms and schemes are removed from QUERY message and processed message is forwarded further to the destination in the case when there is at least one supported value.

When the destination node receives QUERY message, it creates the ACK message which contains $e =$ and $a =$ supported values. The message is stored in an internal buffer where it waits for the first next packet to be sent to the source node. The validity of the message is based on a simple timer, and the message is removed from the buffer after the time interval Δt to release the occupied memory resources. Any additional QUERY messages received from the same sender will be ignored until the previously stored message in the buffer is sent. Finally, after receiving the ACK message at the source node, QSIP session is established using those crypto algorithms and schemes that are listed first in the delivered ACK message (Fig. 1a).

In case when there are no supported crypto algorithms and schemes on the intermediate node, the ACK message with empty $e =$ and $a =$ values is returned to the sender without forwarding the QUERY message to the destination. QSIP aims to minimize key material consumption in a way that the intermediate nodes respond to QUERY messages without forwarding the message to the destination when there are no supported crypto algorithms and schemes as shown in Fig. 1b. The utilized QoS routing protocol may use information about unsupported crypto algorithms and schemes to ignore the previously defined route to the destination and recalculate the route.

In addition to the exchange of information on supported crypto algorithms and schemes along the path between the source and the destination, QSIP seeks to provide additional information on the status of the utilized route. Therefore, each QSIP message is expanded with a $t = timestamp$ value to indicate the time of sending the message. Inserting a timestamp value instead of generating additional probe packet [38–41], provides an elegant way to calculate the delay and evaluate the state of public channels of QKD links which can be of use to for an adequate route calculation.

QSIP Session Parameter Modification. The modification of already established QSIP session can be initiated either by sender or the destination node by resending $QUERY$ message. The response procedure to this message is identical as to initial QUERY message which is used for establishment of QSIP session (Fig. 1c).

QSIP Session Tear down. QSIP does not implement specific messages for tear down of an established QKD session. Since QSIP is not a per-flow reservation protocol, there are no reservations that need to be canceled explicitly.

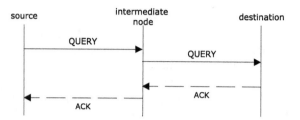

(a) Session setup - the intermediate node forwards QUERY message toward the destination node

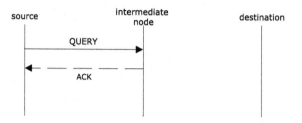

(b) Session setup - the intermediate node response with ACK message without forwarding QUERY message when no values are supported

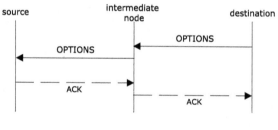

(c) Session modification

Fig. 1. Session setup and session modification QSIP protocol operations.

4 QKD Packet Encapsulation

To facilitate the ease of routing operation, in practice, encryption and authentication are performed between data link (L2) and network (L3) ISO/OSI layer. In the case of realization of QKD network as a network with a single TCP/IP stack, the packet is encapsulated with MAC header and forwarded to the network interface card (Fig. 2). However, in the case of realization of QKD network as an overlay network, MAC header is ommited (Fig. 3).

Since there are no defined standards for QKD network packets [42,43], there are different variants of the QKD header. In this paper, we focus on the solution used in AIT R10 QKD Software [44]. The QKD header which is authenticated

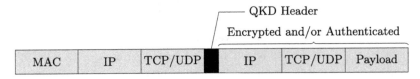

Fig. 2. QKD Packet Encapsulation

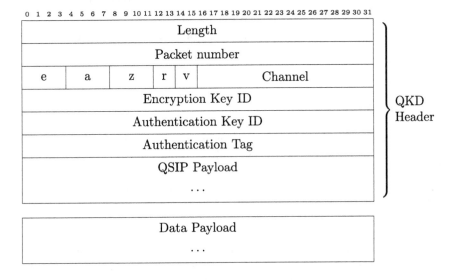

Fig. 3. QKD Packet Encapsulation in overlay network

Fig. 4. The QKD header

but not encrypted by default [16,44,45], is used to carry authentication tag and information about used encryption and authentication scheme as shown in Fig. 4.

Table 1 provides short explanation of the QKD header's fields [44]. The QKD header is extended to carry QSIP message in case when QSIP messages are exchanged.

Table 1. QKD header fields

Field	Length	Description
Length	32 bits	Total packet length in bytes
Packet number	32 bits	The Packet number
e	4 bits	Type of used encryption cipher
a	4 bits	Type of used authentication algorithm
z	4 bits	Type of used compression algorithm
v	2 bits	Version
r	2 bits	Reserved for further use
Channel	16 bits	The Channel ID
Encryption Key ID	32 bits	ID of Key used for Encryption
Authentication Key ID	32 bits	ID of Key used for Authentication
Authentication-tag	32 bits	Authentication tag
QSIP Payload	-	Contains the QSIP message (if any)
Payload	-	Data payload

5 Conclusion

This paper deas with signaling operations in a QKD network, discussing the existing signaling protocols and their limited application in a QKD network. Due to the common realization of a QKD network as an overlay network, reservation of key material resources of quantum channels does not pose any gain. On the other hand, reservation of resources of public channels is usually not feasible in the overlay network while the dynamic nature of QKD network makes the available state information inherently imprecise. Taking into account that network communication for resource reservation and session maintenance consumes a considerable amount of scarce key material, we turn to in-band signaling protocols. We propose a new QKD signaling protocol (QSIP) that aims to establish a session, modify the parameters of the already established session and to carry additional values to evaluate the state of the public channel of QKD link.

Practical implementation of QKD on the data-link network layer provides an elegant way to access those signaling packets that are used to establish a data session on an application network layer, as is the case with the SIP protocol which is commonly used to establish a VoIP call. The establishment of a SIP session at the application level requires the hop-by-hop communication between nodes including bidirectional communication source-destination. Expanding these packets to carry QSIP values placed in the QKD header is considered as an adequate solution to establish a QKD session and minimize consumption of scarce key material.

The main contribution of this paper is the analysis of existing signaling protocols and their limited application in a QKD network as well as the proposal for the use of a new in-band signaling protocol in QKD network. Our future work will focus on the analysis of practical usage of QSIP in QKD testbeds and simulations.

Acknowledgments. The research received a financial support from the SGS grant No. SP2017/174, VSB - Technical University of Ostrava, Czech Republic.

References

1. Maurer, U.M.: Secret key agreement by public discussion from common information. IEEE Trans. Inf. Theor. **39**(3), 733–742 (1993)
2. Shor, P.W.: Algorithms for quantum computation: discrete logarithms and factoring. In: Proceedings of 35th Annual Symposium on Foundations of Computer Science, IEEE Computational Society Press, pp. 124–134 (1994)
3. Bennett, C.H., Brassard, G.: Quantum cryptography: public key distribution and coin tossing. In: Proceedings of IEEE International Conference on Computers, Systems and Signal Processing, vol. 175, New York (1984)
4. Wegman, M.N., Carter, J.L.: New hash functions and their use in authentication and set equality. J. Comput. Syst. Sci. **22**(3), 265–279 (1981)
5. Mayers, D.: Unconditional security in quantum cryptography. J. ACM **48**(3), 351–406 (2001)
6. Shor, P.W., Preskill, J.: Simple proof of security of the BB84 quantum key distribution protocol. Phys. Rev. Lett. **85**(2), 441–444 (2000)
7. Yin, J., Cao, Y., Li, Y.H., Liao, S.K., Zhang, L., Ren, J.G., Al, W.Q.C., Liu, W.Y., Bo Li, H.D., Li, G.B., Lu, Q.M., Gong, Y.H., Xu, Y., Li, S.L., Li, F.Z., Yin, Y.Y., Jiang, Z.Q., Li, M., Jia, J.J., Ge Ren, D.H., Zhou, Y.L., Zhang, X.X., Wang, N., Chang, X., Zhu, Z.C., Liu, N.L., Chen, Y.A., Lu, C.Y., Shu, R., Peng, C.Z., Wang, J.Y., Pan, J.W.: Satellite-based entanglement distribution over 1200 kilometers. Science **356**(6343), 1140–1144 (2017)
8. Wang, S., Chen, W., Yin, Z.Q., Li, H.W., He, D.Y., Li, Y.H., Zhou, Z., Song, X.T., Li, F.Y., Wang, D., Chen, H., Han, Y.G., Huang, J.Z., Guo, J.F., Hao, P.L., Li, M., Zhang, C.M., Liu, D., Liang, W.Y., Miao, C.H., Wu, P., Guo, G.C., Han, Z.F.: Field and long-term demonstration of a wide area quantum key distribution network. Opt. Express **22**(18), 21739–21756 (2014)
9. Sasaki, M., Fujiwara, M., Ishizuka, H., Klaus, W., Wakui, K., Takeoka, M., Miki, S.: Field test of quantum key distribution in the Tokyo QKD network. Opt. Express **19**, 10387–10409 (2011)
10. Xu, F.X., Chen, W., Wang, S., Yin, Z.Q., Zhang, Y., Liu, Y., Zhou, Z., Zhao, Y.B., Li, H.W., Liu, D., Han, Z.F., Guo, G.C.: Field experiment on a robust hierarchical metropolitan quantum cryptography network. Chin. Sci. Bull. **54**(17), 2991–2997 (2009)
11. Elliott, C., Yeh, H.: DARPA Quantum Network Testbed. Technical Report, BBN Technologies Cambridge, New York, USA, BBN Technologies Cambridge, New York, USA, July 2007
12. Alleaume, R., Bouda, J., Branciard, C., Debuisschert, T., Dianati, M., Gisin, N., Godfrey, M., Grangier, P., Langer, T., Leverrier, A., Lutkenhaus, N., Painchault, P., Peev, M., Poppe, A., Pornin, T., Rarity, J., Renner, R., Ribordy, G., Riguidel, M., Salvail, L., Shields, A., Weinfurter, H., Zeilinger, A.: SECOQC white paper on quantum key distribution and cryptography. arXiv preprint quant-ph/0701168 **28** (2007)

13. Alleaume, R., Branciard, C., Bouda, J., Debuisschert, T., Dianati, M., Gisin, N., Godfrey, M., Grangier, P., Länger, T., Lütkenhaus, N., Monyk, C., Painchault, P., Peev, M., Poppe, A., Pornin, T., Rarity, J., Renner, R., Ribordy, G., Riguidel, M., Salvail, L., Shields, A., Weinfurter, H., Zeilinger, A.: Using quantum key distribution for cryptographic purposes: a survey. Theor. Comput. Sci. **560**(P1), 62–81 (2014)
14. Salvail, L., Peev, M., Diamanti, E., Alléaume, R., Lütkenhaus, N., Länger, T.: Security of trusted repeater quantum key distribution networks. J. Comput. Secur. **18**(1), 61–87 (2010)
15. Mehic, M., Niemiec, M., Voznak, M.: Calculation of the key length for quantum key distribution. Elektronika ir Elektrotechnika **21**(6), 81–85 (2015)
16. Mehic, M., Komosny, D., Mauhart, O., Voznak, M., Rozhon, J.: Impact of packet size variation in overlay quantum key distribution network. In: 2016 XI International Symposium on Telecommunications (BIHTEL), Sarajevo, Bosnia and Herzegovina. IEEE pp. 1–6, October 2016
17. Kollmitzer, C., Pivk, M.: Applied Quantum Cryptography. LNP, vol. 797. Springer Science & Business Media, Hiedelberg (2010)
18. Peev, M., Pacher, C., Alléaume, R., Barreiro, C., Bouda, J., Boxleitner, W., Debuisschert, T., Diamanti, E., Dianati, M., Dynes, J.F., Fasel, S., Fossier, S., Fürst, M., Gautier, J.D., Gay, O., Gisin, N., Grangier, P., Happe, A., Hasani, Y., Hentschel, M., Hübel, H., Humer, G., Länger, T., Legré, M., Lieger, R., Lodewyck, J., Lorünser, T., Lütkenhaus, N., Marhold, A., Matyus, T., Maurhart, O., Monat, L., Nauerth, S., Page, J.B., Poppe, A., Querasser, E., Ribordy, G., Robyr, S., Salvail, L., Sharpe, A.W., Shields, A.J., Stucki, D., Suda, M., Tamas, C., Themel, T., Thew, R.T., Thoma, Y., Treiber, A., Trinkler, P., Tualle-Brouri, R., Vannel, F., Walenta, N., Weier, H., Weinfurter, H., Wimberger, I., Yuan, Z.L., Zbinden, H., Zeilinger, A.: The SECOQC quantum key distribution network in Vienna. New J. Phys. **11**(7), 075001 (2009)
19. Zhang, L., Deering, S., Estrin, D.: RSVP: A new resource reservation protocol. Network **7**(5), 8–18 (1993)
20. Sun, J.Y., Lang, J., Miao, C., Yang, N., Wang, S.: A digital watermarking algorithm based on hyperchaos and discrete fractional fourier transform. In: 2012 5th International Congress on Image and Signal Processing, pp. 552–556. IEEE, October 2012
21. Cheng, X., Sun, Y., Ji, Y.: A QoS-supported scheme for quantum key distribution. In: 2011 International Conference on Advanced Intelligence and Awareness Internet (AIAI 2011), Number 2009, pp. 220–224. IET (2011)
22. Mehic, M., Maurhart, O., Rass, S., Komosny, D., Rezac, F., Voznak, M.: Analysis of the public channel of quantum key distribution link. IEEE J. Quantum Electron. **53**(5), 1–8 (2017)
23. Dianati, M., Alleaume, R., Gagnaire, M., Shen, X.S.: Architecture and protocols of the future European quantum key distribution network. Secur. Commun. Netw. **1**(1), 57–74 (2008)
24. Hannes, T., Richard, G.: RSVP Security Properties. Technical report, RFC 4230
25. Chen, S., Nahrstedt, K.: An overview of quality-of-service routing for the next generation high-speed networks problems and solutions. IEEE Netw. **12**(6), 64–79 (1998)
26. Sarkar, K., Basavaraju, T., Puttamadappa, C.: Ad Hoc Mobile Wireless Networks. CRC Press, Boca Raton (2008)

27. Lee, S.B., Ahn, G.S., Campbell, A.: Improving UDP and TCP performance in mobile ad hoc networks with INSIGNIA. IEEE Commun. Mag. **39**(6), 156–165 (2001)
28. Kui, W., Janelle, H.: Qos support in mobile and ad-hoc networks. Crossing Boundaries GSA J. Univ. Alberta **1**(1), 106 (1992)
29. Chlamtac, I., Conti, M., Liu, J.J.N.: Mobile ad hoc networking: imperatives and challenges. Ad Hoc Netw. **1**, 13–64 (2003)
30. Seah, W., Lo, A., Chua, K.: A flexible quality of service model for mobile ad-hoc networks. In: 2000 IEEE 51st Vehicular Technology Conference Proceedings VTC2000-Spring, (Cat. No.00CH37026), vol. 1, pp. 445–449. IEEE (2000)
31. Bennett, C., Bessette, F., Brassard, G., Salvail, L., Smolin, J.: Experimental quantum cryptography. J. Cryptol. **5**(1), 3–28 (1992)
32. Mehic, M., Partila, P., Tovarek, J., Voznak, M.: Calculation of key reduction for B92 QKD protocol. In: Donkor, E., Pirich, A.R., Hayduk, M., eds.: SPIE Sensing Technology + Applications, p. 95001J. International Society for Optics and Photonics, May 2015
33. Elliott, C.: Building the quantum network. New J. Phys. **4**, 346 (2002)
34. Marhoefer, M., Wimberger, I., Poppe, A.: Applicability of quantum cryptography for securing mobile communication networks. In: Emerging Trends in Information and Communication Security, Long-Term and Dynamical Aspects of Information Security, pp. 97–111 (2007)
35. Konig, S., Rass, S.: On the transmission capacity of quantum networks. Int. J. Adv. Comput. Sci. Appl. **2**(11), 9–16 (2011)
36. Franklin, M., Wright, R.N.: Secure communication in minimal connectivity models. J. Cryptol. **13**(1), 9–30 (2000)
37. Desmedt, Y., Wang, Y.: Perfectly secure message transmission revisited. In: Knudsen, L.R. (ed.) EUROCRYPT 2002. LNCS, vol. 2332, pp. 502–517. Springer, Heidelberg (2002). doi:10.1007/3-540-46035-7_33
38. Couto, D.S.J.D., Aguayo, D., Bicket, J., Morris, R.: A high-throughput path metric for multi-hop wireless routing. Wirel. Netw. **11**(4), 419–434 (2005)
39. Javaid, N., Bibi, A., Djouani, K.: Interference and bandwidth adjusted ETX in wireless multi-hop networks. In: 2010 IEEE Globecom Workshops, pp. 1638–1643. IEEE, December 2010
40. Ashraf, U., Abdellatif, S., Juanole, G.: An Interference and link-quality aware routing metric for wireless mesh networks. In: 2008 IEEE 68th Vehicular Technology Conference, pp. 1–5. IEEE, September 2008
41. Mehic, M., Fazio, P., Voznak, M., Partila, P., Komosny, D., Tovarek, J., Chmelikova, Z.: On using multiple routing metrics with destination sequenced distance vector protocol for MultiHop wireless ad hoc networks, 98480F. International Society for Optics and Photonics, May 2016
42. Länger, T., Lenhart, G.: Standardization of quantum key distribution and the ETSI standardization initiative ISG-QKD. New J. Phys. **11**(5), 055051 (2009)
43. Lenhart, G.: QKD standardization at ETSI. In: Qcw 2010, vol. 57, pp. 50–57 (2012)
44. Maurhart, O., Pacher, C., Happe, A., Lor, T., Tamas, C., Poppe, A., Peev, M.: New release of an open source QKD software : design and implementation of new algorithms, modularization and integration with IPSec. In: Qcrypt 2013 (2013)
45. Mehic, M., Maurhart, O., Rass, S., Voznak, M.: Implementation of quantum key distribution network simulation module in the network simulator NS-3. Quantum Inf. Process. **16**(10), 253 (2017)

Distribution of Voice Messages in Crisis or Emergency Situations

Filip Rezac[1(✉)], Miroslav Voznak[1], Jaromir Tovarek[1],
and Jerry Chun-Wei Lin[2]

[1] VSB - Technical University of Ostrava, 17. listopadu 15, 70800 Ostrava,
Czech Republic
filip.rezac@vsb.cz
[2] School of Computer Science and Technology, Harbin Institute of Technology
Shenzhen Graduate School, Shenzhen, China

Abstract. The system which description and realization is presented in this article is intended to expand existing solutions to the emergency services for the distribution of voice messages with pre-recorded content in order to inform target participants about critical events in their surroundings using multimedia tools, based on Session Initiation Protocol. The transmission of information via voice channel has, over other forms of distributed notification, the advantage that the target user is forced to pick up the call and listen to the message - so the information cannot be ignored or overlooked. Another benefit is more accurate addressing of target groups, and ultimately it can ensure the re-delivery of messages to users who have not heard them. The authors present their own method of sending pre-recorded messages, which are then tested in terms of the definition of the performance capabilities of the distribution network. Practical implementation thereafter demonstrates the advantages and use of the proposed solutions in a simulated environment.

Keywords: Distribution of voice messaging · Voice over IP notification · Crisis situation · Network congestion model · Performance testing

1 Introduction

Throughout history, human society has been subjected to devastating disasters, which even today bring a high loss of life, and last but not least, great economic and environmental damage. The increasing number of threats in recent years has increased interest in the issue of early warning and notification, and, for example, according to studies by the World Bank and the United Nations [1], these systems are one of three key factors which may increase investments help to minimize or completely eliminate partial disaster.

On the basis of the above, current systems are designed for warning a wide range of people in danger, or serving as an information source, are widespread, and are used in various fields of human activity. The survey results showed that the vast majority of these systems are based on the principle of sending text messages, or the distribution of voice messages via a central device or equipment (sirens, radio, etc.).

© Springer International Publishing AG 2017
A. Dziech and A. Czyżewski (Eds.): MCSS 2017, CCIS 785, pp. 148–160, 2017.
https://doi.org/10.1007/978-3-319-69911-0_12

This article aims to introduce the implementation of a Voice Distribution System (VDS) based on the idea of using technology, packet-switched networks with Voice over IP (VoIP), and Session Initiation Protocol (SIP) for generating and distribution by sending voice messages via an SIP server directly to the terminal devices - cell phones, landlines, IP phones, etc. The entire VDS is placed in an integrated security center which also operates 112, and is accessible for the emergency center. The employee logs into the created system, inserts a pre-recorded warning message along with other parameters, and sends the request.

Based on the input information, the system develops scenarios and call parameters, which are further sent to the SIP requests generator, which prepares the SIP message in the form of packets to be sent to the SIP server.

The SIP server processes the incoming message and will initiate calls to the end participants. The participant thereby gains better orientation and sufficient information to resolve the situation. If the called party did not receive a call (missed call, the phone is switched off), the VDS arranges to resend the messages and set up a call with that particular participant.

2 Review of the Current State of Alert and Notification Systems

Worldwide, mapping technologies used to distribute messages in emergency situations is rather complicated, since each country uses its own system of protection and informing the population. In an analysis of existing technologies for distributing messages in emergency situations, we focus on selected countries that by their size, geographical location, and economic maturity represent a sufficient sample to explore.

Currently in the United States, the Integrated Public Alert and Warning System (IPAWS) is used, which has been deployed in practical operation since 2012, and is still being developed intensively. All mobile operators have had to provide service in the US in support of their network infrastructures, sending warning messages using technology of the Cell Broadcast Service (CBS) [2], which has a range of 93 characters, and these messages are displayed directly on the screen of a mobile device. The IPAWS system has deployed in full operation since April 2012, and current education of the population in its use is ongoing.

In Japan, after the big earthquake in 2011, the Disaster Voice Messaging System (DVMS) was developed, which is currently the only system using the distribution of voice messages in practical crisis management. The system works on the principle of an answering service, where a user uploads a voice message using the data transmission network, and the user for whom the message is addressed gets a Short Message Service (SMS) notification about picking up the message. The system creates the possibility for the distribution of voice messages in case of overloading of the mobile networks that can deliver messages using the data infrastructure.

In 2006, European Telecommunication Standards Institute (ETSI) started, together with the 3rd Generation Partnership Project (3GPP) project, to define and standardize technology for the subsequent development of a public system of early warning, the Public Warning System (PWS) [3]. The project aims to find suitable technology for distributing warning messages, where the last of the specifications indicate that it seems most appropriate to use CBS technology, which is used in the IPAWS system.

The specific implementation of PWS is being sold by the European Public Warning System (EU-ALERT), under the aegis of ETSI and Holland. In 2009, a letter was also sent to other European countries with applications for participation in the project. The project has been gradually deployed since 2010, but full-featured functionality is prevented mainly by legislation in each country, and the unwillingness of mobile operators to run CBS technology.

In the case of systems used in other countries, disseminating warning information using infrastructure such as sirens and detectors, or used to distribute public media resources, such as radio and television stations, dominate.

3   Voice Distribution System Draft

3.1   Introduction of the System Concept and Applicable Technologies

Because of easier and dynamic development, the intended effort was to design a system so that it could be implemented when using tools coupled and licensed under the General Public License (GPL). Employees of the crisis center work with the system through a web interface. After logging in, the worker marks on the map the area of emergency situations, and the VDS automatically sends a request to provide a list of telephone numbers and participants that have to be addressed, then inserts a pre-recorded warning message and other values into prepared forms.

The assumption is that the system co-operates with mobile operators who are able to supply a list of mobile phone numbers of participants located in the crisis area under the Local Area Code (LAC) in the networks of 2nd and 3rd generation, or Tracking Area Code (TAC) networks in the 4th generation. The list is loaded into the system in the XML format, and contains three attributes - the telephone number of the end user, the TAC or LAC code defining the user's location, and the Cell ID (CID), which specifies the particular base station and its cell. Number of rows in the list is equal to the number of end users.

Voice messages are stored in the system in the .pcap format, and have a maximum length of 30 s, which is derived from the standard length of reporting messages generated by electronic sirens. The .pcap format was chosen because it allows you to save a file for a voice message transmitted in the form of Real-time Transfer Protocol (RTP) packets. VDS also contains a module where the source or warning message text is automatically converted to a voice message in the corresponding format. Input for voice messages can be recorded in the said .pcap or .wav format, or text that subsequently uses Text-To-Speech (TTS) voice synthesis methods, and is converted into a voice sample.

Once the message is ready, it is then sent to all of the target participants, and after answering, the message is played. The crisis center worker can still set the call ringing at 5, 10, or 15 s. If by this time the target participant does not answer the call, it will be considered as non-accepted. If the target participant initiated the call back to the missed number, the Interactive Voice Response (IVR) service is prepared, which offers the caller a list of possible actions, including playing any warning messages.

After sending the request to dispatch the distributed call, it is first necessary to create SIP messages from the individual embedded parameters, which are then processed by the SIP server. To create a messages, system uses the Sipp open-source application. Sipp works with preset XML schemes, which define the format of SIP messages, and messages transmission properties are set using the command line parameters.

The system for dynamic work with parameters specified within the Sipp and XML uses two methods. In the first phase, the values that a worker of the crisis center puts into appropriate forms is assigned to the correct parameter, and it is sent to Sipp. For a dynamic change of telephone numbers based on an embedded target list of participants, it must also dynamically change values in the XML scheme for Sipp. For this purpose, a.csv file is generated by the application immediately upon entering the list of target subscribers. Block diagram of the system is shown in Fig. 1.

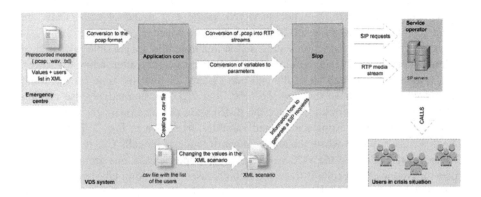

Fig. 1. VDS system concept.

3.2 Management of Call Flows in the Voice Distribution System

In context of VDS realisation, it was necessary to design algorithms and define parameters with which it would work. First, a basic variable had to be made, which defined the maximum amount of calls that the VDS could generate in the distribution network - C_{max}. This variable depends on several factors, which are further discussed. As soon as a worker of the crisis center enters an XML list of target users into the application, it calculates the total amount of calls that it must generate - C_{req}, and the number of groups that the calls will be divided into - G_n. Intervals between individual groups is set at 60 s, and is marked with the parameter - T_{int}. This period is the given value of the maximum length of prerecorded voice messages - 30 s, and the worker must set the time for ringing at a maximum of 15 s. Thereby we achieve a total value of 45 s. This means that the length of the call will never be longer than the aforementioned 45 s. The remaining 15 s represents a reserve period for ending all processes in progress in the given group. At the moment, we can define the expected call time for all of the calls - T_{snd}. The amount of groups G_n can be ascertained as a total number of calls C_{req} divided by the maximum number of generated calls by VDS - C_{max} (Eq. 1). The expected time for sending all calls T_{snd} may be ascertained using Eq. 2.

$$G_n \doteq \frac{C_{req}}{C_{max}} \tag{1}$$

$$T_{snd} \doteq G_n \cdot T_{int} \tag{2}$$

In the event of a real threat of danger or a natural disaster, workers of integrated security centers have exact timing models for the maximum time for everyone of the target participants to be warned. The time data is inserted into the form by the worker, and is referred to as the maximum time to send all planned calls - T_{max}. After entering the values, one of two things will happen. In the first case, where T_{snd} is smaller than T_{max}, after sending all of the calls there will be a time reserve period for re-calling all of the unanswered calls - T_{rem}. In this case, the system generates information about the length of time, and the worker reports that during this time the system will automatically generate calls that were not answered in the first round of calls. Calls are re-generated until T_{rem} is used up. In the second case, where T_{snd} is greater than T_{max}, the system generates information stating that at this time it is not possible to guarantee sending a message to all end participants, or to realize re-calling after failure to answer. If the worker wants to call all of the end participants, or limit the time for re-calling unanswered calls, he must increase the time limit T_{max}, or alternatively use another method for warning distribution. Once the distribution of voice messages starts, these flows can be described using the defined variables, as shown in Fig. 2. The diagram only presents a situation where the total number of requests for calls C_{req} is greater than the maximum capacity of the VDS system C_{max}. In opposite case, one group is created, processing requests and calls is the same in both cases. Generating takes place in each group with an interval of 60 s. Each group is comprised of C_{max} call requests, the last group contains the rest of the requests - C_{rst}. Adding all the C_{max} and C_{rst} in Eq. 3 we get total number of calls requests C_{req}. SIP requests, along with the RTP media flow, are gradually delivered to the SIP server, and then it starts to initialize the calls.

The target participant's device starts ringing for a period which the worker set up in a form on the system. If at that time the participant answers, an embedded voice message is played, which contains information about the crisis and how to deal with this situation. This call is identified as received - C_{answ}. If during the ringing there is no answer, or the end device is unavailable, the call is flagged as unanswered - C_{miss}. Detection of an unanswered or unavailable call is carried out by monitoring incoming SIP responses from each call. Once all of the requirements in all groups have been generated, the system adds up all unclaimed calls using Eq. 4, and if it has time T_{rem}, starts to create SIP requests for these calls again. Unanswered calls are generated until the time T_{req} been used up, or no other unanswered calls exist.

$$C_{req} = \sum_{i=1}^{n} C_{max_{Gi}} + C_{end_G} \tag{3}$$

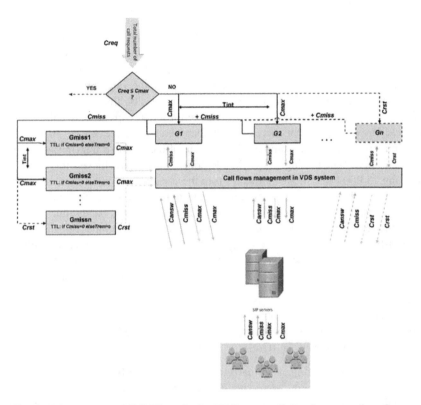

Fig. 2. Management of Call Flows in the VDS system if C_{req} is greater than C_{max}.

$$C_{miss} = \begin{cases} \sum_{i=1}^{n} C_{maxG_{miss_i}} + C_{endG_{miss}} \\ \sum_{i=1}^{n} C_{missG_i} \\ C_{req} - C_{answ} \end{cases} \tag{4}$$

4 Performance Testing and VDS Voice Communication Capacity

The description of the algorithm in the previous text raises an important issue, and this being how many SIP requests and subsequent calls the system is able to generate for a given maximum time interval. This value, referred to in the previous text as C_{max}, depends on several factors:

- Bandwidth and codecs used for the transmission line between the application, SIP request generator, and SIP servers.
- Computational demands of machines that are running SIP servers.
- Computational demands of Sipp call generator and maximum load of this application.

The basic steps prior to sending a voice RTP packet is a encoding with a certain type of a codec and packetization. RTP packets are sent at dedicated intervals and transmission timing which depend on the size of the payload, and also partly on the speed of the output bit rate from the encoder. Knowing the size of the headers for each protocol in the ISO/OSI model, it is possible to express the value of bandwidth of RTP streams for N calls, irrespective of the type of transmission line [4].

For example, the G.711 codec is responsible for 5 000 current VoIP call bandwidth of 452 Mb/s. If there is an increased number of calls, for example 10 000 while maintaining the codec, we would get to the edge of the standard transmission capacity of 1 Gb/s lines. When using the GSM-FR codec, we have achieved this limit when generating 25 000 calls in one moment. From these values, it can be concluded that the bandwidth can be a limiting factor for a finite number of generated calls, and their number is derived from the codec used, as well as the offered bandwidth.

Another factor that is crucial for defining the limit of the number of calls generated by the distribution system are the computing power of the SIP server, as well as the type of SIP solutions. Based on the recommendations, drafts, and previous measurements that are described in [5–7], it was possible to define the monitored parameters:

- Percentage CPU load with respect to the number of processor cores.
- Percentage load of RAM.
- The ratio of successful and unsuccessful calls handled with a limit of 2% of so-called Grade of Service (GoS).

For performance testing, a virtualized environment VMware ESXi 6.0 was used and individual test platforms were created with the following calculation parameters: CPU Intel Xeon E5-2660 2.20 GHz with 2 CPUs and 4 cores per CPU, making a total of 8 cores, RAM 2 GB, 1×1 Gb LAN with Ethernet, HDD 16 GB, OS Ubuntu Server 16.04 LTS 64-bit. These virtual machines to generate calls were installed with Sipp 3.6.0 tools, and platforms were tested following SIP servers - SIP back-to-back user agent (B2BUA) Asterisk 1.8.15 LTS, SIP B2BUA Asterisk 11.6.0 LTS, SIP B2BUA Aster-isk 13.9.1 with SIP PJSIP library and SIP proxy server Kamailio 4.4.1. Asterisk and Kamailio projects were chosen as representatives of open communication solutions that are both in terms of services offered, as well as stability and performance, equivalent rivals to commercial products.

Measurements have shown that computing power is not a crucial factor for defining the limits of simultaneous calls, even with B2BUA Asterisk or Kamailio SIP proxy. A crucial factor limiting the maximum number of simultaneous calls generated is the GoS ratio of 2%. For B2BUA Asterisk, variable values of the maximum number of simultaneous calls occurred, depending on the version, but the highest value at 2% GoS was 950 simultaneous calls. Kamailio SIP Proxy showed a value of 190 simultaneous calls per second at 2% GoS, which during connection of the RTP data amounted to 5 700 simultaneous calls, as can be seen in Fig. 3a and b.

A key part of the VDS is also the call generator, which has the task of creating SIP requests and routes the RTP data to SIP servers. In the test topology, as well as in the VDS draft, Sipp was chosen for the role of call generator. It has been found that Sipp and SIP Proxy are the elements defining limit values for calls simultaneously generated

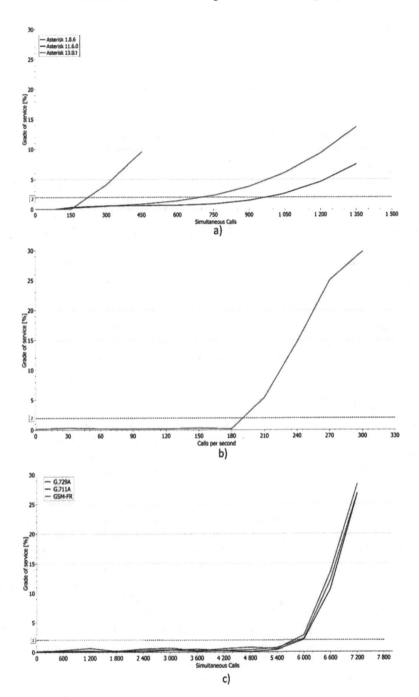

Fig. 3. GoS value depending on: (a) The number of simultaneous calls to SIP B2BUA Asterisk; (b) The number of calls per second to Kamailio SIP proxy; (c) The number of simultaneous calls to a sipp generator.

using selected codecs and the variable C_{max} in Sipp represents 5 800 simultaneous conversations, while maintaining 2% of unchecked calls. See Fig. 3c.

It is clear that the above-measured values are dependent on the hardware and software configuration, but this setting was chosen with regard to the presented design and practical implementation of the voice distribution system.

5   Deployment and Evaluation on a Simulation Model

The main aim of this section is to check whether the implemented VDS core is capable of distributing voice messages within the simulation on a real fragment of the cellular network, and whether there is congestion of the VDS or the network itself.

Required inputs and variables with which the system works have been described above, including the algorithm for call service flows. Practical implementation was carried out using the PHP programming language, its framework Nette, MariaDB database, and other individual tools. Suitable architecture of the application was also designed, including directory and database structures. XML scripts for creating and configuring SIP servers (B2BUA or SIP Proxy) used identical configuration files, such as were used during performance testing.

In context of verifying these assumptions and the functionality of the system itself, it was necessary to design an experiment based on a simulation model created in the simulation environment Riverbed Modeler. Its structure and behavior would corresponded to the real fragment of a mobile network, through which the VDS warning voice messages will be distributed. The area for participants to distribute voice messages to was selected so as to include part of the mobile radio access network, which represents the reference, and a general enough pattern with regard to the rest of the network in the Czech Republic, but also in other countries of the world. The area designated LAC 1713 of the mobile operator O2 has been chosen. The selected part had to meet several key conditions, which included the presence of 2nd, 3rd and 4th generation networking technologies. Furthermore, the area chosen had to contain densely populated conurbation, but also places with weak or no mobile coverage. Finally, it had to be an area with available data on the number of base stations, and the ratio of individual technologies. The measured area is shown in Fig. 4, where dots with numbers represent a greater intensity of base stations in the area, and when zooming in on the interactive map, each station can be observed. The number of cells with unique CIDs in the tested area was as follows: 2G – 237, 3G – 208, 4G – 32. The number of participants was a randomly generated number, in the range of from 12 to 120 participants per cell, with a total of 31 000 mobile subscribers within the simulated field. These values are based on the relationships presented in scientific publications [8–10].

Technologies operated within mobile network allows the transmission of voice calls from VDS to the end user by means of two domains: circuit switched and packet switched. A circuit switched domain guarantees call transmission through a dedicated channel with full bandwidth throughout the entire call. Packet switched domains, on the other hand, split the voice flow into individual packets, and these are transmitted via various channels to the end user. Based on already published studies [11, 12], it could also be possible for both domains express a maximum theoretical capacity of

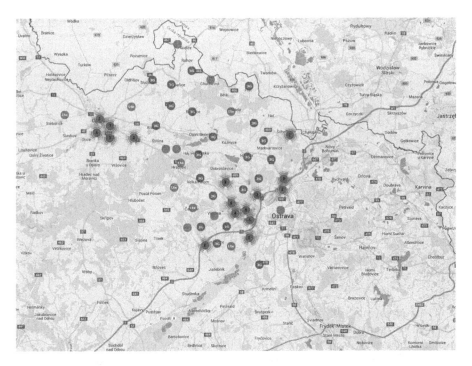

Fig. 4. Map showing areas of base stations under LAC 1713 of mobile operator O2.

simultaneous calls where the circuit switched domain has a value of 24 326 simultaneous calls, and packet switched approximately 35 176. Since the values obtained depend on the fulfillment of ideal conditions, which are in practical use unattainable, the assumption was made, that the real capacity of simultaneous calls, which will be used for distribution of voice messages from the VDS system, will be rapidly lower.

The limit for defining the maximum true capacity of the testing area again formed a GoS value of 2%. From the test results, it was found that for circuit switched domains the optimal load is set at 426 calls per second, equivalent to 15 975 simultaneous calls, and for packet switched networks approximately 764 calls per second, corresponding to 28 650 simultaneous calls (see Fig. 5). Based on the above values, the cause of the increase in the value of GoS to the border limit was also sought.

The results clearly indicate that the capacity of each line access in the core of the mobile network were sufficient, and there was no exhaustion of transmission capacities. Transfer analysis of calls in the radio part of the network has been made based on the results of measurement of end-to-end delay. It was found that according to the assumptions, the key point where the losses appear is the radio area connection between the base stations and the mobile station subscribers. Regardless of the domain used, the maximum number of calls generated per second has been limited by a delay in seconds, according to recommendation G.114 [13], the maximum permissible value of the delay for the telephone call is 500 ms.

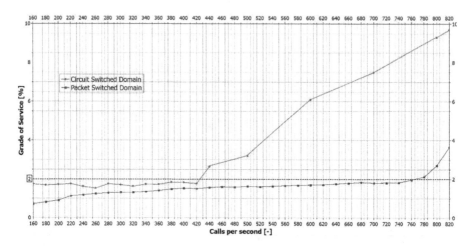

Fig. 5. The number of calls per second for circuit and packet switched domain depending on the GoS ratio.

When deploying VDS in practical operation, it is to be expected, of course, that there will be normal traffic on the mobile networks, and in the event of emergency situations there will also occur overload or inaccessibility of the network. This opens up space for methods to restore network infrastructure, based on the implementation of provisional data networks, as presented, for example by Minh [14]. The simulation results also brought findings that for an unburdened mobile network, the capacity of the embedded VDS core is insufficient when using one SIP requests generator and one SIP proxy server. The VDS system was, however, designed as a scalable solution, so in terms of implementation of core application, the increasing the number of SIP generators or servers does not require fundamental changes in the source code.

6   Discussion

As demonstrated in the previous text, the VDS system is a convenient and comprehensive solution for crisis management, and can supplement or replace the existing systems of warning and informing the population in emergency situations. However, the results presented are only preliminary, and deployment options in the ongoing development of the system must be improved in many incremental steps. The following improvements are planned:

- Guaranteed high availability of individual system elements: Since VDS was primarily designed for operation in the field of crisis management, a necessary condition is to ensure the availability of individual infrastructure elements. In case of failure or interruption of communication, it must not disrupt the distribution of voice messages themselves. Replication capabilities and seamless switching between individual elements have already been presented [15, 16], and their implementation is scheduled in the development of VDS.

- The possibility of selective filtration of participants in the affected area: Currently, VDS works through a list of telephone numbers of participants gradually, and distributes them on the basis of C_{max} into individual groups G_n. The next vision of the system will implement selective filters for individual telephone contacts from a list, with the aim of contacting smaller groups of persons in emergency situations, e.g. for the purpose of informing emergency services.
- Implementation of congestion module on the basis of data from the individual base stations and cells: Above, the possibility of getting up a temporary data network that would serve as an emergency measure to maintain essential communication channels was presented, but also on the side of VDS it is necessary to flexibly regulate traffic on the basis of data from the network.
- Ability to use the system in other areas of human activity: The proposed system aims to provide a broad spectrum of the population with sufficient information to resolve the crisis situation as soon as possible, and in a form that cannot be easily overlooked or ignored. If we look at it in a broker sense, depending on the content of the pre-recorded messages, the system does not always just have to serve as a part of crisis management, but it can provide a basic infrastructure for other fields of human activity, such as information systems, advertising campaigns, reports for the blind and partially sighted, and others.

7   Conclusion

The proposed VDS system brings a new approach to the distribution of warning information in crisis situations using VoIP technology. This solution is not intended to replace the currently used methods and technologies, but its goal is to work as a secondary means of eliminating the weak spots in the coverage of existing systems, with value - added economic savings and efficiency. The emphasis in this article is therefore to design, test, and the subsequent implementation of a comprehensive distribution system of voice messages intended primarily for emergencies and crisis situations. The presented results also showed a possible scalability when using a mobile distribution network, and outlined possible areas for improving the system. The VDS system is currently being actively developed, and it should be noted that interest in a practical output was shown by rescue and emergency services of the Czech Republic, who have been negotiating the terms for deployment in real-world environments.

Acknowledgements. This research was funded by the grant SGS reg. no. SP2017/174 conducted at VSB - Technical University of Ostrava, Czech Republic.

References

1. The United Nations, The World Bank: Natural hazards, unnatural disasters: the economics of effective prevention. http://www.alnap.org/pool/files/nhud-report-full.pdf. Accessed 19 May 2017

2. 3GPP TS 23.041: Technical realization of Cell Broadcast Service (CBS). http://www.etsi.org/dliver/etsi_ts/123000_123099/123041/14.00.00_60/ts_123041v140000p.pdf. Accessed 19 May 2017

3. 3GPP TS 22.268: Public Warning System (PWS) requirements. http://www.etsi.org/de-liver/etsi_ts/122200_122299/122268/13.00.00_60/ts_122268v130000p.pdf. Accessed 19 May 2017

4. Segui Boronat, F., Cebollada Guerri, J.C., Mauri Lloret, J.: An RTP/RTCP based approach for multimedia group and inter-stream synchronization. Multimedia Tools Appl. **40**(2), 285–319 (2008). Springer, Heidelberg

5. Davids, C., Gurbani, V., Poretsky, S.: RFC 7502: Methodology for benchmarking session initiation protocol (SIP) devices: basic session setup and registration. https://tools.ietf.org/html/rfc7502. Accessed 19 May 2017

6. Husic, J., et al.: RFC 6076: Basic telephony SIP end-to-end performance metrics. https://tools.ietf.org/html/rfc6076. Accessed 19 May 2017

7. Voznak, M., Rozhon, J.: Approach to stress tests in SIP environment based on marginal analysis. Telecommun. Syst. **52**(3), 1583–1593 (2013). Springer, Heidelberg

8. Stuckmann, P.: Quality of service management in GPRS-based radio access networks. Telecommun. Syst. **19**(3), 515–546 (2002). Springer, Heidelberg

9. Bhebhe, L., Parkkali, R.: VoIP performance over HSPA with different VoIP clients. Wireless Pers. Commun. **58**(3), 613–626 (2011). Springer, Heidelberg

10. Muhleisen, M., Walke, B., Timm-Giel, A.: Uplink VoIP capacity of 3GPP LTE under power control and semi-persistent scheduling. In: Proceedings of IEEE ATNAC 2013, pp. 69–76. IEEE, Christchurch (2013)

11. Yang, S.-H., Yang, S.-R., Kao, C.-C.: Analyzing VoIP capacity with delay guarantee for integrated HSPA networks. In: Ślęzak, D., Kim, T., Chang, A.C.-C., Vasilakos, T., Li, M.C., Sakurai, K. (eds.) FGCN 2009. CCIS, vol. 56, pp. 316–323. Springer, Heidelberg (2009). doi:10.1007/978-3-642-10844-0_38

12. Pratap, A., Pati, H.K.: Capacity estimation for cellular LTE using AMR codec with semi-persistent scheduling. In: Jain, L.C., Patnaik, S., Ichalkaranje, N. (eds.) Intelligent Computing, Communication and Devices. AISC, vol. 308, pp. 725–736. Springer, New Delhi (2015). doi:10.1007/978-81-322-2012-1_78

13. ITU-T Rec. G.114: International telephone connections and circuits – General recommendations on the transmission quality for an entire international telephone connection. https://www.itu.int/rec/dologin_pub.asp?lang=e&id=T-REC-G.114-200305-I!!PDF-E&type=items. Accessed 19 May 2017

14. Minh, Q.T., et al.: On-the-fly establishment of multi hop wireless access networks for disaster recovery. Commun. Mag. **52**(10), 60–66 (2014). IEEE

15. Leu, J.S., Hsieh, H.-C., Chen, Y.-C.: Inexpensive high availability solutions for the SIP - based VoIP service. Multimedia Tools Appl. **53**(1), 285–301 (2014). Springer, Heidelberg

16. Tomala, K., Rozhon, J., Rezac, F., Vychodil, J., Voznak, M., Zdralek, J.: Interactive VoiceXML module into SIP-based warning distribution system. In: Dziech, A., Czyżewski, A. (eds.) MCSS 2011. CCIS, vol. 149, pp. 338–344. Springer, Heidelberg (2011). doi:10.1007/978-3-642-21512-4_41

Estimation of Call Quality for Low Performance Servers

Jan Rozhon[(⊠)], Jakub Safarik, Erik Gresak, and Lukas Macura

CESNET z.s.p.o., Zikova 4, 160 00 Prague, Czech Republic
rozhon@cesnet.cz

Abstract. The call quality is an important issue of the modern voice over IP (VoIP) networks. This is given by their inherent "best effort" nature and the fact that any packet can be delayed or lost along the transmission path. To ensure sufficient call quality from the customer's point of view a multitude of approaches can be adopted, i.e. dynamic change of routing, codec swap or packet tagging. For these approaches to be efficient call quality information needs to be accessible on the devices through which the call is routed. Since the local area networks (LANs) do not suffer from underperformance the decision about the transmission strategy should be made on the edge of the local network. For the VoIP traffic the place for this decision is the Session Border Controller (SBC). This paper describes a way of speech quality estimation that is both accurate and performance undemanding making it possible to implement and integrate on low performance SBCs based on open-source software. These SBCs find their application mostly in small remote branches of private or academic institutions that do not require complex features of the proprietary hardware solutions but still need the advanced security and call quality monitoring.

Keywords: BeeSIP · Call quality estimation · OpenWRT · Session Border Controller

1 Introduction

The inherent features of the internet connections pose a great challenge for the real-time communication. The packet loss, delay and its variations all introduced by possibly variable path of each packet cause major degradation of the service quality and decrease the customer's satisfaction. Although the evolution of the computer networks made the speech quality issues on the wired lines in local area networks (LANs) rather a history, the high-paced spread of the mobile communication infrastructure reintroduced them again.

This problem is well known, however, and various methods have been developed and can be adopted to tackle it. These methods include:

- Voice/video traffic prioritization – the real-time communications are prioritized in the network by allocating the network devices' resources sooner than to any other traffic. For this purpose, DiffServ Code Points (DSCP) are used [1].

© Springer International Publishing AG 2017
A. Dziech and A. Czyżewski (Eds.): MCSS 2017, CCIS 785, pp. 161–172, 2017.
https://doi.org/10.1007/978-3-319-69911-0_13

- Use of enhanced codecs – voice and video codecs have been enhanced with the packet loss concealment (PLC) algorithms and the required bandwidth of the codec has been reduced [1].
- Load balancing – the Voice/video traffic is distributed among multiple peers to prevent the congestions of both devices and network.

The choice of the correct method and its parameters depends on the network environment and its setup. Moreover, the conditions on the network vary dynamically making the static configuration of the network devices inefficient. Therefore, it is beneficial (especially in case of a failure) to be able to dynamically adjust network configuration and/or call routing.

This sort of dynamic configuration adjustment should, in case of VoIP traffic, take place in the border element called Session Border Controller (SBC) since the problems in the local area networks are unlikely and remote network devices on the internet cannot be controlled or administered. Besides, ensuring service quality is one of the key roles of this element as it is noted in [2].

The relevant information for the policy change is hidden in the level of user's experience and satisfaction. This information, however, is difficult to obtain since the process of speech evaluation requires computationally and/or time expensive mathematical operations (omitting the human-based evaluation) [3–5]. For this reason, low performance devices are not suitable for this kind of evaluation.

However, these devices are commonly used to interconnect remote and small branches of the institutions or companies to the root VoIP infrastructure securely and reliably, since direct IP connections of individual phones can cause compatibility issues and make the configuration of the network complex and difficult. With security being a centrepiece of all modern communication systems and a field of threat detection rapidly developing [6], many private and public institutions employ small low-performance SBCs in increased numbers, the speech quality based policing performed on these devices could have a significant impact on the overall service performance from the user's perspective.

For this reason and because there is an open-source based SBC use case of a project called BeeSIP being developed in the team of authors, we have focused on creating and implementing the simplified speech quality estimation tool for this platform.

Further sections describe the current state of knowledge in the area (Sect. 2), proposed speech quality estimation tool for the field of low-performance SBCs (Sect. 3), the precision and speed performance of the methodology (Sect. 4) and consequent conclusion (Sect. 5).

2 State of the Art

There are two main groups of methods and approaches to measure the quality of call with first one being the subjective methods consisting of human based measurements and second one being objective methods that have their foundations on algorithmic calculation of users satisfaction score. Obviously, the first group is not suitable for the continuous monitoring of speech quality. The need for clean original speech sample for the quality calculation restricts the use of the intrusive objective methods like Perceptual Evaluation of Speech Quality (PESQ) [7] or Perceptual Objective Listening Quality Assessment (POLQA) [8] as well. The nonintrusive objective subgroup of methods is the one providing the feasible combination of speed, accuracy and passable requirements. The most commonly used member of this subgroup is E-model. However, the survey provided in [9] showed that the PESQ algorithm accommodates the effects of packet loss on speech quality better than the E-model. Therefore, it is better suited for the task of making accurate speech quality measurements or estimations. For this reason, several models employing PESQ as the reference basis have been created to enhance the E-model so that the results provided by the system are both accurate and easy to obtain and calculate.

The speech quality estimation system proposed in this paper is an enhancement and general rework of previous work that can be found in [10]. The author of this papers uses 2-state Gilbert Model to generate the losses and tries to fit the observed packet sequence into the model. This, however, proves problematic for the networks with different packet loss distributions and for the systems using the Packet Loss Concealment (PLC) algorithms.

As for the neural networks used in this area, the authors of [11] use the neural networks to map the cepstrum distance for the frame. This approach is one of the first application of the neural networks in the area of speech quality and it leads to a similar error rate as described here and involves the signal analysis of the speech sample, which makes the system much more complex and not suitable for the low performance devices. For this reason, the work has not been used as a basis for this paper.

For the synthesized speech, the recent research presented in [12] has been performed. The authors use neural networks and genetic algorithms to estimate the quality of speech, but again the model-specific approach for the packet loss determination is used.

3   Environment

BeeSIP is an OpenWRT based open-source operating system for embedded devices such as low performance routers or switches. It allows for dynamic operating system image creation that is ready to be deployed in a preconfigured state on vast number of platforms including x86.

One of the use cases of the BeeSIP is a lightweight SBC built on top of the following open-source software elements:

- Asterisk PBX, which handles the media and performs the necessary codec translations,
- Kamailio SIP Proxy, which does security checking of the incoming SIP traffic (DOS protection due to high performance [13], authentication and authorization of users) and performs NAT helper operations,
- SQLite3 database, for low volume information storage such as authentication credential, dynamic call routing, etc.

In this setup, BeeSIP is used in several locations in CESNET network that interconnects the academic institutions in the Czech Republic. Besides providing the security, which is an essential function of SBC that is usually a subject of thorough testing [14], BeeSIP allows to employ dynamic call routing based on the estimated qualitative parameters of the speech. This is made possible by the fact that the routing logic is stored in the database and is fetched by the Kamailio each time an outgoing call is requested and because there is a neural network based module that estimates the quality of call.

This module harnesses the fact that the most computationally expensive part of the neural network usage is training that, in case of BeeSIP platform, has been offloaded to the external server. This way, the module consists of a simple C++ library performing the calculations of the Mean Opinion Score estimation as it is described below. When obtained, MOS value is inserted into the database, where the embedded logic performs a switch to alternate outbound route if the score is below a given threshold (usually, this value is set to 3). The system architecture is depicted in Fig. 1.

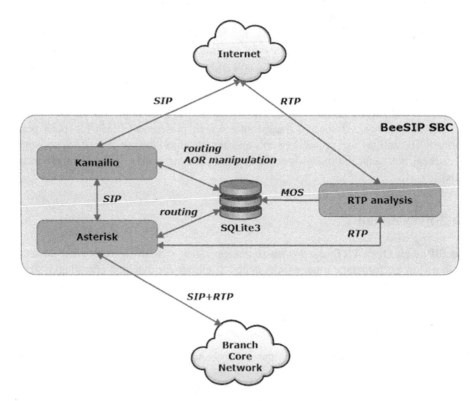

Fig. 1. BeeSIP SBC architecture with RTP analysis module.

4 Speech Quality Estimation

For the purposes of speech quality estimation performed right in the SBC element itself, the methodology must be based on the information already present on the SBC. Since VoIP traffic degradation is tied with the known phenomena of packet loss and delay and these network parameters are easy to monitor, the speech quality system should harness this information. Although this information can be used for speech quality estimation using the E-model's R-factor equation in its simplified form, the neural network model with proper set of training data can perform even more accurately.

The proposed and implemented model has the following key features.

Input parameters are packet loss and delay of the UDP traffic with jitter being transformed into additional packet loss due to the operation of dejitter buffers. The statistics of the packet loss consist of:

- Packet Loss Probability – the overall ratio of the lost packets to the total number of packets sent (RTP sequence numbers are used),

$$P_{PL} = \frac{N_{LOST}}{N_{SENT}} \tag{1}$$

- Packet Loss Probability in Burst – the overall ratio of the lost packets in burst periods (see [15] for burst definition) to the total number of packets,

$$P_{BPL} = \frac{N_{LOST\_IN\_BURST}}{N_{SENT}} \tag{2}$$

- Burst Density – the overall ratio of the lost packets in burst periods to the total number of packets in all bursts,

$$\rho = \frac{N_{LOST\_IN\_BURST}}{N_{BURST}} \tag{3}$$

- Relative Mean Burst Length – the ratio of all packets in bursts (received and lost) to all the packets in the sequence multiplied by the number of bursts in the packet sequence,

$$E'(B) = \frac{N_{BURST}}{N_{SENT} \cdot K_{BURST}} \tag{4}$$

- Relative Mean Gap Length – same as above but with the gaps (see gap definition in [15]),

$$E'(G) = \frac{N_{GAP}}{N_{SENT} \cdot K_{GAP}} \tag{5}$$

All of these parameters are purely numeric and enter the first stage of the model which is implemented by the simple neural network with structure of 5-3-1 (with Elliot activation, see results for comparison of different topologies) and bias neuron in each layer. This structure has been found adequate and most accurate by empirical study with the help of a simple evolution algorithm.

Based on the packet loss statistics, the neural network calculates the MOS value that has the packet loss and jitter effect imprinted in itself. The delay effect is then added using the E-model in these steps:

- Conversion of MOS to R-factor,
- Adding delay impairment,
- Reverse conversion to MOS.

The last missing part required for the model to work is the definition of weights in the neural network. For this, the set of possible and probable packet loss sequences has been created using the 4-state Markov model [16]. The model has been fed with multiple combinations of its transition probabilities settings (see Table 1). Based on these settings, a sequence of ones and zeros has been created with 1 denoting the packet loss event and 0 denoting the transition. This sequence has been applied on the sequence of RTP packets containing the sample speech of length between 20 to 24 s.

Table 1. 4-state Markov model transition probabilities for the loss model.

Probability	Training [%]	Testing [%]
p13	0, 1, 3, 5, 10	1, 3, 7, 15
p14	0, 1, 3, 5, 10	1, 3, 7, 15
p32	0, 1, 3, 5, 10	1, 3, 7, 15
p31	60, 75, 90	50, 80
p23	100	100
p41	100	100

This way a set of approximately 740 000 samples have been created for the group of 10 different speech recordings from the P.862 recommendation. These samples have been used to train and test the neural network (random 80% for training and 20% for testing).

Same procedure has been repeated for both G.711 (A-law) and Speex encoded samples thus creating sets for two distinct neural network models (one for each codec).

5   Results

Since no given structure of the neural network (NN) model is obviously the right one, several network topologies have been tested to select the most accurate one. Based on the training and testing data obtained with the above-described procedure, the topologies have been tested and evaluated based on their statistical performance. From this comparison, topology 5-3-1 resulted as significantly better especially in terms of root mean square error (RMSE).

Table 2. Pearson's correlation coefficient and RMSE for different neural network topologies (G.711 Codec).

Topology	Pearson's correlation coefficient [−]	RMSE [−]
5-1-1	0.952	0.260
5-3-1	0.952	0.200
5-5-1	0.951	0.237
5-3-2-1	0.853	0.341
5-5-3-1	0.899	0.286

Table 3. Pearson Correlation Coefficient and RMSE for different Neural Network Topologies (G.711 Codec).

Relative error [%]	Relative sample count [%]
< 1	10.071
< 5	46.638
< 10	76.521
< 25	98.994
< 50	99.999
≤ 100	100.000

The significance of the results from Table 2 have been tested using the Levene median test and Mann-Whitney-Wilcoxon test.

The distribution of the samples based on their relative error is summarized in Table 3. From there it is obvious that more than 76% of samples are within 10% error interval. This is true for the given topology 5-3-1 and both tested codecs G.711 and Speex. To be able to identify the shortcomings of the method better, the graphical representation of error distribution is depicted in Fig. 2, which provides a basis to compare the results with an ideal Gaussian curve of the normal distribution with same parameters (mean and standard deviation) as the group of results. From there, it is obvious that the model tends to lower the overall MOS score in the units of percent. This fact is not a problem for the implementation, however, since the worse score can only lead to a sooner switch of the outgoing routes.

During the testing, the model resulted in increased accuracy of the speech quality estimation when compared to similar systems and E-model itself. The results comparing PESQ, E-model and neural network model for different settings of the overall and entirely random packet loss is shown in Fig. 3 for G.711 codec and Fig. 4 for Speex codec. Both images show that the loss model performs better than E-model in comparison to PESQ reference.

To complete the picture, Figs. 5 and 6 show the boxplots of Pearson's correlation coefficient and RMSE for various settings of audio codecs.

The codec settings have been chosen based on the inherent features of both codecs with G.711 being the coder of wave and Speex being the hybrid coder. For the former, several packetizations (10, 20 and 40 ms) have been used to widen the validity of the measurement.

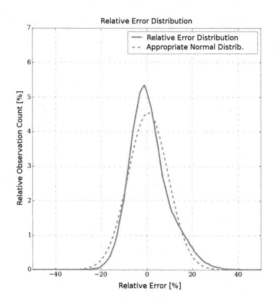

Fig. 2. Relative error distribution for the NN-based model with PESQ as reference.

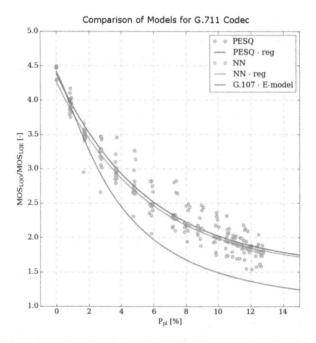

Fig. 3. Comparison of models for G.711 A-law Codec under Random Packet Loss.

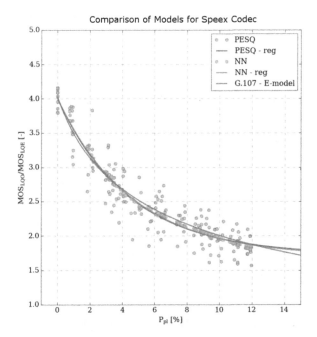

Fig. 4. Comparison of models for Speex Codec under Random Packet Loss.

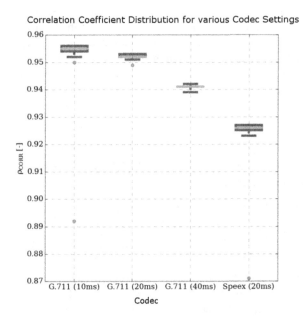

Fig. 5. Boxplots of Pearson's Correlation Coefficient for different Codec Settings.

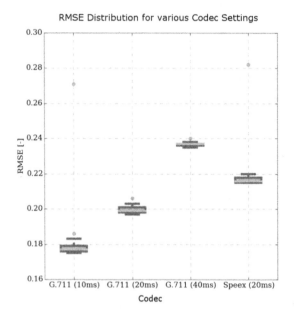

Fig. 6. Boxplots of RMSE for different Codec Settings.

From both the figures (Figs. 5 and 6) it is clear that both statistics are distributed tightly for all the codec settings. The worst score in terms of these two statistics has the setting of communication codec to G.711 with 40 ms with the highest value of RMSE and the second lowest value of Pearson's correlation coefficient. The reason for this is the relatively smaller number of packets in the data stream, which causes higher quality distortions even in situations where low packet loss is experienced. This codec setting is not widely used, though.

6   Conclusion

In this paper, a speech quality estimation methodology has been presented. The one that has the following features:

- High precision in comparison with PESQ,
- Delay sensitivity thanks to the incorporation of delay impairment from E-model,
- Low performance requirements,
- Simple implementation.

All these features make the methodology perfectly suitable to be used in embedded devices such as low cost routers or switches to further enhance the functions and abilities of the SBC element being developed by the team of authors.

Based on the results provided, we can summarize that for an extremely big set of sample sounds (around 740 000 samples per codec) the methodology performs with RMSE as low as 0.2 and very high correlation coefficient, which is in all the cases greater than 0.92. This performance has been validated by appropriated statistical tests and does not degrade significantly because of neither codec nor packetization change.

In future, we plan to create a fully embeddable library that is possible to be used independently of the operating system environment. In terms of methodology, we plan to employ evolution algorithms to test different more complex neural network topologies that could incorporate delay characteristics so that the E-model does not need to be incorporated.

Acknowledgment. This research has been supported by the Ministry of Education of the Czech Republic within the project CZ.02.1.01/0.0/0.0/16_013/0001797.

References

1. Hartpence, B.: Packet Guide to Voice over IP, 1st edn. O'Reilly Media, Sebastopol (2013)
2. Hautakorpi, J., Camarillo, G., et al.: Requirements from Session Initiation Protocol (SIP) Session Border Control (SBC) Deployments, IETF RFC5853 (2010). https://tools.ietf.org/html/rfc5853
3. Kim, D.: ANIQUE: an auditory model for single-ended speech quality estimation. IEEE Trans. Speech Audio Process. **13**(5), 821–831 (2005)
4. Grancharov, V., Zhao, D., Lindblom, J., Kleijn, W.: Non-intrusive speech quality assessment with low computational complexity. In: Ninth International Conference on Spoken Language Processing, INTERSPEECH 2006 – ICSLP, Pittsburgh, PA, USA, 17–21 September (2006)
5. Rozhon, J., Voznak, M.: Development of a speech quality monitoring tool based on ITU-T P.862. In: 2011 34th International Conference on Telecommunications and Signal Processing, TSP 2011 - Proceedings, Art. no. 6043771, pp. 62–66 (2011)
6. Voznak, M., Rezac, F.: Web-based IP telephony penetration system evaluating level of protection from attacks and threats. WSEAS Trans. Commun. **10**(2), 66–76 (2011)
7. Rix, A., Hollier, M., Hekstra, A., Beerends, J.: Perceptual evaluation of speech quality (PESQ) the new ITU standard for end-to-end speech quality assessment part I—time-delay compensation. J. Audio Eng. Soc. **50**(10), 755–764 (2002)
8. ITU-T: P.863: Perceptual objective listening quality assessment, ITU-T Recommendation P.863, ITU-T (2014)
9. Khan, H., Sun, L.: Assessment of speech quality for VoIP applications using PESQ and E-model. In: Proceedings of the Advances in Communications, Computing, Networks and Security, University of Plymouth, Plymouth, United Kingdom, vol. 7, pp. 263–273 (2010)
10. Sun, L.: Voice quality prediction models and their application in VoIP networks. IEEE Trans. Multimedia **8**(4), 809–820 (2006)
11. Meky, M., Saadawi, T.: Prediction of speech quality using radial basis functions neural networks. In: Proceedings Second IEEE Symposium on Computer and Communications, pp. 174–178. IEEE Computer Society (1997)
12. Mrvova, M., Pocta, P.: Quality estimation of synthesized speech transmitted over IP channel using genetic programming approach. In: The International Conference on Digital Technologies, pp. 39–43. IEEE (2013)
13. Voznak, M., Rozhon, J.: Approach to stress tests in SIP environment based on marginal analysis. Telecommun. Syst. **52**(3), 1583–1593 (2013)

14. Voznak, M., Rezac, F., Tomala, K.: SIP penetration test system. In: TSP 2010 - 33rd International Conference on Telecommunications and Signal Processing, pp. 504–508 (2010)
15. Schulzrinne, H., et al.: RTP: a transport protocol for real-time applications, IETF RFC3550 (2003). https://tools.ietf.org/html/rfc3550
16. Clark, A.: Modeling the effects of burst packet loss and recency on subjective voice quality. In: IPtel 2001 Workshop (2001)

Note Onset Detection with a Convolutional Neural Network in Recordings of Bowed String Instruments

Jędrzej Mońko and Bartłomiej Stasiak$^{(\boxtimes)}$

Institute of Information Technology, Łódź University of Technology,
ul. Wólczańska 215, 93-005 Łódź, Poland
bartlomiej.stasiak@p.lodz.pl

Abstract. In this article a convolutional neural network (CNN) is applied to the problem of note onset detection in music recordings. The work is focused on the analysis of pitched, non-percussive (PNP) onsets produced by bowed string instruments. Experimental evaluation is based on three datasets. The neural network has been trained on the largest one, which contains music excerpts of various kind. Two smaller datasets were used for testing. One of them is based on monophonic recordings of solo cello performances, while the other contains only polyphonic pieces for bowed string instruments (a violin duo and string ensembles).

The results obtained in experimental evaluation show that onset detection based on convolutional neural network trained with mixed audio material yields very good results in the case of solo cello recordings. For polyphonic bowed string instrument recordings, the overall detection efficacy is comparable to the general case, i.e. to the results obtained for mixed-genre, heterogeneous material. Detailed analysis shows that the method fails at detecting very "soft" note onsets present in some recordings.

Keywords: Note onset detection · Convolutional neural network (CNN) · Bowed string instruments · Onset detection function (ODF) · Sound spectrogram

1 Introduction

Note onset detection in music recordings is a part of a more general research field known as Music Information Retrieval (MIR). This field comprises several research problems related to extracting useful information from audio recordings, e.g. music genre recognition, tempo detection, rhythm analysis, chord sequence analysis or audio similarity assessment [17]. Onset detection, in particular, is the task of finding the precise time when new "sound events" occur in a recording.

While interesting on its own, the problem plays an important role as a support for methods retrieving higher-level information, including beat/downbeat tracking and decoding the rhythmic structure of a piece of music. This in turn

© Springer International Publishing AG 2017
A. Dziech and A. Czyżewski (Eds.): MCSS 2017, CCIS 785, pp. 173–185, 2017.
https://doi.org/10.1007/978-3-319-69911-0_14

gives a valuable insight into the musical style and genre, facilitating construction of content-based multimedia search engines and recommendation systems. Successful onset detection enables also automatic music transcription or audio-to-score alignment, which may be useful in a wide range of applications, from plagiarism detection to intelligent karaoke or musical training systems [21].

2   Motivation and Previous Work

Existing onset detection algorithms [1, 2, 25, 27] deal well with recognizing new music events exhibiting sudden increase of energy in the sound signal, typical for percussion instruments. However, the situation is completely different in the case when the beginning of a new note is more extended in time and the resulting onset is "soft", which is typical for bowed string instruments.

Generally, new sound events appearing in music recordings may be divided into a few broad categories [17]. Some onsets are characterized by a rapid increase in signal energy while the others do not exhibit this feature (percussive onsets vs non-percussive onsets). Another criterion is whether the new sound has a certain pitch (in other terms, whether the fundamental frequency of the new note may be determined) or not. The classification of the most important note onset types is therefore as follows:

- NPP – non-pitched percussive (e.g. snare drum, cymbals);
- PP – pitched percussive (e.g. piano, xylophone);
- PNP – pitched non-percussive, characterized by ambiguous changes in energy (e.g. violin, cello).

Currently, the problem of onset detection is considered to be resolved for the recordings of percussion instruments, which contain mainly NPP onsets [6]. As recordings of these instruments are characterized by a sudden increase in energy of the sound signal at note onsets, the detection of such sound events is a relatively easy task. Existing methods provide satisfactory efficiency (although not quite enough to consider the problem as fully solved) also for PP onset type detection. The last type of events (the PNP onsets) is typical for bowed string instruments, wind instruments, and also for human voice. The non-abrupt signal energy increase in these events significantly complicates the analysis and automatic note onset detection [6]. The new note may in fact emerge without any significant change in the signal energy [10], especially when legato playing technique is used. Moreover, also the pitch changes may appear quite "fuzzy", especially when accompanied by position shifts and glissandi [22]. Additional difficulties are caused by the presence of vibrato effect, typical for bowed string instrument performances [6]. These problems are the essential inspiration to concern this particular group of instruments in the current research.

The fundamental concept of the *(note) onset* is linked to a specific type of *change* or *novelty* appearing in the sound signal. It should be noted that the character of this change depends not only on the instrument-related rough classification of sound events presented above, but it is also influenced by many other factors, such as sound articulation technique used by the performer or acoustic conditions. Nevertheless, the basic approach is to construct some kind of a novelty measurement indicator – a so-called *onset detection function* (of time), in such a way that it will output high values exactly in the moments when new notes will be played (and low values in the other, quasi-stable segments of the sound signal). Such onset detection function (ODF) may be then simply thresholded – with fixed, or loudness-dependent threshold value – to find the onset positions.

A natural choice for the ODF construction is some kind of a *difference* between consecutive frames of the sound signal, usually computed in the frequency domain [1]. A classical example is the *spectral flux*:

$$\text{ODF}_{\text{SF}}(n) = \sum_k \text{ReLU}(|X_k(n)| - |X_k(n-1)|), \tag{1}$$

where n is the index of the time frame and $|X_k(n)|$ denotes the magnitude of the k-th frequency bin computed for this frame. Application of the *rectified linear unit* (ReLU), being an identity function for all positive arguments and yielding zero for all negative arguments, ensures that only the *increase* of the energy of the k-th spectral component will be taken into account. This gives preference to a percussive, energy-related aspect of new sound events. More subtle spectral changes may be revealed by phase spectrum analysis, e.g. by computing the difference between predicted and actual phase for a given frequency bin:

$$d\varphi_k(n) = \text{princarg}[\varphi_k(n) - 2\varphi_k(n-1) + \varphi_k(n-2)], \tag{2}$$

where $\varphi_k(n)$ is the phase value of the k-th frequency bin of the n-th frame and the princarg properly handles the phase wrapping, yielding a value within the $[-\pi, \pi]$ range. The coefficient $d\varphi_k(n)$ may be further weighted by magnitude change (to ignore it for negligibly low-level spectral components) [23] or it may be used to compute higher-level statistics, useful in the onset detection task [2]. Some more specific methods, robust to particular sound effects that may appear in the sound signal, such as e.g. vibrato, have also been proposed [5,6].

The vibrato effect is a good example of a significant *change* of the sound signal, which does not imply the beginning of a new musical note [22]. This and similar ambiguities, related e.g. to *glissandi*, *tremolo* or various other effects occurring in contemporary music, lead to conclusion, that the aforementioned methods based on simple, deterministically constructed ODFs should be easily outperformed by example-based, machine learning approaches. This thesis has been consistently supported in numerous recent works [3,8,15,20,23,24]. The state-of-art methods are usually based on neural networks, including bidirectional long short-term memory neural networks (LSTM) [8], recurrent neural networks (RNN) [3] and convolutional neural networks (CNNs) [19,20,24]. Besides the solutions based on some kind of intermediate signal representation, such as MLP-based approach cumulating information from several different ODFs [23] or other ODF fusion techniques [18,26], the most flexible and effective methods operate directly on raw sound spectrograms [19,20].

The convolutional neural networks (CNNs) have been designed primarily for image analysis. Their construction have been biologically inspired [9,11] and they show significant similarity, in their architectural and functional principles, to some elements of a human visual system. On this basis, owing to the reduction of neural connections between layers and extensive weights sharing [16], they are capable of processing raw images without any intermediate feature extraction or parameterization stage [14,28]. When applied to sound analysis tasks, they are fed with some form of a time-frequency representation of the sound signal, such as short-time Fourier transform [17], usually scaled logarithmically along the frequency axis [20,24]. The input data is processed by a sequence of consecutive convolutional layers, where each such layer computes its output on the basis of 2D convolution of its input with adaptable kernels. Special data-reduction layers, performing a pooling operation (e.g. max-pooling or mean-pooling), are inserted between the convolutional layers. The last few layers are often densely-connected and they contain standard sigmoidal neurons performing the final data reduction and classification or regression, according to the desired target output.

Despite the huge input data dimensionality and the big number of parameters to optimize, the convolutional neural networks, are being successfully trained and used in complex, real-life challenges, due to application of effective dropout and regularization techniques and the increasing availability of the efficient GPU-based computational platforms. The potential of the CNNs enables to solve more and more high-level problems directly, without the need of using intermediate low-level models. Therefore, in some MIR applications, the onset-detection stage is sometimes omitted and the spectral data are used to train the neural network to perform e.g. the beat/downbeat tracking task directly [4,13]. However, in other problems involving content-based audio analysis the explicit information about location of each onset is still important and necessary, which is the fundamental motivation for our current work.

In this paper we present an extension of our previous research based on the CNN application to the onset detection problem [24]. The next section demonstrates the details of the neural architecture of our network, as well as the input and output data format. In Sect. 4 the dataset including recordings of bowed string instruments is described and the results of the CNN-based onset detection are then presented and discussed (Sect. 5).

3   Neural Network Architecture

The architecture of our convolutional neural network is the same as in [24], where it proved to successfully deal with the onset detection problem on a large heterogeneous database of mixed-genre music material. The input to the network is a matrix of 80 rows and 15 columns representing 15 consecutive time frames of the sound spectrogram, corresponding to ca 175 ms of the audio file. The rows represent 80 logarithmically distributed frequency bands of the spectrogram (up to 16 kHz). The audio files are sampled at 44100 Hz and the spectrogram parameters are: window size $N = 2048$ and the hop-size $K = 512$ samples, which yields time resolution of ca. 11.6 ms per frame. The target (the expected output for a single input matrix) is a single value from the range $[-1, 1]$, indicating the distance between the middle frame of the current input matrix and the nearest onset [23,24]. More precisely, if an onset appears in the center frame of the current input matrix (according to the ground-truth data), we expect the network to produce the maximum output value. For off-center onset location, the output value is expected to drop correspondingly as demonstrated in Fig. 1, where the center frame ($n = 28$) of the input matrix happens to be two frames apart from the onset position ($n = 30$), so the corresponding target value (top plot) is relatively low (-0.6).

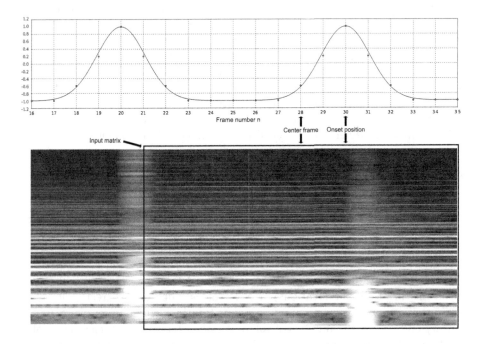

Fig. 1. Bottom plot: the sound spectrogram fragment with a single input matrix indicated (the black box). Top plot: the associated target values [24]. Note, that the spectrogram in the bottom plot has increased resolution – for illustration purposes – with respect to the the matrix that is actually fed to the network input ($w \times h = 15 \times 80$ pixels).

The CNN network structure is as follows [24]:

- Convolutional layer with 10 rectangular filters of size: $w \times h = 7 \times 3$ with ReLU (Rectified Linear Unit) activation function and stride value of 1 in both directions (full overlap). Note that for input size of $w \times h = 15 \times 80$ it yields $w \times h = 9 \times 78$ output.
- Max-pooling layer with non-overlapping kernels of size: $w \times h = 1 \times 3$ (output size $w \times h = 9 \times 26$).

- Convolutional layer with 20 square filters of size $w \times h = 3 \times 3$ and stride value of 1 in both directions (output size $w \times h = 7 \times 24$).
- Max-pooling layer with non-overlapping kernels of size: $w \times h = 1 \times 3$ (output size $w \times h = 7 \times 8$).
- Inner product (i.e. fully connected) layer with 256 hidden neurons and ReLU activation function.
- Inner product (i.e. fully connected) layer with one output neuron and tanh (hyperbolic tangent) activation function.

The output of the trained network may be treated as an onset detection function (ODF) indicating the likelihood of an onset appearing in a particular moment in time. The advantage of thus defined ODF is that it is robust to local changes in the loudness of the sound, which normally requires some form of variable thresholding (based on e.g. moving average or moving median of the signal energy). Here, in contrast to classical ODF functions [1,2,7,17], a fixed threshold T may be used for all the analyzed audio files. After the thresholding, the peak-picking procedure is applied and the peaks found within the range of 50 ms relative to the actual onsets are treated as the correctly detected ones [1].

Objective assessment of note onset detection quality is done with measures used for binary classifiers: precision (Eq. 3), recall (Eq. 4) and F-measure (Eq. 5):

$$P = \frac{TP}{TP + FP} \tag{3}$$

$$R = \frac{TP}{TP + FN} \tag{4}$$

$$F = 2 \cdot \frac{P \cdot R}{P + R} \tag{5}$$

where TP is the number of relevant elements detected (true positives – the actual onsets at proper locations), FP is the number of incorrectly detected elements (false positives – onsets detected at locations where no onsets actually appear) and FN is the number of relevant events omitted by a classifier (false negatives – the undetected onsets). The precision determines how many of all the reported onsets are the correct ones, while the recall – how many of the true onsets have been actually detected. The F-measure is used for representing the balance between the two aforementioned measures. It is defined as harmonic mean of precision and recall.

4   Datasets

The dataset used in our experiments comprises two separate parts. The first one, which has been used to train the network is the same as in our previous work [24], and it contains mixed audio material. The second part of the dataset contains recordings of bowed string instruments only (2005 annotated onsets).

4.1 Training Set

The total duration of audio files in the dataset used in [24] is over 45 min (10939 annotated onsets), covering a wide range of music styles from classical to pop, both polyphonic and monophonic. Here, the training procedure has been conducted with the use of a subset (approximately 75%) of that data, composed of a selection of the (complete) audio tracks – exactly the same as we used for the training process in [24]. However, this time we do not use the remaining files for testing, but we test on a separate audio collection of bowed string instruments.

For training, the spectrograms are cut into overlapping fragments some of which are then rejected, so that the obtained set is balanced, i.e. the number of "onset fragments" (for which the target value is non-zero) is equal to the number of "non-onset fragments". For testing, all possible fragments are used in an ordered sequence.

4.2 Test Set

The dataset used for testing has a different characteristics than the training dataset, mostly because audio material uniformity. It consists of recordings of music pieces performed on bowed string instruments only. About half of the collection (1029 onsets) are recordings of solo cello performances, while the rest (976 onsets) contains polyphonic audio material, mainly a violin duo and string ensembles. The entire set is intended to cover a wide range of musical expression styles (various tempi, dynamics, etc.).

5 Testing Procedure and Results

The training set (Sect. 4.1) was used to train the CNN network with the architecture described in Sect. 3. For training and testing we used Caffe framework [12] installed on two separate machines, for comparison purposes: a CPU-only machine with Intel Core i7-2620M processor and a cluster node with Tesla K20m GPU. The approximate training time was 4 h 30 min in the first case and 20 min in the second one. In the testing phase we used the CPU-only machine where our network achieved processing rate of 1883 frames per second. Considering the sampling frequency of 44,1 kHz and the hop-size of 512 samples, it means that the CNN was capable of analyzing approx. 22 s of a recording per second (not including the time needed for pre-processing and computing the spectrogram).

After the training, the two test subsets – monophonic and polyphonic (Sect. 4.2) – have been used for testing and for computing the detection efficacy. The resulting F-measure for both subsets has been computed for different threshold values from the range of $[-0.8, 0]$. The relationship of threshold value and F-measure is presented in the plots (Figs. 2 and 3). Additional testing procedure also involved artificial onset shifting by a constant factor within a single file to compensate for potential differences in annotation convention and therefore to maximize the F-measure [24]. Obviously the results obtained with shifted onset annotations cannot be treated as objective ones but rather as indication of theoretical neural network capabilities in case of strictly uniform annotation style of the ground-truth data.

5.1   Cello Dataset

Interestingly, the neural network performs very well in the case of solo cello recordings. The peak F-measure of 92%, corresponding to the threshold level of −0.35 (Fig. 2) is better by almost ten percent than the overall 83% detection results achieved (for threshold −0.29) in experiments presented in our previous work [24], where both training and testing dataset contained mixed audio material. Such a high F-measure may result from the fact, that spectrogram of solo bowed string instrument recording contains very clear onset-related spectro-temporal patterns, which can be easily detected by convolutional neural network. Typically an onset is indicated by abrupt wide spectrum burst followed by a harmonic "comb". When there are no other instruments nor additional noise sources present in the recording, then the ambiguity of onset-related pattern is always very little, if any. Our CNN is also quite insusceptible to vibrato effect, which often leads to many false positive detections in the case of classical ODF-based methods.

With onset shifting applied, the result is slightly better – 93.2% (threshold −0.35, Fig. 3). However, the improvement in efficacy is notably lower in comparison with [24] (88.6%, threshold −0.29 with annotation shifting vs. 83% without). This may be due to two factors. Firstly, the solo cello dataset is relatively small and the ground-truth data is annotated by a single person – therefore the annotation convention is kept uniform within the entire dataset. In contrary, the

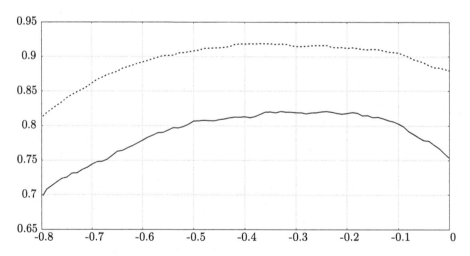

Fig. 2. The overall F-measure (ordinate) with respect to the ODF threshold value (abscissa). String ensembles database (solid line), cello dataset (dotted line), no annotation shifting.

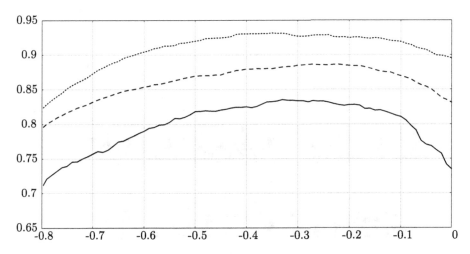

Fig. 3. The overall F-measure (ordinate) with respect to the ODF threshold value (abscissa). String ensembles dataset (solid line), cello dataset (dotted line), mixed audio material [24] (dashed line), annotation shifting applied.

training dataset is merged from several sources, thus the uniformity of annotation style and accuracy cannot be guaranteed. Secondly, cello recordings contain mostly monophonic music material, hence there is almost no uncertainty in precise onset timing as opposed to situation where overlapping melodic lines occur. In the latter case, ambiguities may arise e.g. when two or more instruments do not stay perfectly in rhythm, thus generating a few separate onsets instead of a single one.

5.2   String Ensembles Dataset

The overall detection performance (F-measure) in the tests involving polyphonic audio material reaches the highest value of 82% for threshold level of -0.33 (without shifting the annotations). The score is very close to detection performance for mixed audio material reported in [24] (83%, threshold -0.29). It should be noted that the results are quite stable in the broad range of threshold values. For threshold level of -0.29, used in [24] (instead of -0.33), the F-measure drops by only 0.1%.

These results might lead to assumption, that the CNN performance is similar, regardless of the music material used for testing. Generally that is true, as the various music recordings share common spectro-temporal characteristics. However, the detailed analysis shows that while the overall F-measure is high, the actual detection efficacy may be very poor for specific recordings (Fig. 4). This primarily applies to music pieces of a very "calm" character, i.e. of slow tempo and quiet dynamics. When such music is performed with bowed string or wind instruments, the onsets are usually very "soft" – there is no significant energy increase of spectral components, that might clearly indicate an onset. The worst

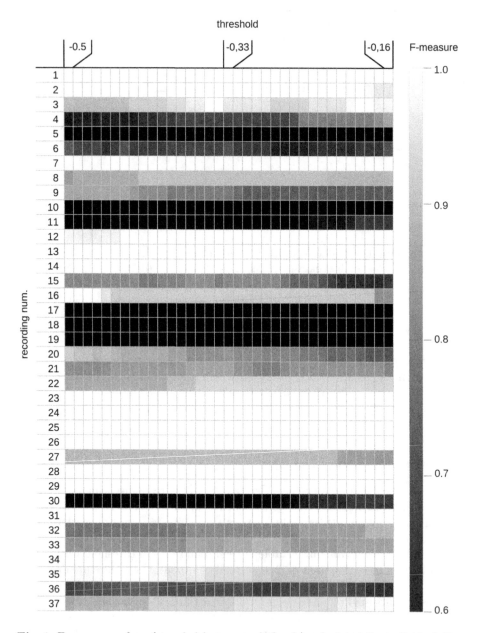

Fig. 4. F-measure values (encoded by grayscale levels) calculated for individual files with respect to ODF peak-picking threshold value (horizontal axis). White and black correspond to boundary F-measure values of 1.0 and 0.6 (or less), respectively. Note that for audio files 10, 17, 18, 19 the result is very poor (below 0.6) for all threshold values presented in the chart, while in most other cases the F-measure is rather good (around 0.9).

F-measure result with threshold level of -0.33 (optimal for the overall case) is only 14% for string quartet recording. Both precision and recall values are very low with just 2 of 14 onsets detected correctly and as many as 12 false positive detections. In the case of other similar recordings the F-measure ranges from ca. 25% to 55%. Another important observation is that changing the threshold value individually does not significantly improve the results. In contrast, for most of the other recordings the F-measure is higher than 84%; in fact, for about half of all the recordings it exceeds 90%.

Low onset detection efficacy in specific cases may result from insufficient training patterns related to "soft" onsets. It is indicated not only by poor detection results but also by insensitivity to changing the threshold value. Majority of music recordings simply does not contain soft onsets, which are rather specific to certain classical music pieces performed with bowed string or wind instruments, or human voice. However the method is surprisingly robust to the vibrato, which is very important in the case of string ensemble music.

Application of optimal onset shift increases the overall F-measure by 1.5%. Again, it is a relatively small improvement. Analysis of the results obtained individually for each audio file with several different shift values shows that annotation shifting does not improve results where original F-measure was high. In fact, shifting annotations by more than 43 ms often reduces the efficacy in such cases. The procedure seems to be advantageous only when original score is low, yet still the improvement is rather moderate.

5.3 Conclusions

The presented convolutional neural network is a very efficient tool for sound analysis and recognition, in particular for the onset detection task. It has been shown, that onset detection with CNN trained on mixed audio material may perform very well even in the case of very specific recordings, containing only excerpts of bowed string instrument pieces. However, because of high degree of generalization, the presented approach fails at detecting very "soft" non-percussive onsets. This limitation comes from the fact that such onsets are specific to certain music styles and instruments. Therefore, it should be concluded, that the applied training dataset based on mixed music material contains too few patterns related to non-percussive onsets.

The presented results are comparable to those obtained by state-of-art methods based on deep learning approach, including RNN [8] (F-measure 87.3%) and CNN [19,20] (F-measure 88.5% and 90.3% respectively). The direct comparison is however difficult as the selection of the training and testing material is very significant, as may be seen from Figs. 2 and 3. Even within the same category, the difficulty level of individual recordings often varies greatly (Fig. 4). The violin recording analyzed by Bello *et al.* in their seminal work [1] with standard ODF-based methods, scores 96.8% (F-measure) there, despite being a representative of a "difficult" PNP class. However, the content of this audio file itself is rather unambiguous, with distinct, precise onsets, which have been almost perfectly detected also by our network.

The obtained results may be improved with a more specialized classifier, i.e. the one trained on a dataset containing relatively more soft onsets, though this would require a careful selection of the recordings and annotating them under strict, uniform rules to avoid temporal ambiguities in the ground-truth data. Due to the fact that our method relies solely on short-time, low-level signal features, another way to improve the soft onset detection efficacy would be to use a detector with prior "knowledge" on music semantics and structure, able to adaptively increase the detection sensitivity in predicted onset locations.

References

1. Bello, J., Daudet, L., Abdullah, S., Duxbury, C., Davies, M., Sandler, M.: A tutorial on onset detection in music signals. IEEE Trans. Speech Audio Process. **13**(5), 1035–1047 (2005)
2. Bello, P., Sandler, M.: Phase-based note onset detection for music signals. In: Proceedings of IEEE Conference on Acoustics, Speech, and Signal Processing ICASSP, vol. 5, pp. 441–444 (2003)
3. Böck, S., Arzt, A., Krebs, F., Schedl, M.: Online real-time onset detection with recurrent neural networks. In: Proceedings of the 15th International Conference on Digital Audio Effects (DAFx 2012) (2012)
4. Böck, S., Krebs, F., Widmer, G.: Joint beat and downbeat tracking with recurrent neural networks. In: Proceedings of the 17th International Society for Music Information Retrieval Conference, ISMIR 2016, New York City, United States, 7–11 August 2016, pp. 255–261 (2016)
5. Böck, S., Widmer, G.: Local group delay based vibrato and tremolo suppression for onset detection. In: Proceedings of the 13th International Society for Music Information Retrieval Conference (ISMIR 2013), Curitiba, Brazil, pp. 589–594, November 2013
6. Böck, S., Widmer, G.: Maximum filter vibrato suppression for onset detection. In: Proceedings of the 16th International Conference on Digital Audio Effects (DAFx 2013), Maynooth, Ireland, pp. 55–61 (2013)
7. Duxbury, C., Bello, J., Davies, M., Sandler, M.: Complex domain onset detection for musical signals. In: Proceedings of the 6th International Conference on Digital Audio Effects (DAFx 2003) (2003)
8. Eyben, F., Böck, S., Schuller, B., Graves, A.: Universal onset detection with bidirectional long short-term memory. In: Neural Networks, 11th International Society for Music Information Retrieval Conference (ISMIR 2010), pp. 589–594 (2010)
9. Fukushima, K.: Neocognitron: a self-organizing neural network model for a mechanism of pattern recognition unaffected by shift in position. Biol. Cybern. **36**, 193–202 (1980)
10. Holzapfel, A., Stylianou, Y., Gedik, A.C., Bozkurt, B.: Three dimensions of pitched instrument onset detection. IEEE Trans. Audio Speech Lang. Process. **18**(6), 1517–1527 (2010)
11. Hubel, D.H., Wiesel, T.N.: Receptive fields and functional architecture in two nonstriate visual areas (18 and 19) of the cat. J. Neurophysiol. **28**, 229–289 (1965)
12. Jia, Y., Shelhamer, E., Donahue, J., Karayev, S., Long, J., Girshick, R., Guadarrama, S., Darrell, T.: Caffe: convolutional architecture for fast feature embedding. arXiv preprint arXiv:1408.5093 (2014)

13. Krebs, F., Böck, S., Dorfer, M., Widmer, G.: Downbeat tracking using beat synchronous features with recurrent neural networks. In: Proceedings of the 17th International Society for Music Information Retrieval Conference, ISMIR 2016, New York City, United States, 7–11 August 2016, pp. 129–135 (2016)
14. Krizhevsky, A., Sutskever, I., Hinton, G.E.: Imagenet classification with deep convolutional neural networks. In: Pereira, F., Burges, C.J.C., Bottou, L., Weinberger, K.Q. (eds.) Advances in Neural Information Processing Systems 25, pp. 1097–1105. Curran Associates Inc., New York (2012)
15. Lacoste, A., Eck, D.: A supervised classification algorithm for note onset detection. EURASIP J. Adv. Sig. Process. **2007**, 153 (2007)
16. LeCun, Y., Bottou, L., Bengio, Y., Haffner, P.: Gradient-based learning applied to document recognition. Proc. IEEE **86**, 2278–2324 (1998)
17. Lerch, A.: An Introduction to Audio Content Analysis: Applications in Signal Processing and Music Informatics. Wiley-IEEE Press, Hoboken (2012)
18. Quintela, N.D., Giménez, A.P., Guijarro, S.T.: A comparison of score-level fusion rules for onset detection in music signals. In: Proceedings of 10th International Society for Music Information Retrieval Conference, ISMIR 2009, pp. 117–121, October 2009
19. Schlüter, J., Böck, S.: Musical onset detection with convolutional neural networks. In: 6th International Workshop on Machine Learning and Music (MML) (2013)
20. Schlüter, J., Bock, S.: Improved musical onset detection with convolutional neural networks. In: Proceedings of the IEEE International Conference on Acoustics, Speech, and Signal Processing (ICASSP 2014), Florence, Italy (2014)
21. Soszyński, F., Wołowski, J., Stasiak, B.: Music games as a tool supporting music education. In: Proceedings of the Conference on Game Innovations, CGI 2016, pp. 116–132 (2016)
22. Stasiak, B., Mońko, J.: Analysis of onset detection with a maximum filter in recordings of bowed instruments. In: Proceedings of the 138th Audio Engineering Society Convention (2015)
23. Stasiak, B., Mońko, J., Niewiadomski, A.: Note onset detection in musical signals via neural-network-based multi-ODF fusion. Int. J. Appl. Math. Comput. Sci. **26**(1), 203–213 (2016)
24. Stasiak, B., Monko, J.: Analysis of time-frequency representations for musical onset detection with convolutional neural network. In: Proceedings of the 2016 Federated Conference on Computer Science and Information Systems, FedCSIS 2016, pp. 147–152 (2016)
25. Thoshkahna, B., Ramakrishnan, K.R.: An onset detection algorithm for query by humming (QBH) applications using psychoacoustic knowledge. In: Proceedings of 17th European Signal Processing Conference, EUSIPCO 2009, pp. 939–942. IEEE (2009)
26. Tian, M., Fazekas, G., Black, D.A.A., Sandler, M.: Design and evaluation of onset detectors using different fusion policies. In: 15th International Society of Music Information Retrieval (ISMIR) Conference, pp. 631–636 (2014)
27. Wang, H., Wang, L.: Onset detection algorithm in voice activity detection for Mandarin. In: Proceedings of International Conference on Computer Science and Network Technology (ICCSNT), pp. 1148–1151 (2013)
28. Zeiler, M.D., Fergus, R.: Visualizing and understanding convolutional networks. CoRR abs/1311.2901 (2013)

Detection of the Incoming Sound Direction Employing MEMS Microphones and the DSP

Grzegorz Szwoch$^{(\boxtimes)}$ and Józef Kotus

Department of Multimedia Systems, Faculty of Electronics,
Telecommunications and Informatics,
Gdańsk University of Technology, Gdańsk, Poland
greg@sound.eti.pg.gda.pl

Abstract. A 3D acoustic vector sensor based on MEMS microphones and its application to road traffic monitoring is presented in the paper. The sensor is constructed from three pairs of digital MEMS microphones, mounted on the orthogonal axes. Signals obtained from the microphones are used to compute sound intensity vectors in each direction. With this data, it is possible to compute the horizontal and vertical angle of an incoming sound. The algorithm was implemented on a low-cost, fixed point TMS320C5535 digital signal processor. The microphone signals are acquired via I2S buses, then the algorithm computes the acoustic pressure, particle velocity and sound intensity components, which are then used to calculate the azimuth and elevation of a sound source. The detection results are exposed via the USB interface. The intensity values are computed in overlapping frames in order to improve the signal-to-noise ratio. In the experimental setup, readouts with a frequency of c.a. 70 Hz, frequency range up to c.a. 9 kHz and the angular resolution of 1 degree, were obtained. Validation of the sensor was performed in an anechoic chamber using a test source with known direction. A comparison of the tested system with a commercial sound intensity probe was also made. Additionally, some preliminary tests in real world conditions were also performed. The obtained results prove that the proposed sensor and the algorithm provide high accuracy of detection of the incoming sound direction, comparable to a commercial device. Therefore, the sensor and the DSP algorithm form a low-cost system that may be used e.g. for acoustic monitoring of traffic.

Keywords: Audio analysis · Detection of sound direction · Acoustic vector sensor · Digital signal processor

1 Introduction

An acoustic vector sensor (AVS) is a device capable of measuring the sound field in terms of acoustic particle velocity and pressure [1]. A typical AVS provides three velocity signals in the orthogonal directions and one pressure signal. One of applications of AVS is detection of direction-of-arrival (DOA) of an incoming sound signal. Thus, an AVS may work as an "acoustic radar" that detects and tracks sound sources. Possible practical application of this systems include e.g. road traffic monitoring, with functions such as vehicle counting and speed detection. The traditional, video-based

© Springer International Publishing AG 2017
A. Dziech and A. Czyżewski (Eds.): MCSS 2017, CCIS 785, pp. 186–198, 2017.
https://doi.org/10.1007/978-3-319-69911-0_15

monitoring fails in difficult lighting conditions. Therefore, other solutions, such as microwave detectors, LIDARs and audio monitoring systems are viable alternatives. However, commercial AVS probes are expensive devices, which limits their implementation on a larger scale.

A thorough review of algorithms used for sound source detection and tracking with AVS can be found in [1]. The first important work in this area was by Nehorai and Paldi [2] who proposed two DOA detection algorithms: one based on the intensity vector and another one using the velocity covariance matrix. Hawkes and Nehorai [3] explored vector-sensor arrays for improved detection of multiple sources. Shujan et al. [4] proposed the speaker tracking algorithm based on the Multiple Signal Classification (MUSIC) method. Zhong and Premkumar [5] used the particle filtering method for simultaneous tracking of multiple sound sources. Awad and Wong [6] proposed the recursive least squares method for the source tracking. Wenzhao et al. [7] used a circular AVS array for detection of the number of sources and their direction. Agarwal et al. [8] perform detection of sound sources in an underdetermined case using the higher order statistics approach. Nagesha et al. [9] used an AVS array for underwater sound source localization.

The main motivation for the research described here was reproducing the AVS function with cheap pressure sensors and an algorithm which computes the velocity and pressure signals from the individual signals recorded by the sensors, and then performs the DOA detection. In our previous works, we have evaluated a commercial AVS probe for localization of multiple sound sources [10]. Application of the sensor in a surveillance system is described in [11]. In [12], we described a custom 3D sound intensity probe built from electret condenser microphones. In this paper, we propose a new, low cost AVS built from digital microphones in MEMS (micro-electro-mechanical system) technology, with an accompanying algorithm for detection of sound direction, implemented on a digital signal processor (DSP). The main intended application of the sensor is acoustic monitoring of road traffic.

2 The Processing Algorithm

The proposed algorithm processes the incoming pressure signals in time domain and computes the angles that indicate the direction of a sound source. First, the pressure signals are recorder by a set of six MEMS sensors, placed in pairs alongside three orthogonal axes that form a Cartesian coordinate system (Fig. 1). The origin of this system is situated in the middle point between a pair of microphones on each axis. The six recorder pressure signals are therefore denoted as $[x_1, x_2, y_1, y_2, z_1, z_2]$. *Acoustic particle velocity* vectors **u** (referred to as 'velocity' further in the text) alongside all three axes may be calculated as:

$$
\begin{bmatrix} \mathbf{u}_x \\ \mathbf{u}_y \\ \mathbf{u}_z \end{bmatrix} = \begin{bmatrix} 1 & 0 & 0 \\ 0 & 1 & 0 \\ 0 & 0 & 1 \end{bmatrix} \cdot \begin{bmatrix} x_2 - x_1 \\ y_2 - y_1 \\ z_2 - z_1 \end{bmatrix}
\tag{1}
$$

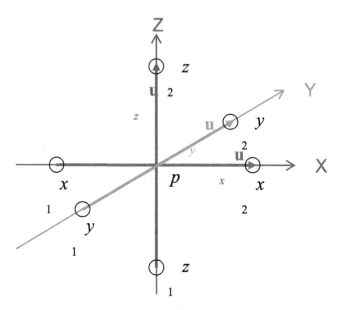

Fig. 1. An acoustic vector sensor built from six MEMS sensors, shown as black circles. Thick arrows depict the velocity vectors.

Pressure p at the origin is computed as the average of all microphone signals:

$$p = \frac{1}{3}\left(\frac{x_1 + x_2}{2} + \frac{y_1 + y_2}{2} + \frac{z_1 + z_2}{2}\right) \qquad (2)$$

Sound intensity vectors $\mathbf{I}$ for each direction may be then computed using the formula [13]:

$$\mathbf{I} = \frac{1}{T}\int_T p(t)\mathbf{u}(t)\,dt \qquad (3)$$

In case of digital signals, the integral in Eq. (3) may be computed by accumulating products of pressure and velocity signals over a number of samples.

Having computed the intensity vectors $(\mathbf{I}_x, \mathbf{I}_y, \mathbf{I}_z)$ and assuming that the coordinate system is oriented so that the XY plane is horizontal and the Z axis is directed upwards (Fig. 1), the *azimuth* (horizontal angle) φ of the incoming sound is:

$$\phi = \arctan\left(\frac{\|\mathbf{I}_y\|}{\|\mathbf{I}_x\|}\right) \qquad (4)$$

and the *elevation* (vertical angle) θ is:

$$\theta = \arctan\left(\frac{\|\mathbf{I}_z\|}{\|\mathbf{I}_x + \mathbf{I}_y\|}\right) \tag{5}$$

In the algorithm, N successive samples are obtained from all six microphones. Each signal is pre-processed by an amplitude correction filter in order to compensate for differences between individual microphones, resulting from variations in their parameters and imperfections in their placement in the system. Next, the velocity and pressure signals are computed from the filtered samples (Eqs. 1 and 2). Each velocity signal is then processed by a phase correction filter. Coefficients of the correction filters are computed during the calibration stage. The details of this process were described in patent application [14]. The intensity values are computed by multiplying the pressure and velocity signals and summing up the results (Eq. 3). Finally, the azimuth and the elevation are computed (Eqs. 4 and 5).

3   Hardware Implementation

The AVS array was constructed using six MEMS sensors, model INMP441 from InvenSense [15]. They are omnidirectional, digital microphones providing 24-bit data, with frequency response from 60 Hz to 15 kHz, SNR of 61 dBA and sensitivity-26 dBFS. The sensor dimensions are $4.72 \times 3.76 \times 1$ mm. Each sensor was mounted on a 10×10 mm board, so that all six boards form a cube (Fig. 2).

Fig. 2. The acoustic vector sensor built from six INMP441 MEMS sensors. Microphone ports are visible as holes in the middle of each board.

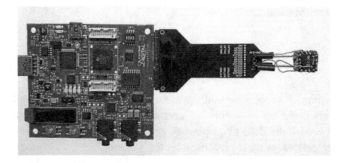

Fig. 3. Acoustic vector sensor connected to the eZdsp5535 board.

A low-power, fixed point TMS320C5535 digital signal processor was chosen for the algorithm implementation [16]. The DSP is mounted on an eZdsp5535 development board [17]. The microphone array is connected to the DSP board via I2S (Inter-IC Sound) buses (Fig. 3). Each I2S bus handles two-channel audio, so each pair of MEMS sensors situated on the same axis is connected to a single bus, forming a stereo pair. One of the buses is designated as the master which receives the clock signal from the DSP. On each pulse in the clock signal, data is read from a microphone and sent to the DSP. For each sample of a stereo signal, two 32-bit values need to be transmitted via the I2S bus. The sampling frequency f_s is related to the DSP clock frequency f_c according to the following formula [18]:

$$f_s = \frac{f_c}{2 \cdot 32 \cdot 2^M} \tag{6}$$

where M defines the frequency divisor. The value of f_c has to be chosen from a set of predefined clock frequencies. For the standard sampling frequency of 48 kHz, the optimal values are f_c = 100 MHz and M = 5, which results in f_s = 48.83 kHz. In our experiments, we wanted to have f_s close to 16 kHz, so the values we used were f_c = 75 MHz and M = 6, resulting in f_s = 18.31 kHz.

After the data is transmitted from the MEMS sensors to the DSP, the I2S buses generate hardware interrupts (IRQ). It is sufficient to handle IRQs from one selected bus only and read data from all three buses within a single interrupt handler. The procedure fills the buffer with successive samples from all six channels, after converting them to 16-bit values by truncating four least significant bits. When the buffer is full, it is put on the queue and a new buffer is created.

The main procedure takes sample buffers from the queue and performs data analysis with a fixed point arithmetic algorithm. First, amplitude correction is performed on the input signals with individual FIR filters of order 128 for each signal. Next, the velocity and pressure signals are computed according to Eqs. 1 and 2. The velocity signals are then processed by phase correction FIR filters of order 128, and the pressure signal is delayed by 65 samples in order to compensate for the filtering delay. Next, the intensity signals are calculated (Eq. 3), and the total intensity values are computed by summing up samples of each intensity signal within the buffer. These values are calculated as 32-bit values which are then scaled down to 16-bit values, with the smallest scaling factor possible, in order to improve the signal-to-noise ratio. The azimuth and the elevation are then obtained according to Eqs. 4 and 5, using the optimized Assembler procedures for computing the square root and the atan2 functions, from the DSPLIB library [19]. The angles are computed as Q15 signed integers, representing values in radians ranging from $-\pi$ to π, and then converted to integer values in degrees, with rounding. Therefore, the final analysis resolution is one degree.

The results of the calculations are put into the output queue. An USB 2.0 full speed host is implemented in the code. When an USB client program makes a request on the USB bus, a single result is sent back, packaged in a 20 byte frame, containing the azimuth, the elevation, three intensity values and a timestamp.

The main problem in the algorithm is determining the buffer length, i.e. the number of samples used for the intensity calculation. If the number is small (e.g. 256 samples), the analysis suffers from low signal-to-noise ratio. Obviously, large buffer sizes (e.g. 4096 samples), while reducing the noise, decrease the time resolution of the analysis. The standard approach is to use overlapping frames. In our first experiments, the following procedure was implemented. The buffer length was set to 256 samples, 13.98 ms for 18.31 kHz sampling frequency. Intensity values are computed in these frames, then the results from the last four frames are combined and used for calculation of the angles. Therefore, the effective buffer length is 1024 samples (55.93 ms) with 75% overlapping. The frequency of readouts is 71.52 Hz.

4 Experiments and Results

The proposed AVS and the algorithm were first tested in an anechoic chamber. The sensor with the DSP board was mounted 1 m above the floor on a tripod which was placed on a turntable. The test sound source was placed 1 m from the sensor, with axis directed towards the sensor cube. In the preliminary tests, various test signals (white noise, tones and chirps) were recorded on the DSP and analyzed on a computer in order to compute the amplitude and phase correction filters and to calibrate the algorithm. Due to inaccuracies in the manufacturing process, each instance of the AVS needs to be calibrated individually.

The same test setup was later used in the experiments in which the DOA detection accuracy was evaluated. The USB client program was written in Python in order to receive the results from the DSP and to perform data recording and visualization. Two test signals were used: white noise and a chirp with linearly increasing frequency. The output signal level on the generator was −12 dBu and the measured sound pressure level at the AVS position was ca. 85 dB SPL (linear). The source position and orientation was constant and the turntable with the AVS was rotated in 15° steps, a separate recording was made for each angle. The results are plotted in Fig. 4 for all measured angles, and additionally, selected characteristics are shown in detail in Fig. 5. It is difficult to establish the ground truth data for this setup because of inaccuracies in the AVS placement relative to the source and also due to directivity of the source. However, it can be observed that for both test signals, the calculated angle characteristics are separated from each other and the readouts are stable within a 3-degree

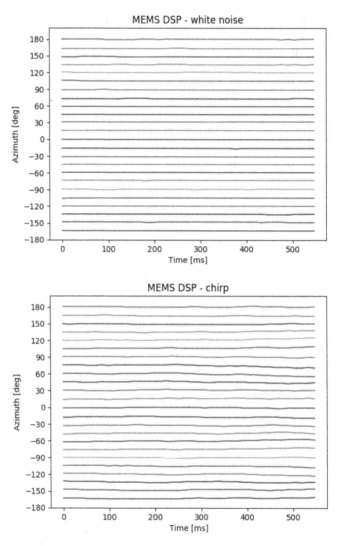

Fig. 4. The results of detection of sound source direction (azimuth) obtained in an anechoic chamber with the custom MEMS AVS and the proposed algorithm, using white noise and the chirp as test signals.

range. Some metrics computed for the results are presented in Table 1. The readouts for the wide-band noise are stable, while some deviations for higher frequencies are observed in the chirp results. However, these deviations remain within reasonable limits. Therefore, the sensor works correctly in the whole tested frequency range up to 9 kHz.

The results of azimuth detection obtained from the fixed point algorithm running on the DSP were compared with the results calculated by a floating point implementation of the same algorithm, running on a PC, using signals recorded from the tested AVS in

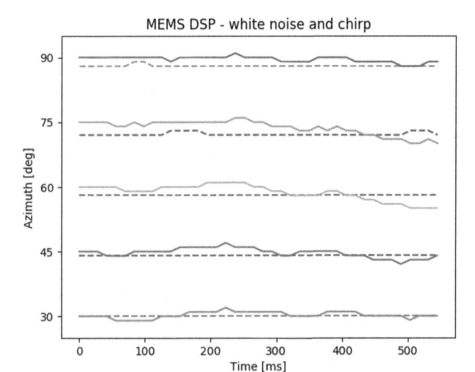

Fig. 5. Results from Fig. 4 shown in detail for selected angles; dashed line: white noise as the test signal, solid line: chirp as the test signal.

Table 1. Comparison of azimuth detection results – root mean squared error and standard deviation of angles

Sensor & algorithm	White noise		Chirp	
	RMSE	Std. dev.	RMSE	Std. dev.
MEMS, fixed p. (DSP)	1.103	0.180	1.555	0.975
MEMS, floating p.	1.457	0.140	1.747	0.784
Reference AVS probe	3.511	0.153	4.642	2.567

an earlier experiment. As it may be observed from Fig. 6 and Table 1, the results from both implementations are consistent. Obviously, the fixed point algorithm provides only integer values, so the floating point results exhibit smoother variations, and deviations for higher frequencies are larger for the fixed point algorithm, but metrics for both cases are similar (Table 1), which proves that the fixed point implementation of the algorithm does not introduce significant errors.

The same experiment was repeated for a commercial, professional acoustic vector sensor, Ultimate Sound Probe (USP) from Microflown [20]. The velocity and pressure signals recorded by the probe were analyzed using the same algorithm, the original amplitude and phase corrections device delivered by the manufacturer was applied in

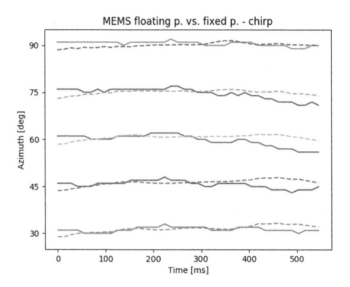

Fig. 6. Comparison of the azimuth detection results using data from the MEMS AVS, computed using the fixed point algorithm on the DSP (solid lines) and the floating point algorithm on a PC (dashed lines), for selected angles in 15 deg steps (with chirp as the test signal).

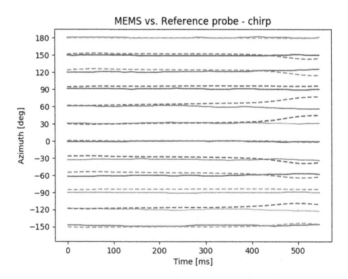

Fig. 7. Comparison of the azimuth detection results using the MEMS sensor and the proposed algorithm (solid lines), with the results obtained using a reference AVS (Microflown USP, dashed lines), with chirp as the test signal (selected angles, 30° steps starting from 0).

this case. The results are presented in Fig. 7 and also in Table 1. It is clearly visible that the results obtained from the reference probe have much larger errors and deviation from the ground truth data than the MEMS AVS, especially for higher frequencies. It is important to emphasize that presented MEMS AVS, for considered signals and frequency range, delivered DOA results with greater accuracy than reference probe.

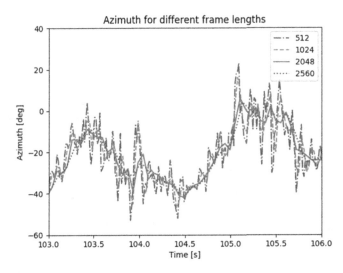

Fig. 8. Comparison of the azimuth detection in the outdoor recording, for different frame lengths

Detection of the elevation angle was also tested. Performing such a test is much more complicated because of problems in mounting the sensor on a tripod in a way that the turntable changes the elevation. When using white noise as a test signal, correct results were obtained. However, with the chirp signal, the results are distorted for high frequencies. The reason is that the DSP board was causing interferences and reflections to sound waves, resulting in incorrect readouts. Therefore, these results are not presented here, because the testing procedure has to be improved.

Finally, an experiment was performed in real world conditions. The probe was placed in outdoor, near a city street, 3 m from the lane edge, with the X axis parallel to the street. Traffic on the street was moderate, with vehicles driving with an average speed of ca. 50 km/h with medium intensity. The DSP was performing the DOA detection and a 10 min recording of the obtained results was made. Figure 8 shows a zoomed-in section of results calculated for different frame lengths. As it can be seen, small frames produce high deviation of the results that require further post-processing, while high frame length does not capture angle changes with sufficient details. Based on this experiment, the value of 2048 was selected for this experiment as an optimal frame length.

An excerpt from the recording is shown in Fig. 9, presenting the detected azimuth and elevation values, and also the intensity radius in the horizontal plane. Passing of several vehicles from left to right was recorded in this section. It may be observed that the movement of sound sources was detected correctly (both the azimuth and the elevation), with readouts having intensity above the noise level in an azimuth range of c.a −50 to 50°. The accuracy of the obtained results was verified using the video recorded during the experiment. It may be concluded that the algorithm works as expected for single vehicles present in the detection field. As expected, the accuracy is limited if e.g. two vehicles are passing in the opposite directions, causing a

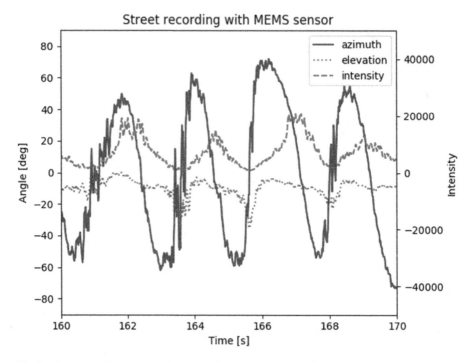

Fig. 9. An excerpt from the outdoor recording near a street – plots of azimuth and elevation (left Y axis) and intensity values returned from the sensor (right Y axis).

superposition of multiple sound sources. Nevertheless, the experiment proves that the proposed AVS and algorithm work properly not only in "acoustically sterile" conditions, but also in real world scenarios, as long as sound level of the detected source exceeds the noise level and there is no significant interference from multiple sources.

5   Conclusion

Intuitively, a custom acoustic sensor built from cheap digital microphones and a low cost DSP evaluation board with a simple processing algorithm is not expected to provide accuracy comparable to an expensive, professional AVS probe. However, the results of experiments performed so far are very promising. In the tests done in an anechoic chamber, the accuracy of the proposed sensor using the DOA detection algorithm presented here was comparable with the reference probe, if not better. The preliminary test made in outdoor conditions also confirmed that the proposed AVS works correctly also in the presence of background noise, and its accuracy is also comparable to that of the reference probe tested in earlier experiments. Therefore, after the first stage of testing, it may be concluded that the idea of constructing an acoustic vector sensor from MEMS microphones and using a fixed point DSP as an analysis platform is justified.

One of the main intended areas of application of the system described here is road traffic monitoring. Video-based monitoring systems fail at night and in difficult weather, and solutions based on radars, LIDARs, microwave sensors, etc. are expensive. Acoustic traffic monitoring is proposed as an alternative. With the low cost AVS described here, it is possible to perform vehicle detection and counting. Currently, we are working on an algorithm that evaluates vehicle speed based on audio recordings, and also on another algorithm that checks whether the road surface is wet or dry. The proposed sensor and the algorithm running on a DSP may be used in practical traffic monitoring systems. Its main advantage is a very good effectiveness-to-cost ratio. The cost is low both in terms of production (cheap microphones, moderately cheap DSP) and usage (low energy consumption), and the accuracy of detection of sound direction is comparable with a commercial sound probe with a significantly higher cost.

In the next phase of research, we intend to focus on improving the processing algorithm (for example, it is possible to limit the analyzed frequency range in order to use only sound from tires and exclude the engine sound) and solving problems with testing the elevation detection. A post-processing stage, using e.g. Kalman filtering, will also be added. We also plan to test AVS setups consisting of two or even more devices working synchronously in order to provide more detailed data on the monitored traffic.

Acknowledgments. This paper is dedicated to the memory of Mr. Wiesław Moskwa who inspired the idea of the AVS described here.

Project co-financed by the Polish National Centre for Research and Development (NCBR) from the European Regional Development Fund under the Operational Programme Innovative Economy No. POIR.04.01.04-00-0089/16 entitled: INZNAK – "Intelligent road signs". The authors also wish to thank Janusz Cichowski for his participation in constructing the sensor.

References

1. Cao, J., Liu, J., Wang, J., Lai, X.: Acoustic vector sensor: reviews and future perspectives. IET Sig. Process. **11**, 1–9 (2017)
2. Nehorai, A., Paldi, E.: Acoustic vector-sensor array processing. IEEE Trans. Sig. Process. **42**, 2481–2491 (1994)
3. Hawkes, M., Nehorai, A.: Acoustic vector-sensor beamforming and capon direction estimation. IEEE Trans. Sig. Process. **46**, 2291–2304 (1998)
4. Shujau, M., Ritz, C., Burnett, I.: Using in-air acoustic vector sensors for tracking moving speakers. In: Proceeding of 4th International Conference on Signal Processing Communication System, pp. 1–5 (2010)
5. Zhong, X., Premkumar, A.: Particle filtering approaches for multiple acoustic source detection and 2-D direction of arrival estimation using a single acoustic vector sensor. IEEE Trans. Sig. Process. **60**, 4719–4733 (2012)
6. Awad, M., Wong, K.: Recursive least-squares source tracking using one acoustic vector sensor. IEEE Trans. Aero. Electr. Syst. **48**, 3073–3083 (2012)

7. Wenzhao, Z., Shengguo, S., Zhongrui, Z., Jinwei, S.: Detection of number of source and DOA estimation in phase-mode space using uniform circular acoustic vector sensor array. In: 6th International Conference on Instrumentation & Measurement, Computer, Communication and Control (IMCCC), pp. 361–365 (2016)

8. Agarwal, A., Kumar, A., Agrawal, M., Fauziya, F.: Higher order statistics based Direction of Arrival estimation with single Acoustic Vector Sensor in the under-determined case. In: OCEANS 2016 MTS/IEEE, Monterey, pp. 1–9 (2016)

9. Nagesha, P.V., Anand, G.V., Gurugopinath, S., Prabhakar, A.: Underwater acoustic source localization by vector sensor array using compressive sampling. In: OCEANS 2016 MTS/IEEE, Monterey, pp. 1–7 (2016)

10. Kotus, J.: Multiple sound sources localization in free field using acoustic vector sensor. Multimed. Tools Appl. **74**, 4235–4251 (2015)

11. Łopatka, K., Kotus, J., Czyżewski, A.: Detection, classification and localization of acoustic events in the presence of background noise for acoustic surveillance of hazardous situations. Multimed. Tools Appl. **75**, 10407–10439 (2016)

12. Kotus, J., Czyzewski, A., Kostek, B.: 3D acoustic field intensity probe design and measurements. Archiv. Acoust. **41**, 701–711 (2016)

13. Jacobsen, F.: Sound intensity and its measurements and applications. Curr. Top. Acoust. Res. **3**, 87–91 (2003)

14. Kotus, J., Szwoch, G., Czyzewski, A.: Sound intensity probe with correction system and calibration system and the method of correction and calibration of this probe. Patent pending, PL, p. 422287, 20 Aug 2017. (in Polish)

15. InvenSense INMP441. https://www.invensense.com/products/digital/inmp441/

16. Texas Instruments: TMS320C5535 Fixed-point digital signal processor. http://www.ti.com/product/TMS320C5535/description

17. Texas instruments: C5535/C5545 eZdsp USB stick development kit. http://www.ti.com/tool/tmdx5535ezdsp

18. Texas instruments: TMS320C5535/34/33/32 Ultra-low power DSP technical reference manual, SPRUH87H. http://www.ti.com/product/TMS320C5535/technicaldocuments

19. Texas instruments: TMS320C55x DSP Library (DSPLIB), SPRC100. http://www.ti.com/tool/sprc100

20. de Bree, H.E.: The microflown: an acoustic particle velocity sensor. Acoust. Aust. **31**, 91–94 (2003)

Performance Evaluation of Selected Parallel Object Detection and Tracking Algorithms on an Embedded GPU Platform

Grzegorz Szwoch$^{(\boxtimes)}$ and Maciej Szczodrak

Multimedia Systems Department, Faculty of Electronics, Telecommunications and Informatics, Gdansk University of Technology, ul. Narutowicza 11/12, 80-233 Gdansk, Poland
greg@sound.eti.pg.gda.pl

Abstract. Performance evaluation of selected complex video processing algorithms, implemented on a parallel, embedded GPU platform Tegra X1, is presented. Three algorithms were chosen for evaluation: a GMM-based object detection algorithm, a particle filter tracking algorithm and an optical flow based algorithm devoted to people counting in a crowd flow. The choice of these algorithms was based on their computational complexity and parallel structure. The aim of the experiments was to assess whether the current generation of low-power, mobile GPUs has sufficient power for running live analysis of video surveillance streams, e.g. in smart cameras, while maintaining energy consumption at a reasonable level. Tests were performed with both a synthetic benchmark and a real video surveillance recording. It was found that the computational power of the tested platform is sufficient for running operations such as background subtraction, but in case of more complex algorithms, such as tracking with particle filters, performance is not satisfactory because of inefficient memory architecture which stalls the processing.

Keywords: Object detection · Object tracking · Object counting · Road traffic monitoring · Parallel processing · Embedded systems · Energy efficiency

1   Introduction

The task of detection and tracking of moving objects in video is an important part of automated video surveillance systems [10] and it may be performed with several approaches. The common feature of most detection and tracking algorithms is their high computational complexity due to amount of data that needs to be processed. This is especially important for live applications, such as video surveillance systems for threats detection or traffic monitoring. A recent trend in surveillance systems are smart cameras that perform video analysis on site [6]. Performing the video analysis with a serial processor requires long computation time and consumes substantial amounts of energy. These factors limit applications of such algorithms in live surveillance systems.

© Springer International Publishing AG 2017
A. Dziech and A. Czyżewski (Eds.): MCSS 2017, CCIS 785, pp. 199–213, 2017.
https://doi.org/10.1007/978-3-319-69911-0_16

Some of the object detection and tracking algorithms process data by performing repeated operations for different items. For example, an object detection algorithm may repeat the same computations for each image pixel. Such algorithms are suitable for implementation on a parallel processor. Graphics Processing Units (GPUs) are popular platforms for parallel processing, using software systems such as CUDA or OpenCL. Due to physical constraints and high energy consumption, their application were limited to desktop stations.

Implementation of parallel algorithms on embedded systems were mainly based on digital signal processors (DSP) and field programmable gate arrays (FPGA) [16]. Due to relatively low number of computing units, such solutions were limited to processing only low video resolutions and low frame rates. The situation started to change around 2014, when NVIDIA released the Tegra K1 chipset and Jetson TK1 development board. This chipset was mainly intended for smartphones, but the development board allowed for implementation and testing of data processing algorithms using the same programming language (CUDA) that desktop GPUs used, so it was possible to translate already existing algorithms to the embedded GPU. A second iteration of the chipset, Tegra X1, was released in 2015, also with the development board, was aimed mainly at automotive systems [2]. Both Tegra chipsets have a relatively high number of processing units and low energy consumption (TDP below 15 W). Parameters of the Tegra X1 chipset make it a suitable solutions for embedded systems, such as smart cameras.

The aim of this paper is to verify whether the computational power and energy efficiency of a mobile GPU chipset in processing video streams with high resolutions is sufficient for considering its implementation in smart cameras, for the purpose of object detection and tracking in video surveillance systems. For this purpose, three computationally complex algorithms were selected for evaluation. One of the most popular approaches to object detection, namely the background subtraction algorithm based on Gaussian mixture models, proposed by Stauffer and Grimson [23] and later extended by Zivkovic [32], was chosen as an implementation of the object detection algorithm. The parallel nature of the algorithm makes it suitable for implementation on various parallel processing platforms, such as GPUs [20,25], FPGAs or supercomputer clusters [27]. For object tracking, different approach has to be taken for scenes with isolated moving objects (such as vehicles in a street) and for scenes with a large number of objects that are impossible to isolate (e.g. spectators at a sport event). For the first case, object tracking is usually performed with Kalman filters [28], with additional algorithms for resolving conflicts when the objects merge or split [10]. The drawback of this approach is its low accuracy when a large number of tracks from moving objects cross and conflict. Another approach to tracking is based on particle filters [5,11] and it proved to be more robust in object tracking in more complex situations [14,18]. No publications on implementation of this approach on a GPU were found, however FPGA optimized approach was recently proposed by Schwiegelshohn et al. [22].

In complex scenes with a high number of moving objects, a different approach is needed. Optical flow methods [4,21,24,29] are commonly used for this task, particularly for obtaining per-pixel motion vectors in crowded scenes usually as the first image processing stage. Many implementations on various devices including FPGAs of optical flow algorithms can be found in the literature. Zach et al. [30] demonstrated variational optical flow computation on a GPU parallelized with a shader. They achieve nearly real time performance for 320×240 resolution. Improved method, also on GPU, has been proposed by Gwosdek et al. [12]. Pauwels et al. [19] implemented modified phase-based Fleet and Jepson method. However, the most popular pixel motion estimation is Lucas-Kanade method [8] with proposed GPU implementation [15]. Apart from FPGAs [17], Lucas-Kanade Optical Flow method was also evaluated on TI C66x digital signal processor [31].

It should also be noted that there are programming libraries that implement common video processing algorithms on a GPU, for example, the OpenCV library has the CUDA module (CUDA-accelerated computer vision) [3] that implements, among others, background subtraction and optical flow. However, these implementations are not optimized for embedded GPUs which results in suboptimal performance on such chipsets, because they have much lower number of processing cores than desktop GPUs. Therefore, it is recommended to perform an independent implementation of the algorithm, optimized for a specific GPU chipset.

Contribution of the research described in this paper to the state-of-art is twofold. First, this paper describes the approach to implementing the selected video analysis algorithm on CUDA-capable parallel devices. Due to significant differences in GPU architecture compared to CPUs, sequential code cannot be simply run on a GPU. In order to benefit from parallel computations, the code must be implemented in a specific way and optimized for the GPU. This paper discusses the most important issues that affect the performance of the GPU implementation of the selected algorithms. Second, the aim of the paper is to evaluate the performance of the selected embedded GPU platforms in complex video analysis. As the Tegra chipsets are still relatively new, there is no sufficient data on their performance in live video surveillance systems. Therefore, the paper aims to answer whether these devices are capable of almost real-time analysis of video streams of different resolutions and frame rates. This information is important for researchers and developers who consider employing such processing platforms for complex video analysis.

In the following Sect. 2, the three selected algorithms mentioned above are described in short and some important features that affect implementation of these algorithms on embedded GPUs, are discussed. In the next Sections, the test methodology (Sect. 3) and results (Sects. 3.1, 3.2 and 3.3) are presented and discussed.

2 Video Processing Algorithms and Their GPU Implementation

This Section describes GPU implementations of three selected algorithms for object detection and tracking. The background subtraction algorithm separates pixels belonging to moving objects from the background. The particle filter performs tracking of a moving object on the background subtraction results. The optical flow algorithm detects and tracks moving objects within a single algorithm. Two different approaches to moving object detection and tracking were chosen because none of them is universal. The method based on background subtraction and particle filter tracking is better suited for scenarios involving a relatively small number of moving objects that may be separated (such as vehicles on a parking). The optical filter approach should be used when a large number of moving objects is present in the scene and it is practically impossible to separate individual objects using the background subtraction method. Examples of typical application of the optical flow algorithm are crowd monitoring, vehicle tracking on a busy urban intersection, etc. All three algorithms exhibit a parallel structure, so that they are suitable for implementation on an embedded GPU. Since these algorithms belong to the state-of-art and they are described in detail in the literature, only the most important features will be presented in this Section, with the focus on parallel implementation of the described methods. References to more detailed descriptions are provided for each algorithm.

2.1 Background Subtraction

The background subtraction (BS) algorithm divides pixels of a single video frame into two classes: the foreground (pixels belonging to moving objects) and the background. The most popular BS algorithm is the one based on Gaussian mixture models (GMM) [23,32], so it was chosen for the GPU implementation. The algorithm is embarrassingly parallel because each pixel is processed independently of the others, and it is well-suited for implementation on parallel platforms [25,27]. A statistical model consisting of N Gaussians (modes, typically, $N = 3$ to 5) is created for each individual pixel. Each mode is described by a weight, means and variances of each RGB channel. The probability that a pixel x_t belongs to a background is [23]:

$$P(x_t) = \sum_{n=1}^{N} w_{n,t} \cdot \eta(x_t, \mu_{n,t}, \Sigma_{n,t}) \qquad (1)$$

where x_T is the pixel value, μ is the mean background vector, Σ is the covariance matrix. Weights w of all modes sum up to one and they are ordered by a decreasing value. The background model of the whole image is a data structure combining the individual pixels models. On a GPU platform, the model is kept in the persistent global memory, so it may be used for processing successive video frames.

In the first detection phase, the algorithm searches for a matching mode that fulfills the condition:

$$\forall k = 1 \ldots 3 : |x_k - \mu_{k,n}| \leq T \cdot \sigma_{k,n} \tag{2}$$

where T is the detection threshold (usually $T = 2.5$) and k is the channel index.

In the next phase, the mean and variance of the matched mode are replaced with:

$$\mu_t = \mu_{t-1} + \rho(x_t - \mu_{t-1})$$
$$\sigma_t^2 = \sigma_{t-1}^2 + \rho[(x_t - \mu_t)^2 - \sigma_{t-1}^2] \tag{3}$$

where σ is the learning factor. If none of the modes were matched, the mode with the lowest weight is removed and replaced by a new one, initialized with the current pixel value. Weights of all modes are then updated:

$$w_t = w_{t-1} + \alpha(M - w_{t-1}) \tag{4}$$

where α is the update factor and M is one if the mode was matched and zero otherwise. The updated weights are normalized so that their sum is equal to one, and the modes are reordered by a decreasing weight. The final result of the GMM procedure is a binary image (the background mask), denoting background and foreground pixels with values of zero and non-zero, respectively.

The GMM algorithm can be implemented as a single GPU kernel. Each pixel is processed independently from the others, so division of data into work groups can be arbitrary (shared memory is not used). Performance of the algorithm is bound by memory access, since reading and writing the pixel models consumes most of the kernel runtime [25]. On most GPU platforms, the speed of memory operations depends on the access pattern, i.e. which memory locations are accessed by work items in a warp [1]. In order to optimize the algorithm, the background model in the GPU memory is ordered by features rather than by pixels. This approach reduces the risk of memory access conflicts, ensuring that consecutive threads access adjacent memory locations. The video frame data is loaded into a 24-bit buffer in the texture memory of the GPU for faster access. The background mask is retrieved from a buffer located in the global GPU memory.

In the post-processing stage, the obtained background mask is cleaned with morphological opening and closing, then connected components are extracted. As a result, a set of image regions, describing positions of moving objects in a single video frame, is created, constituting data needed by the object tracking procedure.

2.2   Object Tracking with Particle Filters

Particle filters are useful in object tracking mainly because they provide multiple hypotheses on the state of moving objects, as opposed to typically used Kalman filters that model a single hypothesis. As a result, the risk of losing the tracked object is reduced. A thorough description of particle filters and their applications for object tracking purposes may be found e.g. in [5,11]. The algorithm is complex is terms of processing, but its parts may be realized with parallel processing. However, its implementation on a GPU platform is much more complicated compared with the GMM algorithm. It is necessary to divide the algorithm into several stages, implemented with individual GPU kernels.

A single iteration of a particle filter consists of a prediction and an update stage. Updating the filter requires a measurement of validity of each prediction. For object tracking in video, color histograms are usually applied for computing the measurement. The implementation described here is partially based on the work by Nummiaro et al. [18] and Isaard [14]. The proposed tracker represents the state of a moving object with a set of particles representing the probability density function of a modeled system. Each particle is described with a weight π and a state vector. Fr the purpose of object tracking in video, the state is described as

$$\mathbf{s} = [x, y, \dot{x}, \dot{y}, h, s] \tag{5}$$

where (x, y) denote the center position of the bounding box of the object, $(\dot{x}, \dot{y})$ is the velocity, (w, h) is the bounding box width and height, s is the scale (size change). After the tracker initialization, all particles have the same weights equal to $1/N$, where N is the number of particles, the same position and size set according to the object detection results, and their initial speed is zero.

During the prediction phase, N samples are drawn from the distribution with replacement. Particle weight influences a chance of a given particle to be selected [14]. A predicted state of each particle is computed by first applying the dynamic model:

$$\begin{aligned}
x^{(t)} &= x^{(t-1)} + \dot{x}^{(t)} \\
y^{(t)} &= y^{(t-1)} + \dot{y}^{(t)} \\
w^{(t)} &= w^{(t-1)} + s^{(t-1)} \\
h^{(t)} &= h^{(t-1)} + s^{(t-1)}
\end{aligned} \tag{6}$$

where t is the frame number. Next, a stochastic component is incorporated by adding random values from independent Gaussian distributions to all state variables. As a result, each particle represents a predicted position, size and velocity of the tracked object.

In the update stage, weights of all particles are recalculated. The approach based on color histograms, suggested by Nummiaro [18], was used. For each particle, its color histogram is computed from the image region described by its state. The weight is computed from the distance between the obtained histogram and the target. Two-dimensional histograms are calculated in the improved HLS (i-HLS) color space [13]. The size of a histogram is 512 bins (64 bins for hue vs 8 bins for saturation). For low saturation, scaled brightness values are used instead of hue. Additionally, color values are weighted by their distance from the area center. The updated value of the particle weight is computed as:

$$\pi = exp\left(\frac{-d^2}{2\sigma^2}\right) \tag{7}$$

where d is the Bhattacharyya distance between the computed and the target histogram and σ is a weighting factor ($\sigma = 0.1$ was used). The new weights are normalized to the unit sum and the current state of the object is computed as a weighted mean of all particles. Finally, if the distance between the histogram of the mean state and the target one exceeds some defined threshold, the target histogram is updated with the current one.

Implementation of the algorithm in CUDA was divided into several kernels. The most difficult part to implement was the update phase which involves computing a large number of histograms. Each histogram requires allocating a memory buffer, and histogram bins are accessed in a non-sequential manner, resulting in a suboptimal memory access pattern. Atomic operations are required for updating the histogram, which slows the algorithm down considerably. The processing scheme that worked best in the experiments was based on work groups of 512 items, that processed image region of 16 x 32 pixels and computed a single particle histogram in the shared memory buffer. Histogram normalization and weight calculation is performed in parallel by the reduction operation, which requires synchronization points, reducing the computation speed. The complete algorithm is mostly memory-bound, and about 87% of the processing time is spent in the kernel that computes color histograms for all particles [26].

2.3 The Virtual Gate Algorithm

The Virtual Gate algorithm performing people counting in a crowd flow is based on the Optical Flow method. The design of the algorithm assumes a top camera view of human silhouettes in places where crowd motion is expected, especially at entrances, stairways, etc. [9].

In order to obtain the motion vectors, an iterative (pyramidal) implementation of the Lucas-Kanade optical flow computation is applied. A pyramid of images is constructed, where each level represents downscaled image. Each level corresponds to 2 times smaller dimensions. Before image subsampling, an antialiasing filtration is applied. The pyramidal representation is good to handle large pixel motion. The pyramidal tracking algorithm working scheme can be described as follows. First, the optical flow is computed at the deepest pyramid level M (the smallest image). Then, the result of the computation is propagated to the upper level $(M-1)$ in a form of an initial guess for the pixel displacement. Given that initial guess, the refined optical flow is computed at level $M-1$, and the result is propagated to level $M-2$ and further up to the level 0 (the original image) [7].

The Virtual Gate is composed of a set of rectangular regions (R_i) situated next to each other and overlapping. The rectangles are identical in size which corresponds to the size of an average human body contour. The motion of objects is estimated in each region R_i using the dense Optical Flow method [7,8]. The set of vectors representing the direction and the velocity of the motion detected is obtained in the result of the above operation. Displacement vectors can be expressed by the planar vector field:

$$\mathbf{V} = V_1(x,y)\mathbf{i} + V_2(x,y)\mathbf{j} = V_\rho(x,y)\mathbf{e}_\rho + V_\varphi(x,y)\mathbf{e}_\varphi \tag{8}$$

where: $\mathbf{i}, \mathbf{j}$ – unit vectors of x and y axes of ground plane, $\mathbf{e}_\rho, \mathbf{e}_\varphi$ – unit vectors related to polar coordinates (the distance from the axis of symmetry, the angle measured counterclockwise from the positive x-axis).

Components of Eq. 8 can be written in the form of polar coordinates:

$$V_1 = V_\rho cos(\varphi) + V_\varphi sin(\varphi) \tag{9}$$
$$V_2 = V_\rho sin(\varphi) + V_\varphi cos(\varphi)$$

Let φ_0 denote the angle corresponding to the direction of y axis. New functions V_1^I, V_2^I, V_1^O, and V_2^O are calculated as given in Eq. 9 in order to obtain the desired direction vectors:

$$V_k^I = \begin{cases} V_k & \text{if } \varphi_2 \leq \varphi \leq \varphi_1 \\ 0 & \text{otherwise} \end{cases} \tag{10}$$

$$V_k^O = \begin{cases} V_k & \text{if } \varphi_2 + \pi \leq \varphi \leq \varphi_1 + \pi \\ 0 & \text{otherwise} \end{cases}$$

where: $k = 1, 2$, $\varphi_1 = \varphi_0 + \alpha$, $\varphi_2 = \varphi_0 - \alpha$, α - tolerance of motion direction.

The number of origins of vectors directed towards "in" (L^I) or "out" (L^O), enclosed in each region R_i is obtained according to Eq. 11:

$$L^{\{I,O\}} = \sum_{i=1}^{I} \sum_{j=1}^{J} \tilde{V}_{i,j}, \quad \tilde{V}_{i,j} = \begin{cases} 1 & \text{if } \left|\mathbf{V}_{i,j}^{\{I,O\}}\right| > T_M \\ 0 & \text{otherwise} \end{cases} \tag{11}$$

where: T_M – vector magnitude threshold,
$\mathbf{V}_{i,j}^{\{I,O\}} = \mathbf{V}^{\{I,O\}}(x_i, y_j)$ – vector with origin at (x_i, y_j), refer to Eqs. 8–10,
I, J – number of points in R_i along x and y axes, respectively.

The obtained L^I and L^O are compared with a threshold value (T_S), proportional to the average area of a human silhouette. If L^I or L^O is greater than T_S, the corresponding counter is incremented. Then, area of region R_i remains filled with zero vectors for the period of C frames, related to the average speed of crowd movement.

3   Experiments

Implementation of the algorithms described in the previous Section was performed using the CUDA language [1] for the GPU part and with C++ for the host code. The aim of the experiments was to assess the performance of the algorithms on the Tegra X1 GPU in terms of processing speed and energy efficiency. The processing speed was measured by computing the total time needed to process all video frames using the system timer of a host device. The timer was started before the image frame was sent to the GPU, and paused after the results were obtained by the host, so the measured scores represent the raw processing time (without input and output operations). As a performance metric, the processing rate, i.e. an average number of video frames processed per second (fps), was used. Energy consumption was evaluated by measuring the electric power drawn by the GPU platform, using the Voltcraft Energy Logger 4000 device. Power was measured in watts with frequency of 1 Hz and the averaged value observed during the processing was reported. In order to compare values obtained from different algorithms and different videos, the measured energy E was normalized to the time needed to process 1000 frames with a given algorithm, and expressed in joules:

$$E = \frac{P \cdot t}{N/1000} = P \cdot \frac{N}{r} \cdot \frac{1000}{N} = P \cdot \frac{1000}{r}, \tag{12}$$

where P is the measured power, t is the measured processing time, r is the calculated processing rate (fps), N is the number of frames processed in t.

The Jetson TX1 development board, equipped with the NVIDIA Tegra X1 GPU chipset, was the testing platform. The main parameters of the device are presented in Table 1. The main aim of the experiments was to evaluate performance of each algorithm for different video resolutions. A synthetic benchmark was created for this purpose. Video frames were generated on the device during the test, showing a colorful target moving along the screen and bouncing off the edges. The velocity and the direction of movement are distorted with a Gaussian noise. The background is a static noise that does not change during the tests. The diameter of the target was always equal to 1/5 of the screen height. A total of 5000 video frames was generated in each run. This approach allowed for comparing the performance of different algorithms in identical conditions. Additionally, in some cases, the tests were also performed on a real video recording. Accuracy of the algorithms was not evaluated in the experiments, it was only ensured that the algorithms produce correct results.

Table 1. Main parameters of the Jetson TX1 platform

Parameter	Jetson TX1
Chipset	NVIDIA Tegra X1
Max TDP	15 W
Processing cores	256
GPU clock rate	72 MHz
GPU memory rate	13 MHz
GPU memory	3854 MB
CUDA runtime	7
Compute capability	5.3
Operating system	Ubuntu 14.04

3.1 Background Subtraction

The processing speed in the GMM algorithm depends on the video resolution, the number of models in each pixel model and on the image content variability. If the image content is stable, the first mode may be matched for most pixels, but if the content changes, all modes need to be evaluated and none of them will match. Image content changes may be caused not only by object movement, but also by lighting changes or camera noise. Table 2 presents the measured values of the processing speed and consumed energy for the synthetic benchmark. The TX1 platform was able to process all video resolutions with the processing rate above 55 fps, which is sufficient for video surveillance applications. Energy consumption for high video resolutions is relatively high.

The same experiment was performed with a real surveillance video recorded in the bank office, with a moderate number of persons. Camera noise and flickering lights introduced variability to the pixel values, which was not present in the synthetic benchmark. The test results shown in Table 3 show that the obtained processing rate is lower than for the synthetic test. Energy consumption is comparable to the previous test, some differences for TX1 may be caused by the fact that some of the total processing time was spent on decoding video frames, which was included in the averaged power measurement.

Table 2. Test results for the GMM algorithm, obtained with the synthetic benchmark

Video resolution	Target area	Processing ratio (fps)	Energy consumption [J]
1920 × 1080	36983	56.87	200.45
1600 × 900	25730	80.14	142.25
1280 × 720	16513	126.24	91.09
1024 × 576	10387	192.86	59.10
800 × 450	6504	299.89	37.01
640 × 360	4185	466.98	24.84
480 × 270	2376	756.25	14.01

Table 3. Test results for the GMM algorithm, obtained with the real recording

Video resolution	Processing ratio (fps)	Energy consumption [J]
1920 × 1080	47.73	173.89
1600 × 900	66.89	121.09
1280 × 720	100.73	80.41
1024 × 576	155.37	51.49
800 × 450	232.16	34.02
640 × 360	350.29	22.55
480 × 270	533.91	14.42

To conclude, the GMM algorithm may be implemented on the TX1 platform and it should process the video with a rate exceeding the source one. Depending on the computational power required by further algorithms in the processing chain, downscaling the video may be advisable. The main factor that limits performance of TX1 is slow memory access. Energy consumption for TX1 is relatively high for larger resolutions, so in terms of energy usage, downscaling the video is also helpful.

3.2 Object Tracking with the Particle Filters

The object tracking algorithm based on the color particle filter was tested using only the synthetic video benchmark, because the video content does not affect the processing speed and energy consumption in a significant way. The results are presented in Table 4. The tracking algorithm required much longer processing time than the GMM. Performance of the TX1 platform in tracking objects in high resolution video was poor. The main problem with TX1 seems to be related to slow memory access. As the video resolution increases, memory operations block the processing and, as a result, TX1 consumes more energy. Therefore, the memory architecture on TX1 limits usability of this platform for real-time tracking applications.

3.3 Object Flow Counting with Virtual Gate Algorithm

The main factors that have influence on the processing speed in the Virtual Gate algorithm are the video resolution, optical flow window size, and the image content variability. Table 5 presents the measured values of the processing speed and consumed energy at window size of 11×11. In the synthetic data, the size of the virtual gate region is the same for all resolutions, and in the real recording, the size is proportional to the video resolution. This is the cause of worse algorithm performance between synthetic and real data. The best energy performance expressed in joules per one pixel is noticed at highest resolution

Table 4. Test results for the particle tracker algorithm, obtained with the synthetic benchmark

Video resolution	Target area	Processing ratio (fps)	Energy consumption [J]
1920×1080	36983	3.29	2368.94
1600×900	25730	6.06	1302.57
1280×720	16513	8.72	928.46
1024×576	10387	17.39	477.42
800×450	6504	34.84	252.57
640×360	4185	57.55	154.65
480×270	2376	91.47	99.48

Table 5. Test results for the Virtual Gate algorithm, obtained with the synthetic benchmark

Video resolution	Processing ratio (fps)	Energy consumption [J]
1920 × 1080	2.24	4336.72
1600 × 900	3.21	3037.76
1280 × 720	4.59	1938.44
1024 × 576	5.78	1305.31
800 × 450	8.60	904.97
640 × 360	11.34	589.81
480 × 270	20.54	353.95

Table 6. Test results for the Virtual Gate algorithm, obtained with the real recording

Video resolution	Processing ratio (fps)	Energy consumption [J]
1920 × 1080	0.75	15371.56
1600 × 900	1.11	10247.24
1280 × 720	1.93	6096.50
1024 × 576	3.05	3853.57
800 × 450	5.10	2220.97
640 × 360	6.21	1459.01
480 × 270	8.44	880.94

$(2.09 \cdot 10^{-3})$, and the worst $(2.73 \cdot 10^{-3})$ for lowest resolution, however processing speed is acceptable only for the latter case (Table 6).

4   Conclusions

The aim of the experiments presented in this paper was to assess whether it is possible to run complex video analysis algorithms on current low-power embedded GPU platforms such as Jetson TX1 from NVidia. The three selected video processing algorithms benefit from the parallel processing, but with some limitations. One of the main features of these algorithms is that they perform a high number of memory operations. Therefore, the embedded GPU chipset for video processing needs both a fast computing unit that performs the actual processing, and a fast memory system, so that the processing is not stalled due to inefficient memory operations. The experiments described in this paper proved that the former requirement is, to some degree, fulfilled in the TX1 chipset, while the latter issue is an important problem. Memory access on a GPU may be optimized in the algorithm code by restructuring the access patterns to achieve coalesced reads and writes [1] and it was done during the implementation. However, the TX1 memory architecture imposes some constraints that limit the achieved processing rate, which was observed in the experiments, and it is most evident for the particle color tracker where the number of memory operations is very large. The Tegra X1 chipset, and other embedded GPUs with a similar architecture, should provide a satisfactory processing speed in these applications that require few memory operations and perform intensive data processing. This is not the case for video analysis algorithms that usually have to read and write a large amount of data. This is why performance of TX1, in terms of both the processing speed and energy consumption, suffer considerably in processing of high resolution video streams. It seems that the designers of these chipsets focused mainly on the computational power (the number of cores, the clock frequency) and they neglected the memory speed. As a result, performance of complex algorithms (such as the particle filter tracker) in this case is poor. However, embedded GPUs, such as TX1, certainly have a great potential in automated video surveillance systems, e.g. for traffic monitoring, but future generations of the embedded GPUs need to improve their memory architecture, so that stalling the processing due to frequent memory operations will no longer be an issue.

Acknowledgment. Project financed partially by the by the Polish National Centre for Research and Development (NCBR) from the European Regional Development Fund under the Operational Programme Innovative Economy No. POIR.04.01.04-00-0089/16 entitled: INZNAK - "Intelligent road signs".

References

1. CUDA C best practices guide. http://docs.nvidia.com/cuda/cuda-c-best-practices-guide. Accessed 30 Dec 2016
2. NVIDIA Jetson TX1 module. http://www.nvidia.com/object/jetson-tx1-module.html. Accessed 30 Dec 2016
3. OpenCV CUDA accelerated computer vision. http://docs.opencv.org/3.0-last-rst/modules/cuda/doc/introduction.html. Accessed 30 Dec 2016
4. Adarve, J.D., Mahony, R.: A filter formulation for computing real time optical flow. IEEE Robot. Autom. Lett. **1**(2), 1192–1199 (2016)
5. Arulampalam, M.S., Maskell, S., Gordon, N., Clapp, T.: A tutorial on particle filters for online nonlinear/non-Gaussian Bayesian tracking. IEEE Trans. Sig. Process. **50**(2), 174–188 (2002)
6. Belbachir, A.N.: Smart Cameras. Springer, Boston (2010). doi:10.1007/978-1-4419-0953-4
7. Bouguet, J.Y.: Pyramidal implementation of the Lucas Kanade feature tracker. Intel Corporation, Microprocessor Research Labs (2000)
8. Burt, P., Adelson, E.: The Laplacian pyramid as a compact image code. IEEE Trans. Commun. **31**(4), 532–540 (1983)
9. Czyżewski, A., Bratoszewski, P., Ciarkowski, A., Cichowski, J., Lisowski, K., Szczodrak, M., Szwoch, G., Krawczyk, H.: Massive surveillance data processing with supercomputing cluster. Inf. Sci. **296**, 322–344 (2015)
10. Czyzewski, A., Szwoch, G., Dalka, P., Szczuko, P., Ciarkowski, A., Ellwart, D., Merta, T., Lopatka, K., Kulasek, L., Wolski, J.: Multi-stage video analysis framework. In: Video Surveillance, pp. 147–172 (2011)
11. Gordon, N., Ristic, B., Arulampalam, S.: Beyond the Kalman Filter: Particle Filters for Tracking Applications. Artech House, London (2004)

12. Gwosdek, P., Zimmer, H., Grewenig, S., Bruhn, A., Weickert, J.: A highly efficient GPU implementation for variational optic flow based on the Euler-Lagrange framework. In: Kutulakos, K.N. (ed.) ECCV 2010. LNCS, vol. 6554, pp. 372–383. Springer, Heidelberg (2012). doi:10.1007/978-3-642-35740-4_29

13. Hanbury, A.: A 3D-polar coordinate colour representation well adapted to image analysis. In: Bigun, J., Gustavsson, T. (eds.) SCIA 2003. LNCS, vol. 2749, pp. 804–811. Springer, Heidelberg (2003). doi:10.1007/3-540-45103-X_107

14. Isard, M., Blake, A.: Condensation-conditional density propagation for visual tracking. Int. J. Comput. Vis. **29**(1), 5–28 (1998)

15. Kim, J.S., Hwangbo, M., Kanade, T.: Parallel algorithms to a parallel hardware: designing vision algorithms for a GPU. In: 2009 IEEE 12th International Conference on Computer Vision Workshops (ICCV Workshops), pp. 862–869. IEEE (2009)

16. Melpignano, D., Benini, L., Flamand, E., Jego, B., Lepley, T., Haugou, G., Clermidy, F., Dutoit, D.: Platform 2012, a many-core computing accelerator for embedded SoCs: performance evaluation of visual analytics applications. In: Proceedings of the 49th Annual Design Automation Conference, DAC 2012, pp. 1137–1142. ACM, New York (2012)

17. Monson, J., Wirthlin, M., Hutchings, B.L.: Implementing high-performance, low-power FPGA-based optical flow accelerators in C. In: 2013 IEEE 24th International Conference on Application-Specific Systems, Architectures and Processors, pp. 363–369. IEEE (2013)

18. Nummiaro, K., Koller-Meier, E., Van Gool, L.: An adaptive color-based particle filter. Image Vis. Comput. **21**(1), 99–110 (2003)

19. Pauwels, K., Van Hulle, M.M.: Realtime phase-based optical flow on the GPU. In: Computer Vision and Pattern Recognition Workshops, CVPRW 2008, pp. 1–8. IEEE (2008)

20. Pham, V., Vo, P., Hung, V.T., et al.: GPU implementation of extended gaussian mixture model for background subtraction. In: 2010 IEEE RIVF International Conference on Computing and Communication Technologies, Research, Innovation, and Vision for the Future (RIVF), pp. 1–4. IEEE (2010)

21. Revaud, J., Weinzaepfel, P., Harchaoui, Z., Schmid, C.: EpicFlow: edge-preserving interpolation of correspondences for optical flow. In: Proceedings of the IEEE Conference on Computer Vision and Pattern Recognition, pp. 1164–1172. IEEE (2015)

22. Schwiegelshohn, F., Ossovski, E., Hübner, M.: A fully parallel particle filter architecture for FPGAs. In: Sano, K., Soudris, D., Hübner, M., Diniz, P.C. (eds.) ARC 2015. LNCS, vol. 9040, pp. 91–102. Springer, Cham (2015). doi:10.1007/978-3-319-16214-0_8

23. Stauffer, C., Grimson, W.E.L.: Adaptive background mixture models for real-time tracking. In: 1999 IEEE Computer Society Conference on Computer Vision and Pattern Recognition, vol. 2, pp. 246–252. IEEE (1999)

24. Sun, D., Roth, S., Black, M.J.: A quantitative analysis of current practices in optical flow estimation and the principles behind them. Int. J. Comput. Vis. **106**(2), 115–137 (2014)

25. Szwoch, G.: Performance evaluation of parallel background subtraction on GPU platforms. Elektronika: konstrukcje, technologie, zastosowania **56**(4), 23–27 (2015)

26. Szwoch, G.: Performance evaluation of the parallel object tracking algorithm employing the particle filter. In: 2016 Signal Processing: Algorithms, Architectures, Arrangements, and Applications (SPA), pp. 119–124. SPA, September 2016

27. Szwoch, G., Ellwart, D., Czyzewski, A.: Parallel implementation of background subtraction algorithms for real-time video processing on a supercomputer platform. J. Real Time Image Process. **11**(1), 111–125 (2016)
28. Welch, G., Bishop, G.: An introduction to the Kalman filter. Technical report TR-95041 (2004). https://www.cs.unc.edu/welch/kalman/kalmanIntro.html
29. Wulff, J., Black, M.J.: Efficient sparse-to-dense optical flow estimation using a learned basis and layers. In: 2015 IEEE Conference on Computer Vision and Pattern Recognition (CVPR), pp. 120–130. IEEE (2015)
30. Zach, C., Pock, T., Bischof, H.: A duality based approach for realtime TV-L^1 optical flow. In: Hamprecht, F.A., Schnörr, C., Jähne, B. (eds.) DAGM 2007. LNCS, vol. 4713, pp. 214–223. Springer, Heidelberg (2007). doi:10.1007/978-3-540-74936-3_22
31. Zhang, F., Gao, Y., Bakos, J.D.: Lucas-Kanade optical flow estimation on the TI C66x digital signal processor. In: 2014 IEEE High Performance Extreme Computing Conference (HPEC), pp. 1–6. IEEE, September 2014
32. Zivkovic, Z., van der Heijden, F.: Efficient adaptive density estimation per image pixel for the task of background subtraction. Pattern Recogn. Lett. **27**(7), 773–780 (2006)

Author Index

Printed in the United States
By Bookmasters